GREAT CANADIAN
WRITING
A Century of Imagination

CLAUDE BISSELL

GREAT

WRI

A Century of Imagination

CANADIAN

PAINTING

THE CANADIAN CENTENNIAL LIBRARY

THE CANADIAN CENTENNIAL LIBRARY

WEEKEND MAGAZINE / MCCLELLAND AND STEWART LIMITED

Pierre Berton, *Editor-in-chief*

Frank Newfeld, *Art Director*

Ken Lefolii, *Managing Editor*

THE CANADIAN CENTENNIAL PUBLISHING CO. LTD.
150 SIMCOE ST., TORONTO, CANADA

6/14/67 *pub.* 4.95

CONTENTS

Introduction 9

Places 11

Action 35

People 59

✿

Politics 79

✿

The Critical and the Contemplative 95

✿

Poetry 111

✿

A Note on the Anthologist

Dr. Claude Thomas Bissell, president of the University of Toronto, is perhaps Canada's leading authority on Canadian literature. Born at Meaford, Ontario, in 1916, he began his career as an Instructor in English at Cornell University in 1938. For most of his life, however (save for World War II service in the Canadian Infantry), he has been associated with the University of Toronto, first in the English department and later in various executive capacities.

Before his appointment to the presidency of the University of Toronto in 1958 he served for two years as president of Carleton University in Ottawa. He was chairman of the Canada Council from 1960 to 1962 and has also recently headed the National Conference of Canadian Universities and Colleges, the Canadian Universities Foundation and the World University Service of Canada. He is well known for his articles on Canadian and English literature in various Canadian and U.S. journals.

INTRODUCTION

This is an anthology of Canadian writing in English during the first century of our existence as a nation. I have included a few selections from Canadian writing in French. Good translations, either from French to English or from English to French, are not numerous. This is regrettable; yet one must remember that a literature and a language are deeply inter-related and cannot be separated without irreparable loss. Canadian writing in French constitutes a distinctive body of literature, and it can be understood and appreciated only in its own cultural and linguistic framework. This anthology, then, is confined almost entirely to one of the two literatures that Canada has produced.

I have arranged my material in six parts. The first five parts are devoted to prose and the sixth to poetry. Each of the first five parts has a distinctive subject matter, and these subjects recur in the same sequence in the sixth part.

The first part, entitled *Places,* consists of passages that tell us something about our physical environment. Indeed, the opening passages might be characterized as a literary geography of Canada. We move across the country from the East to the West, observing the great signatures scrawled by nature. Occasionally man takes over from nature and creates a habitation that arrests the attention of the writer. But even in these instances it is the natural background that releases the imagination. Again and again one is struck by the fact that it is geology, a geology stripped of its detailed scientific content, that provides the major epic note in much Canadian writing, whether it be prose or poetry.

The remaining passages in this part, beginning with Stephen Leacock's account of a rich man's club, from *Arcadian Adventures with the Idle Rich,* evoke a specific place and time, without any precise geographical reference. But the setting is unmistakably Canadian, and may often be pinpointed. What is observed is of less importance, however, than how it is observed. In short, we are, in Robert Frost's phrase, shifting from "outer" to "inner weather".

The second part is entitled *Action.* Here the emphasis is upon physical action, often of a violent nature, in which nature is either a principal participant or an essential background. In Canadian life, as in Canadian literature, nature could bring either balm and healing or terror and destruction. It was nature as instrument of terror and destruction that frequently attracted the writer. Our greatest poet, E. J. Pratt, is constantly concerned with the pathology of power. In his poem "The Shark", for instance, he describes a creature that symbolizes the amoral savagery of nature. But even in a universe that seemed to tower over man with an implacable and baleful intensity, he found a sure place for the human spirit, and his greatest poems are celebrations of man's triumph over a hostile universe. In other selections in this part nature is more benign. In the selection from Hugh MacLennan's *The Watch that Ends the Night* the dark and sinister qualities of nature yield to warmth and protectiveness. It is not nature that is violent and immoral, but man himself.

In the days of settlement, nature provided the test of man's

valour and ingenuity. For a country whose frontiers have not yet been completely explored this remains true. In the settled areas of Canada, ingenuity and strength in mastering the forces of nature have long ceased to be important. But our long heritage of battle with nature remains, particularly in our passion for some of the more violent forms of sport. Ralph Connor's passage on the early days of Canadian football recalls the rugged individualistic days of that sport before, under southern influence, it became a vaudeville branch of General Motors. Morley Callaghan's description of a professional hockey game in the Montreal Forum brings out the violent melodrama of the game. Hockey rightly occupies a central place in the Canadian imagination. It is played on our great universal, ice, and it simulates the most destructive forces in nature at the same time that it evokes skill and artistry. From sport I move on to war. The transition has not been unpremeditated, for man has been able to accommodate himself to the horror of war only by relating it to a sporting code, an accommodation to which the computer and the nuclear bomb are resistant. With their background of physical struggle and of passionate athleticism, Canadians have made excellent soldiers in the non-professional sense. They have been resourceful, determined, brave, and, in so far as the circumstances permitted, exuberant.

The third part is entitled *People.* For some time it has been a basic platitude that the Canadian imagination cannot properly encompass the phenomenon of man. The opening passage from John Robins might be taken as an epigraph for such an argument. It is still true that English-Canadian literature has not produced great characters. Certainly it can be said, however, that our writers have lost their embarrassment and gaucherie in the presence of human beings. It is impossible to demonstrate adequately powers of characterization in an anthology. A proper demonstration would demand the reading of a number of novels, most of them written during the last twenty years. What I have done is to take passages that try to present general aspects of the Canadian character, or that sketch in broad outlines what might be described as recognizable types. There has never been, so far as I know, either in literature or in life, a representative Canadian, although Frank Underhill argues that Mackenzie King is such a phenomenon. We have not had fictional characters recognizably Canadian in the sense that the characters of, say, Henry James, Sinclair Lewis, Willa Cather, Ernest Hemingway, and Saul Bellow are recognizably American. In our approach to definition we tend to be defensive and negative. We define ourselves by what we are not, and we see ourselves in relationship to types that have been more clearly delineated. Not sure of what our own foibles are, we delight in cataloguing those of others.

In the final passages of this section I shift from theoretical and typical to the concrete and specific. Here I draw upon the literary type that has traditionally given strong emphasis to characterization—the short story. (It is a type to which Canadian writers have made notable contributions.) The two stories present vivid people against an environment that is sharply realized. The general flavour is one of irony, not sharp and piercing, or harsh and sardonic, but relaxed, reflective, even gentle; one is left with the feeling that the incongruities in life lie close to both tears and laughter.

The fourth part is entitled *Politics*. The emphasis here is upon the process itself, since Canada is not transparently a political unit. Canadians have been more concerned about the mechanics than about the theory of politics. We have been too busy trying to determine the nature of our identity to indulge in ideological conflict. In consequence, political writing does not have a literary, much less a philosophical, flavour. Indeed, most writing and speaking on political subjects is of a humdrum nature, consisting either of extended inventories of material progress, or of windy rhetoric. But there are exceptions, and I have included two political speeches, each of which in its own way achieves a degree of literary excellence. (It would be a pity, at any rate, to exclude oratory, since the public speech constitutes the staple of the Canadian literary diet—the dutiful porridge of the national mind.) I have included an excerpt from Louis Riel's long speech in his own defence, because in his trial and execution politics brushed close to tragedy, and something of the pathos, if not the nobility, of tragedy infuses his words. Arthur Meighen, from whom I have taken my second selection, was of all our political figures the one most concerned with the nature and power of language. In this excerpt he is at his best, for he unites a concern for democratic responsibility with a closely argued and passionate exposition of a particular issue.

If the Canadian political scene has produced few from among its active participants who deserve a place in a literary anthology, it has inspired, particularly during this century, a group of shrewd and skilful commentators and critics. Indeed, the comment on the political life is far more lively than the political life itself. I should have liked to expand this part greatly in order to do justice to the work of this group.

The fifth part is entitled *The Critical and the Contemplative*, and consists of passages that deal with various aspects of the intellectual life—social philosophy, literature, the arts, education, and religion. If our political life has not been dominated by ideas, the same cannot be said of other areas. Canadians, indeed, have come arguing down through the years. The Canadian periodicals of the 19th century resounded to the major controversies on the continent in religion and science, and to a lesser extent in politics and sociology. In our century the influence of the serious periodical has waned, but its place has been taken by the universities from which in recent years have come a flow of books of a controversial nature. The scholars in universities have been joined by a group of lively journalists who have frequently found a congenial home in one of the major newspapers. Indeed, a good deal of the writing on subjects of intellectual interest is journalistic in nature—topical, argumentative, and unsystematic. Much of it is devoted to the probing of the Canadian soul or to attempts to account for the apparent lack of any soul at all. From time to time we are urged to abjure this national narcissism. But it is not likely that we ever shall. It is a subject in which we have an obsessive interest, and it is moreover a subject upon which only Canadians can speak with full authority. One can see this clearly if one compares Northrop Frye's concluding essay in the recent *Literary History of Canada* with Edmund Wilson's recent collection of essays about Canada. The great American critic reminds one of a four-masted schooner—a noble sight in full sail, but, alas, largely irrelevant to the issues of our age. Mr. Frye's essay reminds one of the most recent spacecraft, its parts beautifully and subtly fashioned, its antennae reaching out to receive and to record the music and the message of the spheres.

Canada has made one important contribution to general speculation, and that is in the area of communication. The two figures here are Harold Innis and Marshall McLuhan, the first coming to his subject by way of economic history, and the second by way of literary criticism. But our intellectual staple has been religion, a concern that manifests itself chiefly in our poets. Occasionally, as in the poetry of Pratt, they are sensitive to the Christian tradition, but the general tone is speculative and agnostic.

The various parts of this anthology are not conceived of as categorical and inflexible units. Occasionally the reader may well be initially puzzled by the placing of a passage in a particular place and wonder why it did not go elsewhere. But I have sought to achieve a sense of continuity so that the reader will be led on from one selection to another. The relationship between passages is often that of contrast and, indeed, opposition. We are a people not easily given to over-mastering national convictions. For every strong national view, it is not difficult to find one diametrically opposed to it.

By selecting poetry about subjects that have already appeared in the prose sections, I have tried to break down the barrier between poetry and prose. Poetry is not something arcane and remote. It is, in one sense, a technique of using words to achieve heightened effects. E. J. Pratt and Thomas Raddall, for instance, both deal with the subject of telegraphic communication at sea. The former uses rhyming verse; the latter prose, and to many it would be difficult to determine which of the two is the more effective. Sometimes a writer will express the same idea in both prose and poetry. Douglas LePan talks about the nature of the Canadian imagination in a piece of discursive prose, and deals with the same subject in his poem "A Country Without a Mythology".

This anthology, as the title indicates, is designed to provide a representation of the best Canadian writing in English. Occasionally I have included passages that have a purely documentary or historical interest and that could not be looked upon as literature by any definition. I have done this in order to show the ingredients that have gone into the making of the Canadian imagination.

In the making of this anthology I have read many new books and I have re-read many old ones. For the most part I have relied upon strong impressions gained during the happy years when my primary concern was the reading and teaching of English-Canadian literature. I have received help from many sources, particularly from colleagues who have given hints and suggestions. I am especially indebted to Frank Underhill, who sent me a long and fascinating bibliographical letter on Canadian writing about politics. I have received great assistance from my wife, who read many of the novels that have in recent years escaped me, and selected a number of passages that I used in this anthology. I am also grateful for her philosophical and cheerful attitude during a "holiday" that was in large part devoted to the preparation of this anthology.

Ultimately an anthology of any lasting worth must be writing that the anthologist selected for the pleasure it gave him long before he thought of being an anthologist. Most of the passages in this anthology gave me such pleasure, and I hope that they will now give pleasure to others.

C.T.B.

1

PLACES

HUGH MacLENNAN

The details of Halifax were dim in the fading light but the contours were clear and he had forgotten how good they were. The Great Glacier had once packed, scraped and riven this whole land; it had gouged out the harbour and left as a legacy three drumlins . . . the hill on which he stood and two islands in the harbour itself. Halifax covers the whole of an oval peninsula, and the Citadel is about in the centre of it. He could look south to the open Atlantic and see where the park at the end of the town thrusts its nose directly into the outer harbour. At the park the water divides, spreading around the town on either side; to the west the inlet is called the North West Arm, to the east it is called the Stream, and it is here that the docks and ocean terminals are built. The Stream bends with the swell of Halifax peninsula and runs inland a distance of four miles from the park to a deep strait at the northern end of town called the Narrows. This strait opens directly into Bedford Basin, a lake-like expanse which bulges around the back of the town to the north.

He followed the footpath and looked for familiar landmarks, walking around the moat until he had boxed the compass. From here even a landsman could see why the harbour had for a century and a half been a link in the chain of British sea power. It is barricaded against Atlantic groundswells by McNab's Island at the mouth of the outer harbour, and by the smaller bowl of George's Island at the entrance to the Stream. It was defended now against enemy battle squadrons by forts set on rocky promontories running over the horizon into the sea. It was fenced off from prowling submarines by a steel net hung on pontoons from McNab's to the mainland. This harbour is the reason for the town's existence; it is all that matters in Halifax, for the place periodically sleeps between great wars. There had been a good many years since Napoleon, but now it was awake again.

The forests to the far west and north were nothing but shadows under the sky at this time of day. Above the horizon rim the remaining light was a turmoil of rose and saffron and pallid green, the colours of blood and flowers and the sheen of sunlight on summer grass. As his eyes shifted from the dull floor of the distant sea to this shredding blaze of glory crowning the continent, he felt an unexpected wave of exultation mount in his mind. Merely to have been born on the western side of the ocean gave a man something for which the traditions of the Old World could never compensate.

This western land was his own country. He had forgotten how it was, but now he was back, and to be able to remain was worth risking everything.

After sunset the hilltop grew colder. The colours died quickly and as the landscape faded into darkness the street lights of the city came on. They made bluish pools at intervals along the narrow thoroughfares that fanned away from the roots of the hill, and all the way down to the waterfront the life of Halifax began to reveal itself in flashes. Barrington, Granville, and Hollis Streets, running north and south, were visible only at the intersections where the inclines plunging from the hill to the waterfront crossed them, and at these corners pedestrians could be seen moving back and forth, merged in irregular streams.

Children were playing a game with a whole block of a George Street slum for their playground. They darted in and out of his vision as they pursued each other in and out of doorways and back and forth across the street. Here and there in the withered grass along the slope of the Citadel the forms of men and girls lay huddled, scarcely moving; they clung together on the frozen ground in spite of the cold, sailors with only a night on shore and local girls with no better place to be.

Halifax seemed to have acquired a meaning since he had left it in 1914. Quietly, almost imperceptibly, everything had become harnessed to the war. Long ribbons of light crossed on the surface of the water from the new oil refinery on the far shore of the Stream, and they all found their focus in himself. Occasionally they were broken, as undiscernible craft moved through the harbour, and he suddenly realized that this familiar inlet had become one of the most vital stretches of water in the world. It still gleamed faintly in the dusk as its surface retained a residual glow of daylight. Ferryboats glided like beetles across it, fanning ruffled water in their wake. A freighter drifted inland with a motion so slight he had to watch a full minute before it was perceptible. Its only identification was riding lights; no one but the port authorities knew its home port or its destination. While he watched, its anchor ran out with a muted clatter to the bottom and its bow swung to the north.

Then the Stream became static. The smoke of Halifax lay like clouds about a mountain; the spire of St. Mary's Cathedral cut George's Island in two; the only moving object was the beam of the lighthouse on McNab's, circling like a turning eye out to sea, along the coast and into the harbour again.

Barometer Rising, New York, 1941

DONALD CREIGHTON

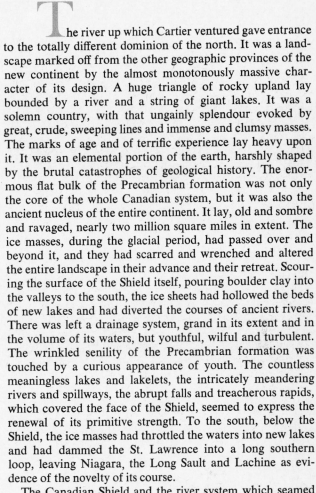

The river up which Cartier ventured gave entrance to the totally different dominion of the north. It was a landscape marked off from the other geographic provinces of the new continent by the almost monotonously massive character of its design. A huge triangle of rocky upland lay bounded by a river and a string of giant lakes. It was a solemn country, with that ungainly splendour evoked by great, crude, sweeping lines and immense and clumsy masses. The marks of age and of terrific experience lay heavy upon it. It was an elemental portion of the earth, harshly shaped by the brutal catastrophes of geological history. The enormous flat bulk of the Precambrian formation was not only the core of the whole Canadian system, but it was also the ancient nucleus of the entire continent. It lay, old and sombre and ravaged, nearly two million square miles in extent. The ice masses, during the glacial period, had passed over and beyond it, and they had scarred and wrenched and altered the entire landscape in their advance and their retreat. Scouring the surface of the Shield itself, pouring boulder clay into the valleys to the south, the ice sheets had hollowed the beds of new lakes and had diverted the courses of ancient rivers. There was left a drainage system, grand in its extent and in the volume of its waters, but youthful, wilful and turbulent. The wrinkled senility of the Precambrian formation was touched by a curious appearance of youth. The countless meaningless lakes and lakelets, the intricately meandering rivers and spillways, the abrupt falls and treacherous rapids, which covered the face of the Shield, seemed to express the renewal of its primitive strength. To the south, below the Shield, the ice masses had throttled the waters into new lakes and had dammed the St. Lawrence into a long southern loop, leaving Niagara, the Long Sault and Lachine as evidence of the novelty of its course.

The Canadian Shield and the river system which seamed and which encircled it were overwhelmingly the most important physical features of the area. They were the bone and the blood-tide of the northern economy. Rock and water complemented each other, fought each other's battles and forced each other's victories. The Shield itself, a huge lopsided triangle, whose northern points were Labrador and the Arctic east of the Mackenzie, occupied over one-half of the land area which was to become the Dominion of Canada. For the French and for their successors it was unescapable and domineering. It hugged the north shore of the St. Lawrence as the river issued from the continent. Westward, in the centre of the lowlands of the St. Lawrence, the good lands began to peter out a hundred miles north of Lake Ontario in the scarred, blank rock, thin soil sheet and towering evergreens peculiar to the Shield. Relentlessly it followed the north shore of Lakes Huron and Superior and at last struck north and west for the Arctic Ocean. Its long, flat, undeviating plateau effected the complete severance of the St. Lawrence lowlands from the western plains. In the east it helped, with the northern spurs of the Appalachians, to cut off Acadia from Quebec. Settlement starved and shrivelled on the Shield; it offered a sullen inhospitality to those occupations which were traditional in western Europe and which had been transferred by the first immigrants to the Atlantic seaboard of North America. But from the beginning it exercised an imperious domination over the northerners, for

". . . from the river there rose, like an exhaltation, the dream of western commercial empire."

though it was a harsh and an exacting country, it offered lavish prizes to the restless, the ambitious and the daring. It was an area of staples, creating simple trades and undiversified extractive industries; and its furs, its forests and its minerals were to attract three great assaulting waves of northerners. Fur was the first great staple of the north. And with the fur trade, the Precambrian formation began its long career in the Canadian economy as a primary, instead of as a subsidiary, economic region. It was upon these ancient rocks that the central emphasis of the Canadian system was placed at first, and the initial importance of the Shield is of deep significance in the history of the economy of the north.

To the south lay the lowlands of the St. Lawrence. Here the intense winters of the Precambrian formation were softened and the hot, bright summers flamed more slowly out of long springtimes and faded gradually into reluctant autumns. North of the lakes, the lowlands stretched from Quebec city to Georgian Bay—a narrow but slowly broadening band of fertility, crowded a little oppressively by the sombre masses of the Shield. South and west, beyond the river and the lakes, they lapsed easily into the central lowlands of the continent and the basin of the Mississippi. In the centre of this rich region lay that immense organization of waters which issued from the continent by the river of Canada; and this drainage system, driving seaward in a great, proud arc from Lake Superior to the city of Quebec, was the fact of all facts in the history of the northern half of the continent. It commanded an imperial domain. Westward, its acquisitive fingers groped into the territory of the plains. Aggressively it entrenched upon the dominion of the Mississippi. It grasped the Shield, reached southward into the valley of the Hudson and at last rolled massively seaward between sombre approaches which curved away southward into the Maritimes and rose northeastward past Quebec and Labrador to Newfoundland.

It was the one great river which led from the eastern shore into the heart of the continent. It possessed a geographical monopoly; and it shouted its uniqueness to adventurers. The river meant mobility and distance; it invited journeyings; it promised immense expanses, unfolding, flowing away into remote and changing horizons. The whole west, with all its riches, was the dominion of the river. To the unfettered and ambitious, it offered a pathway to the central mysteries of the continent. The river meant movement, transport, a ceaseless passage west and east, the long procession of river-craft —canoes, *bateaux*, timber rafts and steamboats—which followed each other into history. It seemed the destined pathway of North American trade; and from the river there rose, like an exhalation, the dream of western commercial empire. The river was to be the basis of a great transportation system by which the manufactures of the old world could be exchanged for the staple products of the new. This was the faith of successive generations of northerners. The dream of the commercial empire of the St. Lawrence runs like an obsession through the whole of Canadian history; and men followed each other through life, planning and toiling to achieve it. The river was not only a great actuality: it was the central truth of a religion. Men lived by it, at once consoled and inspired by its promises, its whispered suggestions, and its shouted commands; and it was a force in history, not merely because of its accomplishments, but because of its shining, ever-receding possibilities.

For something stood between the design and its fulfilment. There was, in the very geography of the region itself, a root defect, a fundamental weakness, which foreshadowed enormous difficulties, even though it did not pre-determine defeat. In the centre, by Lake Ontario and the lower reaches of the river, the drive of the great waterway was unquestioned and peremptory. But this power was not indefinitely transmissible, and the pull of a system stretching over two thousand miles was at long last relaxed and weakened. The outer defences of the St. Lawrence contradicted its inward solidity; its boundaries were not bold and definite, but a smudged faint tracery. Between the valley of the St. Lawrence on the one hand and the valleys of Hudson Bay, the Mississippi and the Hudson river on the other, the separating heights of land were low and facile; and over these perfunctory defences invasions might pass as easily as sorties. The river's continuity was broken at Niagara: it stumbled and faltered at the Cascades, the Cedars and Lachine. As it drove east and north past Quebec and into its immense estuary, the river was caught, its influence narrowed and focused by the uplands of the Shield to the north and the rolling highlands of the Appalachians below. There were breaks and obstacles; and over both its seaward approaches and its continental extremities the hold of the river closed and again relaxed, uncertainly and unconvincingly. Yet for all its inward contradictions and its outward weakness, the river was a unit, and its central entrance was dominated by the rock of Quebec and the island of Montreal.

The Commercial Empire of the St. Lawrence, 1760-1850, Toronto, 1937

ETHEL WILSON

The forests bordered the railway tracks and ran away up the hills. The forests were more brilliant in colour than any that the travellers had ever imagined. Sunlight was reflected from the gold and flame of each leaf of each tree. The forests seemed to blaze with harmless fire. The travellers' vision was intent on the rose, flame, and yellow that shot towards them, passed them, and fell behind them, remaining stationary and identifiable only on the distant hills; they could not see and did not know that away towards the north (and southwards too) beyond and beyond the northern horizon there was a still world of red, rose, and yellow trees, and they did not think that in a few weeks these forest branches would be thin and bare. And because Time was bounded by yesterday, today, and tomorrow as the train slid and rocked along paralleling Time, they could not know that, decades later, a young grandson of the Grandmother's (not yet imagined, not yet born) would be a bush pilot and would fly in a slow, rather rackety plane above such forests. He would fly above the brilliant woods of the Maritime Provinces, and of Quebec, and of Ontario, and would see below him a flaming earth of boundless maple trees, coloured the tender warm rose and fabulous crimson of a carpet of Ispahan; and he would see small and great rivers shining like steel, widely curving through the bright trees; and he would look down on lonely lakes, great and small, shining like mercury, lying as mirrors to the clouds and the blue sky, and reflecting the rose and flame of the maple woods.

"He would fly above the brilliant woods . . . and see below him a flaming earth of boundless maple trees. . . ."

The grandson would see all this in a newly discovered dimension as old as Time; yet it would be the same brilliance which they now saw with amazement, and which had transformed autumnal Canadian forests for centuries unknown.

The Innocent Traveller, Toronto, 1949

HUGH MacLENNAN

Northwest of Montreal, through a valley always in sight of the low mountains of the Laurentian Shield, the Ottawa River flows out of Protestant Ontario into Catholic Quebec. It comes down broad and ale-coloured and joins the St. Lawrence, the two streams embrace the pan of Montreal Island, the Ottawa merges and loses itself, and the mainstream moves northeastward a thousand miles to the sea.

Nowhere has nature wasted herself as she has here. There is enough water in the St. Lawrence alone to irrigate half of Europe, but the river pours right out of the continent into the sea. No amount of water can irrigate stones, and most of Quebec is solid rock. It is as though millions of years back in geologic time a sword had been plunged through the rock from the Atlantic to the Great Lakes and savagely wrenched out again, and the pure water of the continental reservoir, unmuddied and almost useless to farmers, drains untouchably away. In summer the cloud packs pass over it in soft, cumulus, pacific towers, endlessly forming and dissolving to make a welter of movement about the sun. In winter when there is no storm the sky is generally empty, blue and glittering over the ice and snow, and the sun stares out of it like a cyclops' eye.

All the narrow plain between the St. Lawrence and the hills is worked hard. From the Ontario border down to the beginning of the estuary, the farmland runs in two delicate bands along the shores, with roads like a pair of village main streets a thousand miles long, each parallel to the river. All the good land was broken long ago, occupied and divided among seigneurs and their sons, and then among tenants and their sons. Bleak wooden fences separate each strip of farm from its neighbour, running straight as rulers set at right angles to the river to form long narrow rectangles pointing inland. The ploughed land looks like the course of a gigantic and empty steeplechase where all motion has been frozen. Every inch of it is measured, and brooded over by notaries, and blessed by priests.

You can look north across the plain from the river and see the farms between their fences tilting towards the forest, and beyond them the line of trees crawling shaggily up the slope of the hills. The forest crosses the watershed into an evergreen bush that spreads far to the north, lake-dotted and mostly unknown, until it reaches the tundra. The tundra goes to the lower straits of the Arctic Ocean. Nothing lives on it but a few prospectors and hard-rock miners and Mounted Policemen and animals and the flies that brood over the barrens in summer like haze. Winters make it a universe of snow with a terrible wind keening over it, and beyond its horizons the northern lights flare into walls of shifting electric colours that crack and roar like the gods of a dead planet talking to each other out of the dark.

But down in the angle at Montreal, on the island about which the two rivers join, there is little of this sense of new and endless space. Two old races and religions meet here and live their separate legends, side by side. If this sprawling half-continent has a heart, here it is. Its pulse throbs out along the rivers and railroads; slow, reluctant and rarely simple, a double beat, a self-moved reciprocation.

Two Solitudes, New York, 1945

MORDECAI RICHLER

The ghetto of Montreal has no real walls and no true dimensions. The walls are the habit of atavism and the dimensions are an illusion. But the ghetto exists all the same. The fathers say: "I work like this so it'll be better for the kids." A few of the fathers, the dissenters, do not crowd their days with work. They drink instead. But in the end it amounts to the same thing: in the end, work, drink, or what have you, they are all trying to fill in the void.

Most of the Jews who live at the diminishing end of the ghetto, on streets named St. Urbain, St. Dominic, Rachel, and City Hall, work in textile or garment factories. Some are orthodox, others are communist. But all of them do their buying and their praying and their agitating and most of their sinning on St. Lawrence Boulevard, which is the aorta of the ghetto, reaching out in one direction towards Mount Royal, and past that (where it is no longer the ghetto) into the financial district and the factory slums, coming to a hard stop at the waterfront. In the other direction, northwards, St. Lawrence Boulevard approaches the fields at the city limits; where there is a rumour of grass and sun and quick spurious lovemaking.

All day long St. Lawrence Boulevard, or Main Street, is a frenzy of poor Jews, who gather there to buy groceries, furniture, clothing and meat. Most walls are plastered with fraying election bills, in Yiddish, French and English. The street reeks of garlic and quarrels and bill collectors: orange crates, stuffed full with garbage and decaying fruit, are piled slipshod in most alleys. Swift children gobble pilfered plums, slower cats prowl the fish market. After the water truck has passed, the odd dead rat can be seen floating down the gutter followed fast by rotten apples, cigar butts, chunks of horse manure and a terrifying zigzag of flies. Few stores go in for posh window displays. Instead, their windows are jammed full and pasted up with streamers that say ALL GOODS REDUCED or EVERYTHING MUST GO.

Every night St. Lawrence Boulevard is lit up like a neon cake and used-up men stumble out of a hundred different flophouses to mix with rabbinical students and pimps and Trotskyites and poolroom sharks. Hair tonic and water is consumed in back alleys. Swank whores sally at you out of the promised jubilee of all the penny arcades. Crap games flourish under lamp posts. You can take Rita the Polack up to the Liberty Rooms or you can listen to Panofsky speak on Tim Buck and The Worker. You can catch Bubbles Dawson doing her strip at the Roxie Follies. You can study Talmud at the B'nai Jacob Yeshiva, or you can look over the girls at the AZA Stag or Drag.

Conditions improve on the five streets between St. Lawrence Boulevard and Park Avenue. Most of the Jews who live on these streets market what is cut or pressed by their relations below St. Lawrence Boulevard. Others, the aspiring, own haberdashery stores, junk yards and basement zipper factories.

The employer and professional Jews own their own du-plexes in Outremont, a mild residential area which begins above Park Avenue. They belong to the Freemasons, or, if they can't get into that organization, to the Knights of Pythias. Their sons study at McGill, where they are Zionists and opposed to anti-semitic fraternities. They shop on St. Lawrence Boulevard, where the Jews speak quaintly like the heroes of nightclub jokes.

In the spring of 1952 the B'nai B'rith published a report saying that anti-semitism was on the decline in Canada and that the Jews joined with the great prime minister of this great country in the great fight against communism. The uranium market boomed. Dr. S. I. Katz, OBE, told the Cana-dian Club that "The Jewish beavers of this land will help make the Maple Leaf a symbol of greatness." But the spring passed fast. Those balmy days which had accounted for the melting of the snows turned longer and more hard. The sun swelled in the sky and a stillness gripped the ghetto. When the heat was but two days old everyone seemed to have for-gotten that there had ever been a time of no heat. This was partly sham. For, secretively, the people of the ghetto gloated over every darkening cloud. They supposed that to-morrow there would be rain, and if not tomorrow then at least the day after that. But the sky was a fever and there was no saying how long a day would last or what shape the heat would assume by night. There were the usual heat rumours about old men going crazy and women swooning in the streets and babies being born prematurely. When the rains came the children danced in the streets clad only in their underwear and the old men sipped lemon tea on their balconies and told tales about the pogroms of the czar. But the rains didn't amount to much. After the rains there was always the heat again. The flies returned, the old men re-treated to their beds, and all the missing odours of the heat reappeared with a new intensity.

The heat first appeared in June when it was still too soon to send the family up north for the summer. But, just the same, things were not too bad. Not too bad until the week-ends came along. The weekends were hell. All week long you could at least work but when the weekends came along there was nothing to do. You were on your own. You were free, so to speak.

So on Saturday afternoons the well-to-do Jews walked up and down Decarie Boulevard, which was their street. A street of sumptuous supermarkets and banks built of granite, an aquarium in the lobby of the Snowdon Theatre, a syna-gogue with a soundproof auditorium and a rabbi as modern and quick as the Miss Snowdon restaurant, neon drugstores for all your needs and delicatessens rich in chromium plat-ing. Buick convertibles and Cadillacs parked on both sides: a street without a past. Almost as if these Jews, who had prospered, craved for many lights. Wishing away their past and the dark. Almost as if these Jews, who had prospered, regretted only the solemn sky, which was beyond their reach. Sunny by day, and by night—star-filled: a swirl of asking eyes spying down on them. Watching. Poking fun at their ephemeral lights.

The neither rich nor poor Jews walked up and down Park Avenue—a few of the nervy ones attempting Decarie Boule-vard. The poor and the elderly kept to St. Lawrence Boule-vard. Each street had its own technique of walking, a tech-nique so finely developed that you could always tell a man off his own street.

"Each street had its own technique of walking. . . ."

The Decarie Boulevard Jews walked like prosperity, grinning a flabby grin which said money in the bank. Notaries, lawyers, businessmen, doctors. They wore their wives like signposts of their success and dressed them accordingly. The children were big and little proofs, depending on the size of their achievements.

"Lou, meet the boy. Sheldon. He just won a scholarship to McGill."

"Don't say eh? Mm. Hey, I hear talk you're gonna expand the factory. That increases your risk, Jack. You come round first thing Monday morning and I'll fix you like a friend. For your own good. You owe it to your family to protect yourself."

The wives exchanged small flatteries.

"Jack's going to buy a Cadillac. *You* try to stop him."

"Me, I don't live for show. Lou doubled his life insurance instead of buying a new car this year. He says you can never tell. . . ."

Park Avenue was different. It had once been to the prospering what Decarie Boulevard was to them now. But the prospering had built a more affluent street for themselves to walk on, a bigger proof, where, twenty years hence, they would again feel the inadequacy of the neon, the need to push on and to flee the past and install brighter lights again. Meanwhile, the new ones, the intruding *greeners*, were beginning to move in around Park Avenue. Here, they mixed with the middling Jews. Knowing the right people was important. The aspiring walked without certainty, pompous and ingratiating by turns.

On St. Lawrence Boulevard the Jews, many of them bearded, walked with their heads bent and their hands clasped behind their backs. They walked looking down at the pavement or up at the sky, seldom straight ahead.

Son of a Smaller Hero, London, 1955

To understand what a fine place Montreal is when spring is coming you must know the winters that come first. Chill grey mornings; sun bright in the cold noon sky but giving off no heat to speak of; skies darkening again early in the afternoon; long frosty nights with that window-banging wind whipping in burning hard from the north, pushing people before it like paper, making dunes and ridges that hurt the eye to look at on the mountain snows, burning children's cheeks red and cutting like a knife across flat frozen ponds. Old men blowing on their wrinkled hands, boys with blue lips and women with running noses all huddled up and knocking their feet together in the bitter cold waiting for liquor commissions to open and banks to shut, late dates, streetcars. . . .

So when the first rumours of thaw reach the city everybody is glad. That first rumour, coming towards the end of February, is usually hidden away in the back pages of the newspapers. It says that two government icebreakers, the *d'Iberville* and the *Ernest Lapointe*, have started poking their way down the frozen St. Lawrence towards Montreal. That's a while before the NHL hockey playoffs, and most people on the streetcars are talking about how the players are moving slow because of the heat. The resorts up north stop advertising themselves as the St. Moritz or Davos of Canada: they begin to talk of the sun, their pamphlets saying how so many

happily married couples first fell on their beaches. That first thaw is a glory. The big snow heaps on Fletcher's Field and a whole winter's caboodle of snowmen begin to shrivel and shrink away. Giant sweepers roar up and down the streets wiping a winter's precautionary sands off the pavement. You can make out chunks of yellow grass here and there like exposed flesh under the shrinking slush that still sticks to the flanks of Mount Royal. Occasionally it snows: but noon comes and all the gutters are gurgling again. There is a green, impolite smell to the streets.

With the first thaw the change takes hold: there is a difference to everything, the difference between a clenched fist and an open hand. The kids get out on their roller-skates and make most side-streets a hazard. Belmont Park opens, so do the race tracks. Ships steam into port from Belfast and Le Havre and Hamburg and Liverpool and Archangel and Port-of-Spain. NDG organizes softball teams, the ladies of Westmount plan their flower-shows, and the Jr. Chamber of Commerce sets aside one week as Traffic Safety Week. The man who reviews books for the *Star* will say that spring is here but J. P. Sartre is without that traditional Gallic charm, and young writers aren't cheerful enough. But best of all is St. Catherine Street on an April evening. Watch the girls, eh, their hair full of wind, as they go strolling past in their cotton print dresses. Men, sporting smart suits and spiffy ties, waving enticingly at them. See the American tourists having a whale of a time frantically, a Kodak strapped to one arm and a lulu of a wife to the other. . . . Kids wandering in and out of the crowds yelling rude things at girls older than themselves. . . . Sport fans clustering at corners waiting for the *Gazette* to appear. . . .

In parks, playgrounds, and on Mount Royal, tattered men with leather faces loll on benches, their faces upturned to the sun. Maiden aunts hopeful again after a long winter's withering knit near to baby carriages which hold the children of others. Come noon, lovers freed from the factory sprawl on the green mountainside while the children tease and the tattered men watch laconically and the maiden aunts knit near to baby carriages that hold the children of others.

Everybody is full.

Son of a Smaller Hero, London, 1955

WILLIAM WEINTRAUB

The bus sped through the Quebec countryside, with its rich architectural variety—the austere classicism of buildings covered in tar paper, the romantic antiquity of unpainted wood, the baroque splendour of stucco houses with thousands of tiny mirrors set into their walls to glint in the sun.

Enlivening the bleak snowscape were the purple neons of gas stations and funeral parlours and, amid majestic groves of pine, there were elfin touches, like a war-surplus Liberator bomber that was now a hot-dog stand. *Le Roi des Chiens Chauds* said the lettering on the silvery fuselage, where the Air Force roundels had been replaced by new insignia—enormous, juicy frankfurters oozing yellow mustard and green relish.

Why Rock the Boat, Boston, 1961

"... the retreat of Montreal's aspiring middle class, ... prone to all the faults and virtues of that group."

MORDECAI RICHLER

Soon after St. Jerome, a prosperous French-Canadian mill town with a tall grey church, the horizon widens and the highway begins to rise, rise and dip, rise again from the valley and into higher hills. Sloping easily on all sides are the slow, pine-rumpled hills. Old and shrivelled cliffs appear like bruised bones here and there, and in the valleys below, the fertile fields are yellow and green and brown. There is the occasional unpainted barn or silo—blackened by the wind and the rain—rising out of the landscape as natural as rocks. Billboards, more modern, stick out of the earth incongruously. The slim and muddy river, sheltered from the sun by birch and bush, winds northwards drowsily but insistent between the still hills. Cottages—a mess strewn on a hilltop or a pile of them spilled sloppily into a valley— appear every ten miles or so. From time to time, as the highway climbs higher north, some ambitious cliff or hill pokes into the soft underbelly of a low grey cloud. These higher hills, sometimes called mountains, are often ribbed by ski-

tows, trails, and the occasional derelict jump. Bears, the stray deer or two, are often rumoured in these parts, but, like the pretty girls who beckon from the travel brochures, they are seldom seen.

About forty-five miles north of Montreal a side-road turns up off into Ste Adèle en Haut. It's about three miles to the lake. Ste Adèle is the retreat of Montreal's aspiring middle class, and, as a resort town, is prone to all the faults and virtues of that group. The cottages are clean but prosaic: no Jews are wanted, but, on the other hand, they are dealt with diplomatically. The French-Canadians tolerate the Presbyterians from the city because they have brought prosperity to their village, and the Presbyterians find that the French-Canadians add spice to their holiday: they accept their haughtiness as philosophically as rain on Sundays. Few on either side are bilingual.

Son of a Smaller Hero, London, 1955

East of Kingston the islands—more than eleven hundred of them—begin to sprout in and all around the ship channel, choking and diverting the immense river for forty amazing miles, eastwards past Gananoque, almost down to Stoverville. But a third of the continent leans pushing behind the lakes and the river, the pulse, circulation, artery, and heart, all in one flowing geographical fact, of half the North Americans, the flow we live by all that long way from Minnesota to the Gulf.

St. Lawrence's Gulf, martyr roasted on a gridiron, Breton saint, legend imported by the French to name the life's current of a hundred million industrious shore-dwellers, drinking the water, lighting their houses by it, floating on it in numberless craft. "Seas of Sweet Water," the Indians called the lakes, and to the east the marvellous St. Lawrence with the weight of the American Northeast inclining to the Gulf.

So the channel must be cut, though the islands press against the current in resistance, cut sometimes through needles' eyes and wearing deep, deep, through solid pressed ancient rock a hundred and fifty feet down, two hundred, icy cold ten feet below the surface. A holidaying swimmer floats up half-frozen in the narrow channel from a shallow dive, swept forty feet downstream in three seconds by the drive of the current, lucky to catch an exposed tree-root at the edge of a corroded island and haul himself ashore, the water sliding and driving beneath him two hundred feet down to the anonymous rock.

Try to swim upstream, brother, at Flowerlea! And feel yourself carried backwards through your best stroke, feel yourself whipped out of yourself as the river pulls at your thighs, hauling you down away eastwards as though you were falling helpless down a chute. Then grab at the skeletal roots, hang on, swing in the water and ride an eddy ashore! Fight the weight of eleven states and half of Canada, something to think about swinging on your sodden shredded branching root while fifty feet away—not an inch more—a ship seven hundred and fifty feet long glides ghostly past, soundless, what a thing to meet on a holiday beach! Not a thing to swim too close to, glistening black walls rising out of the water above you like an apartment building—SCOTT MISENER on the bows and the name of the line reading backwards to the stern in letters twice your height, swimmer, and not a sound from the ship, the current moving the ship as easily as it moves you. A deckhand leans incuriously at the rail, lifting a friendly hand, and is gone, whirled away eastwards while he lowers his arm.

SCOTT MISENER, ERIKA HAMBURG, TOSUI MARU, BRISTOL CITY, MORMACGLEN—they hail from everywhere, upper lakers, tankers, the few remaining canallers, ocean-going freighters built by thrifty Danes for the lakes trade, drawing twenty-seven feet precisely, up and down all day and all night with their myriads of sirens sounding the whole range of the tempered scale. The shipmaster confers anxiously with his pilot through the forty perilous miles, threading needle after needle. At Flowerlea the channel is so narrow the summer cottagers can lean over and assess the deckhands' breakfast bacon. In the fall the last of the cottagers sit around their barbecue pits with a liner in the front yard,

the shipmaster pacing about above them, cursing them and their hot-dogs, the handiest things to curse. He is afraid of the Flowerlea channel, so narrow, and of the weight of water astern hurrying him along, the navigation season waning and his insurance rate about to jump skyhigh if he doesn't clear the locks by the appointed day.

Late last autumn a shipmaster drove aground off Stoverville at the end of the season; he lost the closing date at the locks and passed the winter iced into the river with a ruined cargo. Each day the sailors walked to Stoverville over the three feet of ice, but the captain, a ruined man, brooded in solitary humiliation all winter in his cabin. He was never seen in Stoverville, although hysterical cables addressed to him arrived daily from Oslo.

He was unlucky, mistrusted his pilot, didn't know the river, hated it, and the river ruined him. He missed all the signs, the waning of the islands, the widening of the channel, the three trees—tamaracks with fifty feet of bare trunk and perky coronas on top—that stand on the promontory west of Stoverville. Making his move to starboard towards the New York shore minutes too late, he felt the current drive his bows so deep into the river bottom he knew he'd never haul her off. He stared at the three tamaracks all winter, counting them and counting them and there were never more than three. This summer, in Oslo, he killed himself.

The tamaracks mark the end of the islands, the beginning of the river's free run from Stoverville to the Atlantic, nothing in the way but the mammoth new locks, then Montreal, Quebec, wider and wider until you can't see across, at last the sleety Gulf. But at Stoverville the river's freedom is a newborn thing, the mass of water has just begun to run, eroding, finding the fastest way down. At Stoverville it's hardly two miles across.

Over there on the New York shore are the old resort towns, fading now, the gingerbread hotels coming down, their gilt furnishings sold off. Now and then a welterweight contender trains here and sometimes a powerboat regatta invites the curious. But the real tourist money goes to Europe or Montego Bay and the old millionaires, who found their way upstate in the seventies from Saratoga, are dead and gone. Between Watertown and Plattsburgh, back a few miles from the river, there's nothing. An Army camp, a Nike site, trees and woods and dunes and the snow belt. And that's it.

On the Canadian side there's Highway Number Two, the worst main highway in the world, with the small river towns dotted along it—Kingston, Gananoque, Stoverville, Prescott—dreaming their dreams dating from the eighteen-thirties of a prosperity which never came. Yet they sleep there along the shore waiting for things to pick up when the hundred and fifty years' slack season shall be over, an occasional coalboat putting in and water-buses running thrice-daily tours of the islands up to the bridge and back.

Twenty miles north of the riverfront strip the towns begin to shrink in size—Tincap, Newboro, Athens; the farms are scrubbier and smaller and hillier. You still see television aerials but now the rocks begin to stick up through the thin topsoil and you are into the Laurentian Shield with a rocky uninterrupted thousand miles clear to James Bay of round old rock, polished by the last Ice Age. St. Lawrence again but this time choking off life, not conferring it. And from this hinterland, from the little towns like Athens, people have been moving back down to the shore for sixty years, as soon as they broke their first ploughshares on the intractable rock humping up out of the hill-sides. They come back to

Stoverville and cherish their disappointments, the growth of their numbers limited by their situation between the river and the rock, the same smooth incredibly ancient rock which beds the river. Life and power flowing beside them and old impregnable rock, out of which nothing can be forced to grow, above them northerly, so they come back one by one into Stoverville from Athens and the other little towns, and here they fashion their lamentations.

"Three Halves of a House" in *Flying a Red Kite*, Toronto, 1962

ETHEL WILSON

The train ran on and the countryside ran to meet them and was left behind. The comfortable farms and broad meadows of Ontario, which now they saw, pleased the Grandmother. She understood them and the human toil and planning and thrift which had given them their prosperous dignity. They had a look of home. Here were elms. Here were sheep and cattle. Here was lazy smoke rising from chimneys of white farms. The sheep grazed in an international manner. They did not seem to know or care that they were Canadian sheep and should perhaps behave differently in a characteristic way, like the bison. They might indeed have been sheep of Staffordshire. Neither were the cows different from English beasts in their behaviour, the dear familiar cows. And the horses gossiped silently together as they did in the fields of England, communing secretly head to head through the soft intimate skin of their noses as the train fled past them.

The Innocent Traveller, Toronto, 1949

MAZO DE LA ROCHE

Philip Whiteoak bought from the Government a thousand acres of rich land, traversed by a deep ravine through which ran a stream lively with speckled trout. Some of the land was cleared, but the greater part presented the virgin grandeur of the primeval forest. Tall, unbelievably dense pines, hemlocks, spruces, balsams, with a mingling of oak, ironwood, and elm, made a sanctuary for countless song birds, wood pigeons, partridges, and quail. Rabbits, foxes, and hedgehogs abounded. The edge of the ravine was crowned by slender silver birches, its banks by cedars and sumachs, and along the brink of the stream was a wild, sweet-smelling tangle that was the home of water rats, minks, raccoons, and blue herons.

Labour was cheap. A small army of men was employed to make the semblance of an English park in the forest, and to build a house that should overshadow all others in the county. When completed, decorated, and furnished, it was the wonder of the countryside. It was a square house of dark red brick, with a wide stone porch, a deep basement where the kitchens and servants' quarters were situated, an immense drawing-room, a library (called so, but more properly a sitting-room, since few books lived there), a dining-room, and a bedroom on the ground floor; and six large bedrooms on the floor above, topped by a long, low attic divided into two bedrooms. The wainscoting and doors were of walnut. From five fireplaces the smoke ascended through picturesque chimneys that rose among the treetops.

In a burst of feeling, Philip and Adeline named the place Jalna, after the military station where they had first met. Everyone agreed that it was a pretty name, and Jalna became a place for gaiety. An atmosphere of impregnable well-being grew up around it. Under their clustering chimneys, in the midst of their unpretentious park, with its short, curving drive, with all their thousand acres spread like a green mantle around them, the Whiteoaks were as happy as the sons of man can be. They felt themselves cut off definitely from the mother country, though they sent their children to England to be educated.

Jalna looked very mellow in the golden sunlight, draped in its mantle of reddening Virginia creeper and surrounded by freshly clipped lawns. One of Wake's rabbits was hopping about, and Renny's two clumber spaniels were stretched on the steps. A pear tree near the house had dropped its fruit in the grass, where it lay richly yellow, giving to the eyes of a town dweller an air of negligent well-being to the scene. Alayne thought that Jalna had something of the appearance of an old manorial farmhouse, set among its lawns and orchards. The spaniels lazily beat their plumed tails on the step, too indolent to rise.

It was warm enough to have tea on the lawn, Meg announced, and when she and Alayne returned from their tour of the mass of overgrown lilacs, syringas, and guelder-rose trees that was called "the shrubbery", and the sleepy kitchen garden where the rows of cabbages and celery and rank bed of parsley were flanked by scarlet sage and heavy-headed dahlias, they found that Rags had arranged the tea-things on the wicker table. Some of the family were already disposed about it in deck-chairs or on the grass, according to their years.

Alayne's eyes missed no detail of the scene before her: the emerald-green lying in rich shadow, while the upper portions of the surrounding trees were bathed in lambent sunshine which so intensified their varying autumn hues that they had the unreal splendour of colours seen under water. Near the tea-table Grandmother dozed in her purple velvet tea-gown. Nicholas was stretched, half recumbent, playing idly with the ears of Nip, whose pointed muzzle was twitching expectantly toward the plates of cakes; Ernest stood courteously by his chair; on the grass sprawled bare-kneed Wake with a pair of rabbits, and bony long-limbed Finch, whom she now saw for the first time. Eden, Piers, and Renny did not appear, but before the second pot of tea was emptied young Pheasant slipped into the scene, carrying a branch of scarlet maple leaves, which she laid across the knee of Nicholas.

Jalna, Boston, 1927

21

". . . the repetition of a single house,

VINCENT MASSEY

Toronto, where I was born in 1887, was in my early years a small, quiet, coherent town; it was far from today's shapeless city, with its pulsating, insistent activity. Then, as now, it escaped the guidance of the planner. Motor-cars had, of course, not yet made their appearance, and there were countless horses. In the older parts of Toronto, known as "residential", you can still see, behind many of the houses, buildings that were at one time stables, and later were converted into flats. As a boy I could hear, after I was tucked in bed, the romantic sound of trotting horses on the pavement and I knew that there must be a special party that night, probably a ball at Government House, round which the social life of the city revolved. I could imagine a scene of gaiety still far beyond my years. The Lieutenant-Governor in those days had little concern with the province outside Toronto, and there was a preferred list of those who had the entrée to Government House, which then stood in pleasant grounds on King Street. There were four buildings on this corner—Government House itself, Upper Canada College, a church, and a saloon (to use the venerable term); a pale little joke of the time was that the four buildings represented legislation, education, salvation and damnation.

The winter climate has not changed, although our approach to it has. In those days there was no snow removal; runners took the place of wheels on all vehicles. Everyone had sleighs of one sort or another. Loads of hay on sledges, coming from farms to stables in the city, offered good sport to boys and girls who clambered aboard them and stole rides. Men so inclined indulged in racing on Sunday afternoons between trotting horses drawing light cutters. Mounted policemen made a half-hearted effort to stop this form of

sport, possibly because of its danger to pedestrians, but particularly because of the desecration of the Sabbath. The city policemen wore black Persian lamb caps of an attractive cut; their uniforms were not yet defaced by garish shoulder badges in an alien tradition. We went to school in moccasins, wearing on our heads knitted tuques. On Saturday afternoons a driving club had its meet at "The Guns" in Queen's Park, and a long line of cutters and sleighs of all sorts, some drawn by tandems, wound its way through the city to the pleasant chime of sleigh-bells on the horses. Winter brought many pleasures. New Year's Day, under the prevailing Scottish influence, was a festival of importance. Those of us who were old enough would hire sleighs and call on the young ladies of our acquaintance. Mamma was always in the drawing-room; tea was probably the best we could hope for. Our aim was to accomplish as many calls as possible, and the climax was reached at Government House where there was always something stronger than tea.

Sunday sixty years ago was a sombre day. Paterfamilias, in top hat and frock coat, with his domestic brood, found his way to one or other of the many churches (as many as there were saloons, it was said)—generally on foot, because for long no street-cars ran on Sunday. The sidewalks, for the most part, were made of boards. The streets were generally paved with wooden blocks, sections of logs, with a persistent inequality of surface. Red brick was the prevailing material for buildings. Electricity was far from universal. Our house, like many, was lit by gas. I can remember my father generating current by rubbing his shoes on the carpet and lighting the jet by touching the burner with his finger and creating a spark. The streets in those days were rich in trees not yet sacrificed to the demands of the motorist, the traffic engineer, or the hydro-electrician. Their loss has made Toronto streets in our subtropical summer hotter than they need be. They were always hot; one way of cooling off in the evening used to be to ride on an open street-car. I remember the

even if bizarre in design, on a street of limited length can give pleasure."

circular run on the four streets which constituted the "belt line" through which we passed (for a single fare) at an unbelievable speed. Motor-cars began to appear as a startling innovation while I was still at school; ours was among the first. Nowhere in Toronto were you far from open country. I could reach it on foot from my father's house on Jarvis Street in a few minutes. The country meant much to us, especially on holidays. Of these, the twenty-fourth of May was the entrance-gate to spring. It had the aroma of tradition. It brought the excitement of fireworks. No one today seems to know its meaning any more.

What's Past is Prologue, Toronto, 1963

ERIC ARTHUR

Repetition of a dwelling or a commercial unit on a street of "infinite" length like Yonge Street would be boring to a degree, but the repetition of a single house, even if bizarre in design, on a street of limited length can give pleasure. This is especially true where the vista is terminated by a building, or what is all too rare in modern Toronto, where the ultimate in enclosure is achieved by a square or a cul-de-sac. We still have streets where the Victorian rhythm of bay windows, whimsical porches and fretted gables seen through elms or flowering chestnuts can give real aesthetic enjoyment, an enjoyment that can never be evoked in the dreary lines of strawberry boxes in our newer subdivisions, or in the serried ranks of ranch houses in the more salubrious areas developed for the well-to-do.

Toronto: No Mean City, Toronto, 1964

JAMES SINCLAIR ROSS

We walked as far as the last grain elevator again, and then sat down on the sheltered side and watched a freight train shunting up and down the yard. A man appeared with a lantern, walking like a pair of legs without a trunk. The headlight for a moment swung on him and made him whole, swung off and left him walking cut in two. The locomotive hissed out clouds of steam that reddened every time the fireman stoked. It started backing up presently, and the dead, clugging sound of car on car ran through the night like a mile of falling dominoes. El Greco all the while sat motionless, his muzzle in my lap. The drizzle thickened till the sound of it on the high expanse of elevator wall was like a great rushing wind.

Then all assembled, the train pulled slowly past us. There seemed something mysterious and important in the gradual, steady quickening of the wheels. It was like a setting forth, and with a queer kind of clutch at my throat, as if I were about to enter it, I felt the wilderness ahead of night and rain. There were two long whistle blasts that instantly the wet put out. The engine left a smell of smoke and distance.

The wind keeps on. When you step outside its strong hot push is like something solid pressed against the face. The sun through the dust looks big and red and close. Bigger, redder, closer every day. You begin to glance at it with a doomed feeling, that there's no escape.

The dust is so thick that sky and earth are just a blur. You can scarcely see the elevators at the end of town. One step beyond, you think, and you'd go plunging into space.

The days are blurred too. It's wind in the morning, wind at bedtime. Wind all through the night—we toss and lie listening.

"... the wind wings on,
   bereft and wild its lonely song.
   It ridges drifts and
   licks their ripples off;
   it smoothens crests,
   piles snow against the fences."

There was a hot dry wind that came in short, intermittent little puffs as if it were being blown out of a wheezy engine. All round the dust hung dark and heavy, the distance thickening it so that a mile or more away it made a blur of earth and sky; but overhead it was thin still, like a film of fog or smoke, and the light came through it filtered, mild and tawny.

It was as if there were a lantern hung above you in a darkened and enormous room; or as if the day had turned out all its other lights, waiting for the actors to appear, and you by accident had found your way into the spotlight, like a little ant or beetle on the stage.

I turned once and looked back at Horizon, the huddled little clutter of houses and stores, the five grain elevators, aloof and imperturbable, like ancient obelisks, and behind the dust clouds, lapping at the sky.

Then the bridge over us picked up the coming of a train. It was there even while the silence was still intact. At last we heard a distant whistle-blade, then a single point of sound, like one drop of water in a whole sky. It dilated, spread. The sky and silence began imperceptibly to fill with it. We steeled ourselves a little, feeling the pounding onrush in the trestle of the bridge. It quickened, gathered, shook the earth, then swept in an iron roar above us, thundering and dark.

It's an immense night out there, wheeling and windy. The lights on the street and in the houses are helpless against the black wetness, little unilluminating glints that might be painted on it. The town seems huddled together, cowering on a high, tiny perch, afraid to move lest it topple into the wind. Close to the parsonage is the church, black even against the darkness, towering ominously up through the night and merging with it. There's a soft steady swish of rain on the roof, and a gurgle of eave troughs running over. Above, in the high cold night, the wind goes swinging past, indifferent, liplessly mournful. It frightens me, makes me feel lost, dropped on this little perch of town and abandoned.

As For Me and My House, New York, 1941

W. O. MITCHELL

High above the prairie, platter-flat, the wind wings on, bereft and wild its lonely song. It ridges drifts and licks their ripples off; it smoothens crests, piles snow against the fences. The tinting green of Northern Lights slowly shades and fades against the prairie nights, dying here, imperceptibly reborn over there. Light glows each evening where the town lies; a hiving sound is there, with now and then some sound distinct and separate in the night: a shout, a woman's laugh. Clear—truant sounds.

As clouds' slow shadows melt across the prairie's face, more nights slip darkness over. Light then dark, then light again. Day then night, then day again. A meadow lark sings and it is spring. And summer comes.

A year is done.

Another comes and it is done.

Where spindling poplars lift their dusty leaves and wild sunflowers stare, the gravestones stand among the prairie grasses. Over them a rapt and endless silence lies. This soil is rich.

Here to the West a small dog's skeleton lies, its rib bones clutching emptiness. Crawling in and out of the teeth an ant casts about; it disappears into an eyesocket, reappears to begin a long pilgrimage down the backbone spools.

The wind turns in silent frenzy upon itself, whirling into a smoking funnel, breathing up topsoil and tumbleweed skeletons to carry them on its spinning way over the prairie, out and out to the far line of the sky.

Who Has Seen the Wind, Boston, 1947

MARGARET LAURENCE

Winter was the right time to go. A bell-voice, clear in the cold air, cried "All aboard!" and the train stirred and shook itself like a drowsy dragon and began to move, regally slow, then faster until it was spinning down the shining tracks. We passed the shacks and shanties that clustered around the station, and the railway buildings and water tower painted their dried-blood red. Then we were away from Manawaka. It came as a shock to me, how small the town was, and how short a time it took to leave it, as we measure time.

Into the white Wachakwa valley then, past the dump grounds and the cemetery on the hill. Peering, I could see on the hill brow the marble angel, sightlessly guarding the gardens of snow, the empty places and the deep-lying dead.

Many a mile, manyamile, manyamile, said the iron clank of the train wheels, and we perched, as unaccustomed travellers do, on the edges of the dusty green plush seats and looked out the rattling windows at the winter. The farms were lost and smothered. Emaciated trunks of maple and poplar were black now and the branches were feathered with frost. The sloughs were frozen over, and the snow was banked high against the snow-fences and shadowed blue in the sun. Everything was blue-bleak and white for distances, until we came to some little whistle-stop where bundled children with scarves up to their noses pranced on the slippery platform and brushed pink bubbles of ice and wool from their red-mittened fists, and the breath of barking dogs gushed white and visible into the dry air snapping with cold.

The prairie had a hushed look. Rippled dust lay across the fields. The square frame houses squatted exposed, drabber than before, and some of the windows were boarded over like bandaged eyes. Barbed-wire fences had tippled flimsily and not been set to rights. The Russian thistle flourished, emblem of want, and farmers cut it and fed it to their lean cattle. The crows still cawed, and overhead the telephone wires still twanged all up and down the washboard roads. Yet nothing was the same at all.

The wind was everywhere, shuffling through the dust, wading and stirring until the air was thickly grey with grit.

25

John met me at the station. He had an old car, but he wasn't using its engine. It was hitched to a horse. He saw my astounded stare.

"Gas is expensive. We save the truck for emergencies."

At the Shipley place the rusty machinery stood like aged bodies gradually expiring from exposure, ribs turned to the sun. The leaves of my lilac bushes were burnt yellow, and the branches snapped if you touched them. The house had never been anything but grey, so it wasn't any different now, except that the front porch, which had been made of green lumber when the house was built and had been warping for years, now had been given a final pliers twist by frost and wore a caved-in look, like toothless jaws.

Our horse-drawn car pulled into the yard, and the dust puffed up around us like flour. My marigolds were a dead loss by this time, of course. I'd planted them behind the house to use as cutting flowers and they'd kept on seeding themselves, but now only a few wizened ones remained, small unexpected dabs of orange among the choking weeds, dry sheepfoot and thistle. The sunflowers had risen beside the barn as always, fed by the melting snow in spring, but they'd had no other water this year—their tall stalks were hollow and brown, and the heavy heads hung over, the segments empty as unfilled honeycombs, for the petals had fallen and the centres had dried before the seeds could form. In the patch where I had grown radishes and carrots and leaf lettuce, only the grasshoppers grew, leaping and whirring in the bone-dry air.

Stone Angel, Toronto, 1964

FREDERICK PHILIP GROVE

The air is breathless: even the slight, wafting flow from the east has ceased. Nature lies prostrate in expectation of the scourge that is coming, coming. The wall of cloud has differentiated: there are two, three waves of almost black; in front, a circling festoon of loose, white, flocculent manes, seething, whirling . . . A winking of light runs through the first wave of black. A distant rumbling heralds the storm . . .

The two have squatted down in the hay, forgetting themselves. They sit and look. Then a noise as of distant breakers in the surf; the roar of the sea, approaching nearer, nearer.

The bush in front through which they have come stands motionless, breathless, blackening as the sun is obscured. Birds flit to and fro, seeking shelter, silent . . .

Then a huge suction soughs through the stems. But already the lash of the wind comes down: like the sea in a storm tree tops rise and fall, the stems bending over and down and whipping back again, tossed by enormous pressures. They dance and roll, tumble and rear, and mutely cry out as in pain. And the very next moment the wind hits the stack, snatching the breath from the lips of the two who sit there crouching. A misty veil rushes over the landscape, illumined by a bluish flash which is followed by nearer and nearer growlings and barkings.

Up rises the girl in the storm, holding on to her bonnet with both her hands, leaning back into the wind, her skirt crackling and snapping and pulling at her strong limbs. Once more she laughs, laughs into the storm and sweeps her arm over the landscape, pointing.

The first rain drops, heavy, large, but few, strike against her body. She looks at the man, the boy still crouching at her feet and calls, "Now down!"

They run to the edge of the stack, squat, slide, and make for the shelter which the boy has prepared.

Down comes the rain in a cloud-burst, forming a wall in front of them where they sit in the sheltering cove in which all the fragrance of the meadow is concentrated. Flashes of lightning break on the slough like bomb-shells; rattling thunder dances and springs.

On sweeps the storm; less and less rain falls; the drops begin to sparkle and glitter; the sun bursts forth. Over the bush huge clouds are lifting their wings; and a playful breeze strikes into the cave where Niels and Ellen still crouch silent . . .

Settlers of the Marsh, New York, 1925

ETHEL WILSON

And the next day they still ran along the prairie, but now the land broke into rolling country ("This *must* be the Rolling Prairie!"), and the world became lightly wooded again. Then, beyond increasingly high hills they looked westward and saw, coldly blue and white against the sky, a tumult of mountains.

In the gullies of the little hills through which they now passed there were aspens and birches whose leaves the early frost had turned from green to gold. The birches with their white maidenly stems and honey-yellow leaves shone against the dark conifers. Far to the north of them, but still east of the Rockies, east of Jasper House, the Athabasca River flowed widely through a land that was all gold. Golden golden golden shone the birch trees in the sunshine in that northern land from north to south, from east to west, spiked here and there by dark conifers. Few travellers along the brave steel way had ever heard of this golden world. But here, as the train hurried towards the mountains, Rachel looked up at the railway cutting and saw, for one moment, poised alone against the blue sky, a single slender white-stemmed aspen tree whose golden leaves trembled and shone and sang in the sunshine. It was there. It was gone. It was hers.

Quickly the mountains were upon them. Each of the travellers had been to Switzerland and the word "Alps" sprang from mouth to mouth, but soon they ceased to speak of the Alps. "This ain't all of it, no, ma'am," said the coloured porter huskily. "It goes 'way 'way up north and down south. This ain't only a little patch of it."

The great peaks advanced upon them and they were as nothing amongst the confusion and welter of the mountains. The train began to pant and toil. What wild extravagance of nature was this. Mist came down, or was it rain or snow, and sometimes blotted the great indifferent torrent-spilling mountains from their sight. "I think, love, that they are rather too big! I could appreciate the mountains better if we had come upon them before we'd seen all the other bignesses. I think," laughing a little, "that my appetite for big things is gone," said the Grandmother.

The mountains ranged themselves on either side of the railway track, peak after peak. The Grandmother looked up murmuring vaguely, "The mountains skip like rams." She would have regarded this statement as hyperbole if the Bible had not said it first. But that is exactly what the mountains did. Silently, silently, they moved one behind the other with surprising speed considering their age and size. They changed their positions as the pushing train sped curving along their bases; so that first one mountain, then another, moved silently, in order, one behind another. The mountains only remained static when the train stood still; but when the train raced along their bases the mountains skipped like rams. "The Lord doeth wonderful things," marvelled the Grandmother, gazing up at the moving peaks as they re-arranged themselves against the sky, and then gave place to still more mountains which behaved in the same way. This occurred for a whole day, for these were the Rocky and Cascade Mountains. They did not see the gorges of the Thompson River (for night had fallen) nor Hell's Gate.

Morning came in the widening Fraser Valley. The train was running for home now, and the long journey was nearly done. It ran along the shores of Burrard Inlet. As the travellers approached Vancouver they hardly saw the swelling line of the mountains across the Inlet, nor the first waters of the Pacific Ocean, nor the masted schooners and brigs which stood off from Hastings Mill, nor the sea-gulls wheeling and wheeling above the salt water—they sat there ready with their gloves on and their handbags on their knees and their minds forerunning them.

The Innocent Traveller, Toronto, 1949

Every town that stands at a confluence of rivers has something over and above other towns. This is true whether the town is little or big. Lytton was so small that relatively it was a village. But relative to the surrounding solitudes it was a town. Roads converged there. The railroad passed through it, trains stopped there, it was fed by this system and it fed the surrounding solitudes for a long radius, especially northwards into the hills.

But what gives Lytton its especial character, lying there at the fringe of the sage-brush carpet in a fold of the hills at the edge of the dry belt and the coast area, is that just beside the town the clear turbulent Thompson River joins the vaster opaque Fraser. The Fraser River, which begins as a sparkling stream in the far northern mountains, describes a huge curve in northern British Columbia, and, increased in volume by innumerable rills and streams and by large and important tributary rivers, grows in size and reputation and changes its character and colour on its journey south.

Long before the Fraser reaches Lytton it has cut its way through different soils and rocks and has taken to itself tons of silt, and now moves on, a wide deceptive flow of sullen opaque and fawn-coloured water. Evidences of boil and whirlpool show the river to be dangerous. At Lytton it is refreshed and enlarged by the blue-green racing urgent Thompson River. This river in the course of its double journey from north and east spreads itself into lakes and gathers itself together again into a river, until as it approaches Lytton it manifests all its special beauty and brilliance.

The sun dipped behind the hills across the river and the windows of the bungalow ceased blazing with evening sunlight. At once you felt the cool air as if it were the earth's cool breath. Anybody looking out of the front windows of Mrs. Dorval's bungalow could look down on to the racing Thompson River. Perhaps the water was emerald, perhaps it was sapphire. It is both. It is neither. It is a brilliant river, blue-green with lacings of white foam and spray as the water hurls itself violently along in rapids against hidden or projecting rocks, a rapid, racing, calling river. The hills rise high and lost on each side of the banks. These hills are traversed hardly at all. There is no reason to climb, to scale the top, to look down. In the sunlight the dun-coloured gorges of the blue-green river look yellow and ochreous, and in some places there are outcroppings of rock that are nearly rose red. Large dark and solitary pine trees give landmark and meaning. Here and there in a gully an army of these dark pointed pine trees marches up an ancient waterway of the hill-side, static. How do they grow on stone? A figure of man or of beast crawling distant across the great folds and crevasses of these sprawling hills would make you stop, look, point with surprise, and question. One is accustomed to their being empty of life. As evening comes on, the hills grow dove grey and purple; they take on a variety of surprising shapes and shades, and the oblique shafts of sunlight disclose new hills and valleys which in daylight merge into one and are not seen. It is the sage-brush that covers nearly everything, that helps to transform everything, and that in the mutations of sunlight and moonlight helps to change the known hills to the unfamiliar. Because the hills are so desolate, strange and still, without movement, the strong brilliant water in headlong motion at their base holds your eyes with its tumult.

Hetty Dorval, Toronto, 1947

MALCOLM LOWRY

A loudspeaker, enthroned on a wagon, barked from the city of Enochvilleport composed of dilapidated half-skyscrapers, at different levels, some with all kinds of scrap iron, even broken airplanes, on their roofs, others being mouldy stock exchange buildings, new beer parlours crawling with verminous light even in mid-afternoon and resembling gigantic emerald-lit public lavatories for both sexes, masonries containing English tea-shoppes where your fortune could be told by a female relative of Maximilian of Mexico, totem pole factories, drapers' shops with the best Scotch tweed and opium dens in the basement (though no bars, as if, like some hideous old roué shuddering with every unmentionable secret vice, this city without gaiety had cackled "No, I draw the line at that.—What would our wee laddies come to then?"), cerise conflagration of cinemas, modern apartment buildings, and other soulless behemoths, housing, it might be, noble invisible struggles, of literature, the drama, art or music, the student's lamp and the rejected manuscript; or indescribable poverty and degradation, between which civic attractions were squeezed occasional lovely dark ivy-clad old houses that seemed weeping, cut off from all light, on their knees, and elsewhere bankrupt hospitals, and one or two solid-stoned old banks, held up that

"... *anyone who had ever really been in hell must have given Enochvilleport a nod of recognition....*"

fair city," mills that shook the very earth with their tumult, filling the windy air with their sound as of a wailing and gnashing of teeth: all these curious achievements of man, together creating as we say "the jewel of the Pacific," went as though down a great incline to a harbour more spectacular than Rio de Janeiro and San Francisco put together, with deep-sea freighters moored at every angle for miles in the roadstead, but to whose heroic prospect nearly the only human dwellings visible on this side of the water that had any air of belonging, or in which their inhabitants could be said any longer to participate, were, paradoxically, a few lowly little self-built shacks and floathouses, that might have been driven out of the city altogether, down to the water's edge into the sea itself, where they stood on piles, like fishermen's huts (which several of them apparently were), or on rollers, some dark and tumbledown, others freshly and prettily painted, these last quite evidently built or placed with some human need for beauty in mind, even if under the permanent threat of eviction, and all standing, even the most sombre, with their fluted tin chimneys smoking here and there like toy tramp steamers, as though in defiance of the town, before eternity. In Enochvilleport itself some ghastly-coloured neon signs had long since been going through their unctuous twitching and gesticulations that nostalgia and love transform into a poetry of longing: more happily one began to flicker: PALOMAR, LOUIS ARMSTRONG AND HIS ORCHESTRA. A huge new grey dead hotel that at sea might be a landmark of romance belched smoke out of its turreted haunted-looking roof, as if it had caught fire, and beyond that all the lamps were blazing within the grim courtyard of the law courts, equally at sea a trysting place of the heart, outside which one of the stone lions, having recently been blown up, was covered reverently with a white cloth, and inside which for a month a group of stainless citizens had been trying a sixteen-year-old boy for murder.

"The Bravest Boat" in *Hear Us O Lord from Heaven Thy Dwelling Place*, Philadelphia, 1961

In our part of the world the days are very short in winter, and often so dark and grey it is impossible to believe the sun will ever shine again; weeks of icy drenching rain, interspersed by the savage storms that sweep down the inlet from the mountains when the sea roared around and under us and battered our shack until it seemed sometimes January would never end, though once in a long while would come a day of blinding sunlight and clarity, so cold the inlet fumed and the mist rose from the water like steam from a boiling cauldron, and at night my wife said of the stars, "Like splinters of ice in a sky of jet."

The wintry landscape could be beautiful on these rare short days of sunlight and frostflowers, with crystal casing on the slender branches of birches and vine-leaved maples, diamond drops on the tassels of the spruces, and the bright frosted foliage of the evergreens. The frost melted on our porch in stripes, leaving a pattern against the wet black wood like a richly beaded cape flung out, on which our little cat tripped about with cold dainty paws and then sat hunched outside on the windowsill with his tail curled round his feet.

afternoon; and among which appeared too, at infrequent intervals, beyond a melancholy never-striking black and white clock that said three, dwarfed spires belonging to frame façades with blackened rose windows, queer grimed onion-shaped domes, and even Chinese pagodas, so that first you thought you were in the Orient, then Turkey or Russia, though finally, but for the fact that some of these were churches, you would be sure you were in hell: despite that anyone who had ever really been in hell must have given Enochvilleport a nod of recognition, further affirmed by the spectacle, at first not unpicturesque, of the numerous sawmills relentlessly smoking and champing away like demons, Molochs fed by whole mountainsides of forests that never grew again, or by trees that made way for grinning regiments of villas in the background of "our expanding and

28

But then at night sometimes the elemental despair would begin again and we would lose all hope for terror at the noise, the rending branches, the tumult of the sea, the sound of ruination under the house, so that we clung to one another like two little arboreal animals in some midnight jungle—and we were two such animals in such a jungle—until we could laugh again at the very commotion, the very extremity of duty to a house filled with an anxiety of love like that of officers for a sailing ship in a gale. Though it was in the early mornings of high tide when getting breakfast that this wild elemental menace often proved the most unnerving, with the grey sea and whitecaps almost level with the windows, and the rain dashing against them, the sea crashing and hissing inshore under the house, causing horrible commotions of logs, jarring thunders dithering the whole little shack so that the lamp brackets rattled with the windows, past which a drifting timber sailed threatening the pier, and beyond the smoke of the factories in Port Boden was just a rainy grey, while leaves were falling into the sea; then our boat hurling itself about down below would seem in jeopardy, at the same time there would be the sound of breaking branches in the forest, the great maple tree would seethe and roar, while the tossing floats squealed piteously, and the loops of Mauger's fishing nets hung on the porch would flap like mad ghosts; and then be motionless; and all the anxiety that had been stretched to its utmost tension repeating, would the poor boat be hurt, the pier against which a thud was like a blow at the heart, relaxed too: though only an instant, the next moment it had all started again, so that what with the wind, the thunderous boomings, the delight in the swiftness outside, the anxiety within and without, the pride that one had survived, the sense of life, the fear of death, the appetite for breakfast as the bacon and coffee smells went singing down the gale every time one opened the door—I was seized sometimes with an exuberance so great that I wanted to dive swiftly into that brimming sea to acquire a greater appetite still, either that or because the sea seemed safer than the house.

But then we went out to a morning of wild ducks doing sixty downwind and golden-crowned kinglets feeding in swift jingling multitudinous flight through the leafless bushes, and another day of winter companionship would draw down to an evening of wind, clouds, and seagulls blowing four ways at once, and a black sky above the trembling desolate alders, the heart clothed already in their delicate green jewellery I had never really seen, and the gulls whitely soaring against that darkness, where suddenly now appeared the moon behind clouds, as the wind dropped, transilluminating its own soaring moonshot depths in the water, the moon reflected in the half-moonlit clouds in the water down there, and behind, in the same translunar depths, the reflection of the struts and cross-braces of our simple-minded pier, safe for another day, disposed subaqueously in some ancient complex harmony of architectural beauty, an inverse moonlight geometry, beyond our conscious knowledge.

With February the days were noticeably longer and brighter and warmer, the sunrise and sunset were sometimes bright and beautiful again, there would be a sudden warm bright noon, or even a whole day that melted the ice in the brooks and set them running, or a day of sunlight when one could look through the trees at heaven, where luminous Aconcaguas sailed God's blue afternoon.

"The Forest Path to the Spring" in *Hear Us O Lord from Heaven Thy Dwelling Place*, Philadelphia, 1961

FARLEY MOWAT

The storm that had heralded my arrival lasted for three full days, but on the fourth day the weather changed abruptly and the arctic spring exploded in a violent eruption. On June the first, the sun shone down upon me with a passion that it hardly knows even in the tropics. And it kept on shining for eighteen hours out of every twenty-four.

I climbed a ridge beside the cabin on the second day of spring and I was awed by what I saw. Thin sheets of water were sliding out from under all the mighty drifts along the shore, and there were already telltale mumblings from under the river ice. Above the ice a good-sized stream was bawling down upon the bay and spreading a lake above a lake, that was soon too deep to wade across.

In half a day the snow that lapped my observation ridge retreated a dozen feet, leaving the exposed gravel and dead moss to steam away like an overanxious kettle. It was a queer thing to see, and I felt as if I were sitting on the summit of a frozen world that inexplicably, and with an unbelievable swiftness, had decided to collapse and melt away.

Every hollow and low-lying spot harboured a freshet that quickened and murmured without pause for rest, even during the brief twilight period that passed for night. The ice began to rot. The shining surfaces turned leaden, dulled and fractured into countless millions of tiny, separate rods that were held upright and together only by their mutual pressure on one another. It was no longer possible to crawl about the drifts in search of wood, for the wet snow refused my weight. After twice plunging over my head into the snow I gave up the search for fear of suffocating in that wet and cold embrace.

And the birds arrived. One morning I was wakened from an uneasy sleep by the mad laughter of many voices chuckling in zany mirth. I flung open the door and found myself staring into the brilliance, and meeting the eyes of half a hundred disembodied heads. The heads were chickenlike, but stained dull red as if by the lifeblood of the bodies they had been parted from.

With something approaching horror I stared at the weird visitors and they stared back from maniac little eyes, and laughed until the whole valley rang with sound. I flung a piece of ice at one, and the whole flock suddenly took flight. As they cleared the ground, their trim white bodies that had been invisible against the snow were projected into view, and I knew them then for ptarmigan, the partridge of the arctic.

People of the Deer, Boston, 1952

STEPHEN LEACOCK

The Mausoleum Club stands on the quietest corner of the best residential street in the City. It is a Grecian building of white stone. About it are great elm trees with birds—the most expensive kind of birds—singing in the branches.

The street in the softer hours of the morning has an almost reverential quiet. Great motors move drowsily along it, with solitary chauffeurs returning at 10:30 after conveying the earlier of the millionaires to their downtown offices. The sunlight flickers through the elm trees, illuminating expensive nursemaids wheeling valuable children in little perambulators. Some of the children are worth millions and millions. In Europe, no doubt, you may see in the Unter den Linden avenue or the Champs Elysées a little prince or princess go past with a clattering military guard of honour. But that is nothing. It is not half so impressive, in the real sense, as what you may observe every morning on Plutoria Avenue beside the Mausoleum Club in the quietest part of the city. Here you may see a little toddling princess in a rabbit suit who owns fifty distilleries in her own right. There, in a lacquered perambulator, sails past a little hooded head that controls from its cradle an entire New Jersey corporation. The United States attorney-general is suing her as she sits, in a vain attempt to make her dissolve herself into constituent companies. Near by is a child of four, in a khaki suit, who represents the merger of two trunk-line railways. You may meet in the flickered sunlight any number of little princes and princesses far more real than the poor survivals of Europe. Incalculable infants wave their fifty-dollar ivory rattles in an inarticulate greeting to one another. A million dollars of preferred stock laughs merrily in recognition of a majority control going past in a go-cart drawn by an imported nurse. And through it all the sunlight falls through the elm trees, and the birds sing and the motors hum, so that the whole world as seen from the boulevard of Plutoria Avenue is the very pleasantest place imaginable.

Just below Plutoria Avenue, and parallel with it, the trees die out and the brick and stone of the City begins in earnest. Even from the Avenue you see the tops of the sky-scraping buildings in the big commercial streets, and can hear or almost hear the roar of the elevated railway, earning dividends. And beyond that again the City sinks lower, and is choked and crowded with the tangled streets and little houses of the slums.

In fact, if you were to mount to the roof of the Mausoleum Club itself on Plutoria Avenue you could almost see the slums from there. But why should you? And on the other hand, if you never went up on the roof, but only dined inside among the palm trees, you would never know that the slums existed—which is much better.

There are broad steps leading up to the club, so broad and so agreeably covered with matting that the physical exertion of lifting oneself from one's motor to the door of the club is reduced to the smallest compass. The richer members are not ashamed to take the steps one at a time, first one foot and then the other; and at tight money periods, when there is a black cloud hanging over the Stock Exchange, you may see each and every one of the members of the Mausoleum Club dragging himself up the steps after this fashion, his restless eyes filled with the dumb pathos of a man wondering where he can put his hand on half a million dollars.

But at gayer times, when there are gala receptions at the club, its steps are all buried under expensive carpet, soft as moss and covered over with a long pavilion of red and white awning to catch the snowflakes; and beautiful ladies are poured into the club by the motorful. Then, indeed, it is turned into a veritable Arcadia; and for a beautiful pastoral scene, such as would have gladdened the heart of a poet who understood the cost of things, commend me to the Mausoleum Club on just such an evening. Its broad corridors and deep recesses are filled with shepherdesses such as you never saw, dressed in beautiful shimmering gowns, and wearing feathers in their hair that droop off sideways at every angle known to trigonometry. And there are shepherds, too, with broad white waistcoats and little patent leather shoes and heavy faces and congested cheeks. And there is dancing and conversation among the shepherds and shepherdesses, with such brilliant flashes of wit and repartee about the rise in Wabash and the fall in Cement that the soul of Louis Quatorze would leap to hear it. And later there is supper at little tables, when the shepherds and shepherdesses consume preferred stocks and gold-interest bonds in the shape of chilled champagne and iced asparagus, and great platefuls of dividends and special quarterly bonuses are carried to and fro in silver dishes by Chinese philosophers dressed up to look like waiters.

But on ordinary days there are no ladies in the club, but only the shepherds. You may see them sitting about in little groups of two and three under the palm trees drinking whiskey and soda; though of course the more temperate among them drink nothing but whiskey and Lithia water, and those who have important business to do in the afternoon limit themselves to whiskey and Radnor, or whiskey and Magi water. There are as many kinds of bubbling, gurgling, mineral waters in the caverns of the Mausoleum Club as ever sparkled from the rocks of Homeric Greece. And when you have once grown used to them, it is as impossible to go back to plain water as it is to live again in the forgotten house in a side street that you inhabited long before you became a member.

Thus the members sit and talk in undertones that float to the ear through the haze of Havana smoke. You may hear the older men explaining that the country is going to absolute ruin, and the younger ones explaining that the country is forging ahead as it never did before; but chiefly they love to talk of great national questions, such as the protective tariff and the need of raising it, the sad decline of the morality of the working man, the spread of syndicalism and the lack of Christianity in the labour class, and the awful growth of selfishness among the mass of the people.

So they talk, except for two or three that drop off to directors' meetings, till the afternoon fades and darkens into evening, and the noiseless Chinese philosophers turn on soft lights here and there among the palm trees. Presently they dine at white tables glittering with cut glass and green and yellow Rhine wines; and after dinner they sit again among the palm trees, half-hidden in the blue smoke, still talking of the tariff and the labour class and trying to wash away the memory and the sadness of it in floods of mineral waters. So the evening passes into night, and one by one the great motors come throbbing to the door, and the Mausoleum Club empties and darkens till the last member is borne away and the Arcadian day ends in well-earned repose.

Arcadian Adventures with the Idle Rich, London, 1914

The university, as everyone knows, stands with its great gates on Plutoria Avenue, and with its largest buildings, those of the faculties of industrial and mechanical science, fronting full upon the street.

These buildings are exceptionally fine, standing fifteen stories high and comparing favourably with the best departmental stores or factories in the City. Indeed, after nightfall, when they are all lighted up for the evening technical classes and when their testing machinery is in full swing and there are students going in and out in overall suits, people have often mistaken the university, or this newer part of it, for a factory. A foreign visitor once said that the students looked like plumbers, and President Boomer was so proud of it that he put the phrase into his next Commencement address; and from there the newspapers got it and the Associated Press took it up and sent it all over the United States with the heading, "Have Appearance of Plumbers; Plutoria University Congratulated on Character of Students," and it was a proud day indeed for the heads of the Industrial Science faculty.

But the older part of the university stands so quietly and modestly at the top end of the elm avenue, so hidden by the leaves of it, that no one could mistake it for a factory. This, indeed, was once the whole university, and had stood there since colonial days under the name Concordia College. It had been filled with generations of presidents and professors of the older type with long white beards and rusty black clothes, and salaries of fifteen hundred dollars.

But the change both of name and of character from Concordia College to Plutoria University was the work of President Boomer. He had changed it from an old-fashioned college of the by-gone type to a university in the true modern sense. At Plutoria they now taught everything. Concordia College, for example, had no teaching of religion except lectures on the Bible. Now they had lectures also on Confucianism, Mohammedanism, Buddhism, with an optional course on atheism for students in the final year.

And, of course, they had long since admitted women, and there were now beautiful creatures with Cléo de Mérode hair studying astronomy at oaken desks and looking up at the teacher with eyes like comets. The university taught everything and did everything. It had whirling machines on the top of it that measured the speed of the wind, and deep in its basements it measured earthquakes with a seismograph; it held classes on forestry and dentistry and palmistry; it sent life classes into the slums, and death classes to the city morgue. It offered such a vast variety of themes, topics, and subjects to the students, that there was nothing that a student was compelled to learn, while from its own presses in its own press-building it sent out a shower of bulletins and monographs like driven snow from a rotary plough.

In fact, it had become, as President Boomer told all the businessmen in town, not merely a university, but a *universitas* in the true sense, and every one of its faculties was now a *facultas* in the real acceptance of the word, and its studies properly and truly *studia*; indeed, if the businessmen would only build a few more dormitories and put up enough money to form an adequate *fondatum* or *fundum*, then the good work might be looked upon as complete.

Arcadian Adventures with the Idle Rich, London, 1914

ETHEL WILSON

"I'll come along," said Mort. "I never seen an undertaker's place. Behind the scenes as you might say. I'll come along with you."

So the two friends got up, and took their time and walked together along Hastings Street and took the street car and changed twice and got off at a very chic building which was large and spreading and of white stucco with window boxes, and a grass plot all around; the kind of building that caused tourists driving in from Bellingham to say "Oh let's stop here, Momma. This looks like a nice kind of place!" You cannot blame these tourists because it does indeed look like a nice kind of place to stay, but it is not, it is not, it finally and inescapably is not. It is a mortician's place, it is a funeral parlour, it is a funeral home, it is the undertaker's, and people who approach meditatively and a bit early for the funeral wonder How on earth did we manage in the old days! Back east when Grampa died it doesn't seem to me we had anything swell like this. We just had the funeral right in the house and old Miss Foster came in to help.

The hot sun was setting, and Mort felt very much at peace as he followed his friend Pork into the side door of the funeral home. A young man in black with a gentle demeanour approached Pork and gave him some instructions, pointing here and there, taking Pork into an inner office and showing him something, and then taking him into another room and showing him something else, and Pork received his nightly instructions, and nodded and said "Yes, Mr. Pontifex, I certainly will. No, Mr. Pontifex, I certainly won't. Well I don't think she can have left that neckpiece in the chapel because I'd have found it last night when I was cleaning, but I'll have another look and if I see it I'll give her a ring, and if I hear anything from the Pinkham family I'll let you know."

All this time Mort effaced himself from the conversation and stood with a great deal of interest in a very handsome kind of parlour lavishly upholstered and hung and carpeted in an anonymous tasteless fashion. There was nothing to induce reverence in this room, but Mort felt a kind of reverence stealing over him like a scent.

The sun, at that time of the year, goes down suddenly, and then it is night before you know it. Pork began turning lights on in various places and this of itself changed the autumn afternoon into night in a funeral home. The young man in black with the gentle demeanour came through the reception parlour with his things on. He nodded kindly to Mort who wondered Does he think I'm one of the relatives, and went out into the street, closing the outside door after him with a soft click. Pork seemed to be somewhere else.

Mort thought Well, I might as well sit down, so he tried a rocking chair as he was partial to rocking chairs. Not a twinge of thought reminded him—at least hardly a twinge—that he should have been home to supper long ago. The gentle influence of the beer, and Pork, and the funeral home, had the assuaging effect on him—and on his angel—of a warm beach on a starred summer night, or of a soft bed on Sunday morning. You do not want to leave it; it is good enough for you.

After a time the door of the reception parlour opened and Pork came in. He was wearing a janitor's overalls and he had a small fur neckpiece in his hand. He said, "Just wait till I put this in the office." When he returned he said, "D'you want to see something?"

Mort nodded. He was pleasantly apprehensive. He had—years ago—seen death many times and in many forms, but this was different. "Is it a stiff?" he asked.

Pork seemed a little shocked. "It wouldn't be my place to show you that . . ." he said, and Mort said, "Of course not." They went along a lighted hall and then they went up a finely carpeted flight of stairs. There was a door. Pork opened the door wide, went inside, clicked lights on, stepped back, and said, "Well, what do you think of *that* . . . !"

Mort went in.

"Well, whaddaya know!" he said.

The coffins stood row behind row in a large oval space; nothing in the room but coffins. Majestic and inescapable they stood, waiting all together. Mort felt stunned by the sudden silent sight of all these coffins. In this room the fact of mortality was delivered straight with a hammer blow, and there was no evasion. There seemed to Mort to be hundreds of coffins. There were only forty-two. Every taste, except those concerned with doom, shape and cost, every aesthetic taste, was catered for. Mort snatched off his hat, which he had put on again, with a vague feeling of reverence for the dead.

"Well well well, whaddaya know," he said again to the coffins in general; and Pork watched his friend, and was gratified with Mort's response.

Mort's eyes began to differentiate between the coffins. Some were open, some were closed, some were half open, some were certainly for the ladies. All seemed to be lined with lavish crinkles of satin arranged by a master. This was nice.

"I guess there'd be quite a bit of money tied up in them coffins," he enquired, turning to Pork, "they'd be worth quite a bit?"

"Caskets," corrected Pork.

"Well, they're coffins to me. But they sure are pretty!" He advanced towards the coffins, tiptoeing uneasily, vigorous but subdued among their horizontal shapes.

A bell whirred somewhere. Pork turned and left, saying "I'll be back." Mort heard him going down the stairs. He began to move from coffin to coffin. He stood and pondered each one. They became less dreadful. He began to enjoy himself. He began to choose his pick.

I guess by the looks these would all be for society people, he thought as he surveyed them. There didn't seem to be a plain working man's coffin in the lot. He was divided between a forbidding box covered with elephant grey and lined with off-white, and a fine job covered with purple brocaded velours and lined with heliotrope satin. Either of these coffins was suited to a certain aspect of Mort's temperament, but he preferred the richness of the purple. There'd be some satisfaction in being buried in something like that. If he wasn't afraid of Pork coming back he'd get in, just for the feel, but he knew Pork wouldn't like it. He now thought of Myrtle. He would choose one for her. After some difficulty and much sticking out of his lower lip and pinching his chin, he chose a coffin prettily lined with shining blue, and stood over it, looking down. He became sentimental, and then he became unhappy. He became luxuriously unhappy, and mysteriously elevated. He looked down into the soft blue satin and—plain as day—he saw Myrt lying there. This, then, was really the end of everything. This was what we come to; and then—no more; this—and no other. He saw Myrt's thin occasionally pretty face with its well-known look, the eyelids closed; and the circumstances of Myrt's death and funeral rose and encompassed him. Easy tears filled his eyes and he dried them with the back of his hand. He thought I haven't always been so good to Myrt as I ought to been, though God knows she'd drive you mad the way she acts sometimes but I bet I'll be sawry sometime for the things I done. Mort was softening up considerably so his angel took advantage of this to start the thought that he'd better not stay here thinking up funerals when nobody was even dead, and he'd better get home to supper because Myrt would be mad. Mort took one more look at Myrtle in her coffin, but she had faded, so he tiptoed noisily to the door, and went out with a farewell look at all the beautiful coffins (I'd sure like to pick one for little Horse Dunkerley with splinters in), closed the door quietly and met Pork on the landing.

"I certainly enjoyed that," said Mort in his pleasant hoarse voice, "I never seen such a sight before! That sure was a very interesting sight . . . I must be getting along home or there'll be hell popping. Now looka here, Pork, you come around and see the wife and me one of these days. Mind you do. Come any time, any time . . ." and Mort waved his big hands this way and that, welcoming Pork in.

"I sure will, I sure will," said Pork heartily. "Would ya like a few flowers for the wife? There some fine gladioluses come too late today and I can't do nothing but throw 'em out."

"*Would* I!" said Mort gratefully and thought to himself Say if that isn't a break! Myrt'll be crazy about the flowers; she'll forget all about me coming in late.

Pork led the way to back premises where there were mops and brooms and pails and a heap of flowers, some fresh, some faded. "If you look among these," said Pork, bending down, "you'll find plenty fresh. The cards is off. They're all in sprays and wreaths and it's no good sending 'em to hospitals . . . You break off the good ones and take 'em along home. I'll only have to throw 'em out anyway," and the two men went down on their hunkers and fumbled clumsily amongst the flowers—chiefly, as Pork had said, gladioluses—and by selection and rejection and careful breaking-off, Mort got a *bo*kay of real nice flowers, although some of the stems were short. He was pleased.

"Well, it certainly has been fine seeing you again, Pork, you sure must come around . . ." and in his mind Mort began seeing his old friend nearly every day. "Thanks for the *bo*kay," he said, turning it about admiringly, "my wife's crazy about flowers. She sure will be pleased. Well, I'll be seeing you," and Pork let Mort out into the dark street and said goodbye again several times, and Pork went back into the funeral home and shut the door, and Mort went down the street and got on a street car and paid his ticket and sat down and looked at his pretty flowers.

The Equations of Love, Toronto, 1952

ERNEST BUCKLER

There were the three days: the day before Christmas, the day of Christmas, and the day after. Those three days lamplight spread with a different softness over the blue-cold snow. Faces were all unlocked; thought and feeling were open and warm to the touch. Even inanimate things came close, as if they had a blood of their own running through them.

On the afternoon of the first day the cold relaxed suddenly, like a frozen rag dipped in water. Distances seemed to shrink. The dark spruce mountain moved nearer, with the bodies of the trees dark as before rain.

Martha had done up all her housework before noon, and the afternoon had the feel of Saturday. It was a parenthesis in time—before the sharp expectancy began to build with the dusk and spark to its full brightness when the lamp was lit. There were so many places it was wonderful to be that afternoon that David was scarcely still a minute.

He went outside and made a snowman. The snow was so packy it left a track right down to the grass roots. It was a perfect day to be alone with, the only confidant of its mysteries. Yet it was equally nice to be with people. The claim of their ordinary work was suspended today, no one's busyness was any kind of pushing aside.

He went inside and sat close to his grandmother. He asked her a string of questions; not for information, but because he was young and she was old. To let her feel that she was helping him get things straight was the only way he knew to give her some of the splendid feeling he had so guiltily more of.

He went out again where Chris was sawing wood. How could Chris *stand* there like that, today . . . his shoulders moved so patiently, the saw sank with such maddening slowness. Yet because he did, he was somehow wonderful. When a block fell, David would thrust the stick ahead on the saw-horse with such a prodigal surge of helpfulness beyond what the weight of the wood asked for that Chris would have to push it back a little before he made the next cut.

He went back into the house and stood at the table where his mother was mixing doughnuts.

Everything was clean as sunshine. The yellow-shining mixing bowl in the centre of the smooth hardwood bread board; the circles of pure white where the sieve had stood; the measuring cup with the flour-white stain of milk and soda on its sides; and the flat yellow-white rings of the doughnuts themselves lying beside the open-mouthed jug that held the lard, drift-smooth at the centre and crinkled like pie crust along the sides. His mother carried the doughnuts to the stove, flat on her palm, and dropped them one by one into the hot fat. He followed her, watching. They'd sink to the bottom. Then, after a fascinating second of total disappearance, they'd loom dark below the surface, then

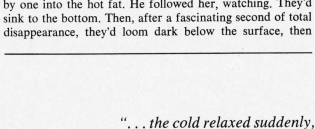

"*. . . the cold relaxed suddenly,
like a frozen rag dipped in water.*"

33

float all at once, brown and hissing all over. It had never been like this, watching her make doughnuts before.

He went into the pantry and smelled the fruit cakes that lay on the inverted pans they'd been cooked in. He opened the bag of nuts and rolled one in his palm; then put it back. He put his hand deep down into the bag and rolled all the nuts through his fingers: the smooth hazelnuts that the hammer would split so precisely: the crinkled walnuts with the lung-shaped kernels so fragile that if he got one out all in one piece he'd give it to Anna: the flat black butternuts whose meat clove so tightly that if you ever got one out whole you saved it to the very last.

Then he leaned over and smelled the bag of oranges. He didn't touch it. He closed his eyes and smelled it only. The sharp, sweet, reminding, fulfilling, smell of the oranges was so incarnate of tomorrow it was delight almost to sinfulness.

He went out and sat beside Anna. She was on her knees before the lounge, turning the pages of the catalogue. They played "Which Do You Like the Best?" with the coloured pages. Anna would point to the incredibly beaded silk dress that the girl wore standing in a great archway with the sunlight streaming across it, as her choice. He'd say, "Oh I do, too." And as his hand touched Anna's small reaching hand and as he looked at her small reaching face, he almost cried with the knowing that some Christmas Day, when he had all that money he was going to have, he'd remember every single thing that Anna had liked the best. She'd find every one of them beneath the tree when she got up in the morning.

He went out where his father was preparing the base for the tree. All the work-distraction was gone from his father today, and David knew that even if so few pieces of board were to be found as to defeat anyone else, his father would still be able to fix something that was perfect.

Joseph laid one crosspiece in the groove of the other. He said to David, "Think you could hold her just like that, son, till I drive the nails?"

"Oh yes," David said, "yes." He strove with such intense willingness to hold them so exactly that every bit of his strength and mind was soaked up. He touched the axe that would cut the tree. The bright cold touch of it shone through him.

He ran in to tell Anna it was almost time. He waited for her to button her gaiters. He was taut almost to pallor when Joseph stepped from the shop door, crooked the axe handle under one arm, and spat on the blade for one final touch of the whetstone.

"Chris," he called, "we're *goin!*"

"All right," Chris said. "You go on. I guess I'll finish the wood."

How *could* Chris stay here? How could anyone *wait* anywhere today? It was almost impossible to be still even in the place where the thing was going on.

Joseph walked straight toward the dark spruce mountain. David and Anna would fall behind, as they made imprints of their supine bodies in the snow; then run to catch up. They would rush ahead, to simulate rabbit tracks with their mittens—the palms for the parallel prints of the two back feet, the thumb the single print where the front feet struck together; then stand and wait. Their thoughts orbited the thought of the tree in the same way their bodies orbited Joseph's.

"Anna, if anyone walked right through the mountain, weeks and weeks, I wonder where he'd come out . . ."

"Dave, hold your eyes almost shut, it looks like water . . ."

"There's one, there's one . . ." But when they came to it the branches on the far side were uneven.

Joseph himself stopped to examine a tree.

"Father, the best ones are way back, ain't they?" David said quickly. This *was* a good tree, but it wouldn't be any fun if they found the perfect tree almost at once.

"There's one . . ." But it was a cat spruce.

"There's one . . ." But the spike at the top was crooked.

"There's one, Father . . ." But a squirrel's nest of brown growth spoiled the middle limbs.

Joseph found the perfect fir, just short of the mountain. The children had missed it, though their tracks were all about. He went to it from the road, straight as a die. The bottom limbs were ragged, but those could be cut off; and above them, the circlets of the upward-angling branches were perfect. The trunk was straight and round. The green of the needles was dark and rich, right to the soft-breathing tip.

"How about this one?" Joseph said.

The children said nothing, looking at the lower limbs.

"From here up," Joseph said. He nicked the bark with his axe.

"Yes, oh yes," they cried then. "That's the best tree anyone could find, ain't it, Father?" The ridiculous momentary doubt of their father's judgement made them more joyous than ever.

They fell silent as Joseph tramped the snow about the base of the tree, to chop it. David made out he was shaking snow from his mitten. He took off Anna's mitten too, pretending to see if there was any snow in hers. He stood there holding her mitten-warmed hand, not saying anything, and watched his father strike the first shivering blow.

The tree made a sort of sigh as it swept through the soft air and touched the soft snow. Then the moment broke. The children came close and touched the green limbs. They thrust their faces between them—into the dark green silence. They smelled the dark green, cosy, exciting smell of the whole day in the balsam blisters on the trunk.

Joseph stood and waited: the good kind of waiting, with no older-hurry in him. Then he lifted the tree to his shoulders, both arms spread out to steady it at either end.

The twins walked close behind him. They let the swaying branches touch their faces. They walked straight now, because the first cast of dusk had begun to spread from the mountain. The first dusk-stiffening of the snow and a shadow of the first night-wonder were beginning. Now the things of the day fell behind them; because all that part of the day which could be kept warm and near was in the tree, and they were taking the tree home, into the house, where all the warm things of after-dark belonged.

Anna whispered to David, "I got somethin for you, Dave."

And he whispered, "I got somethin for you, too."

"What?"

"Oh, I can't tell."

Then they guessed. Each guess was made deliberately small, so there'd be no chance that the other would be hurt by knowing that his present was less than the vision of it. Each of them felt that whatever they had for each other all their lives would have something of the magic, close-binding smell of the fir boughs somewhere in it, like the presents for each other of no other two people in the world.

The Mountain and the Valley, New York, 1952

2

ACTION

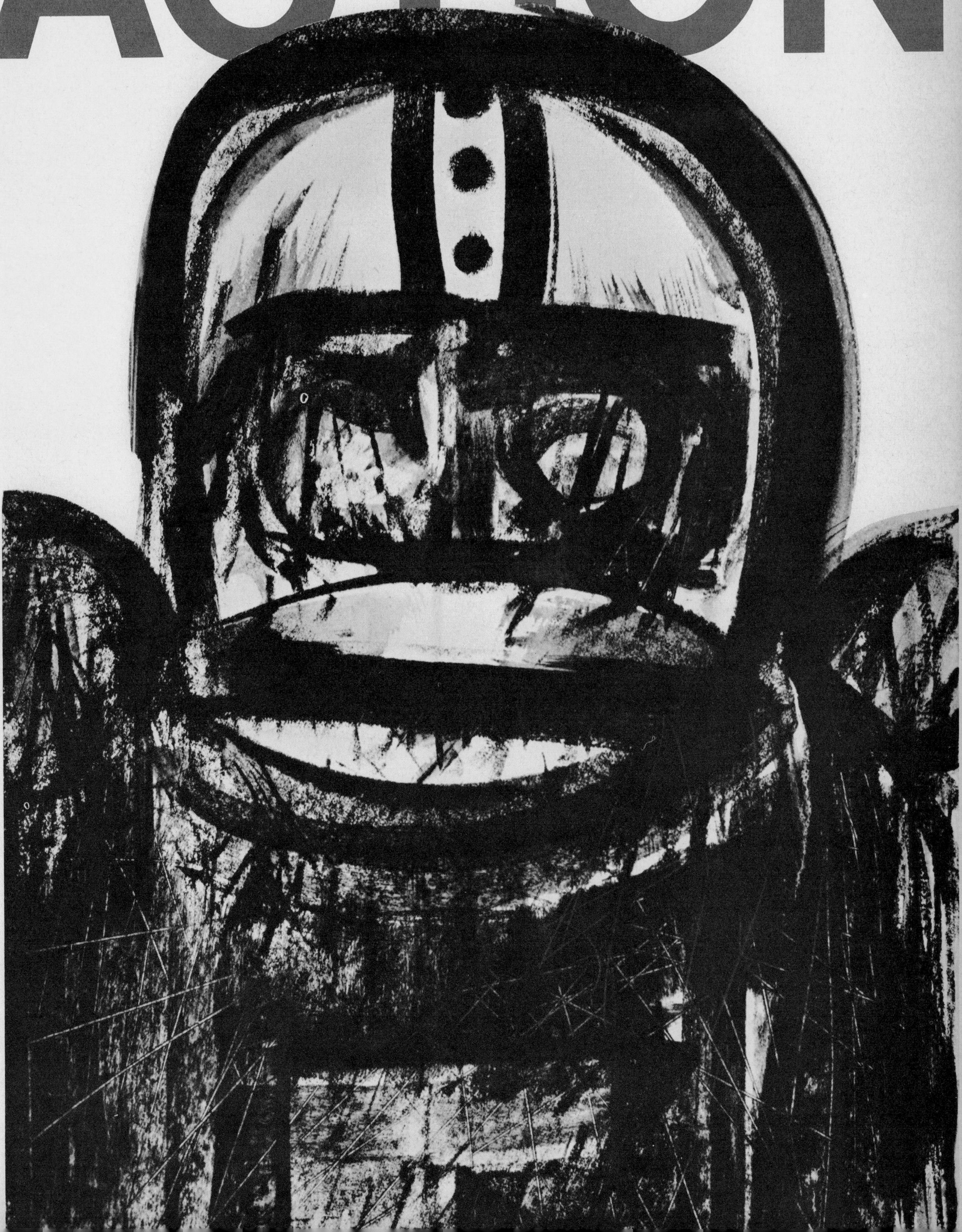

RODERICK L. HAIG-BROWN

Feeding or resting, the migrant schools held well together, usually within a few feet of the surface of the water. In the Canyon Pool, Spring had always sunk down among the rocks on the bottom to rest. Now, whenever her belly was full and the strong urge to feed had briefly left her, she rested with the school in mid-water, cushioned and drifting in the gentle subsurface swell from the violent winter storms. Over them, in the quick and scattering waves, there were nearly always ducks—goldeneyes, mergansers, butter-balls, mallard, teal, bluebills, harlequins and many others, driven in by the greater storms outside. High above these there were birds of prey at most times of the daylight; occa-sionally grey-blue darting peregrines that chased the strong-est flocks to the water just for the sport of it, because their fierce, quick brains and pulsing muscles craved instant satis-faction of the urge that sight of movement stimulated in them; Cooper's hawks, less wanton in their lesser strength, but sure and deadly when a weak or crippled bird came within reach; the bald eagles, ponderously efficient in finding cripples, always ready to battle for the kill of a swifter, more successful hunter; and the ospreys, strong keen hunters of fish, whose prowess served the eagles best of all.

The ospreys ranged widely over the estuary, searching for slow-moving coarse fish but plunging down upon young salmon whenever the schools offered themselves too near the surface. The bright clear days were best for them and a spell of frosty weather in February set them working keenly over the rippled blue surface of the bay. Almost in the breaking of the brittle waves there were copepod larvae, drawn up by the sunlight. Spring fed upon them with her school, cruising easily along close under the surface. An osprey slid down from the Oregon shore, riding into the strengthening north-west breeze. He soared on it, for love of the day and his living, graceful and harmless five hundred feet above the water. He set his wings and slid away half the height, soared briefly and slid away again to within fifty feet of the water. Then he began to hunt in earnest, working over the bay on long smooth strokes of his big wings. His neat white head, with a crest of dark feathers and the sharp, curved beak, turned this way and that as he flew. His pale eyes, small-pupiled in the bright light, saw movement of many things in the water below him. He changed his flight suddenly, hover-ing, rising a little in the wind, then his straightly upstretched wings and long downward-straining legs converted his body from plane into plummet and he drove down. He hit the water and disappeared into the splash. A moment later he was in the air again, flying on slow wings a few feet above the water. A few yards from his dive he checked his flight briefly and with a strong tremor of wings and body shook the water from his feathers.

He rose again to a fair height above the water, still head-ing into the wind; he moved ahead slowly, swinging back and forth in searching. He saw the school of feeding mi-grants, side-slipped directly over it, hovered briefly and made his dive. Spring had seen the shadow of the osprey's coming and had darted away from it. All around her she saw the flashes of the flight of the other migrants. Behind her, under the shattered surface of the waves, she saw the long legs and pale-grey reaching talons. Fully two feet under water the bird's strong claws gripped into the back of a nine-inch chinook. The small fish struggled, but the rough underside of the osprey's feet and the curve of the claws held him firmly. The osprey beat his wings and rose from the water.

The wind had freshened strongly and he tried to rise into it, but the added surface of the flat side of the fish slowed him down. He shook the water from his wings, struggled a little farther, then dropped back to the reaching waves. He lay there for a few moments, resting on outspread wings, his head raised and his fierce eyes looking about him in every direction. He rose again more easily and made headway into the wind. His grip on the fish was changed so that he now held it along the line of his body, its head towards the wind.

He had risen to a good height before he saw the eagle. He slid away instantly, downwind and towards the shore. But the eagle was an old bird, wise in his method of hunting. His fine head and broad tail shone brilliantly white in the sun-light and his broad black wings were carrying him swiftly to intercept the osprey before the sliding turn was fully made. The eagle came up to him and drove down. The osprey dipped, tumbled away, recovered. He was down within fifty feet of the water, but the eagle came at him again. The osprey dropped his fish and half turned in the air to defend himself. The eagle was past him with a rush of wings, intent upon the fish as it shone silver in the sunlight. He caught it easily above the water and swung upward. The osprey went back to his ranging search of the bay and in a little while stooped again, killed again and kept his prey.

Return to the River, New York, 1941

"He rose again more easily and made headway into the wind. His grip on the fish was changed so that he now held it along the line of his body, its head towards the wind. He had risen to a good height before he saw the eagle."

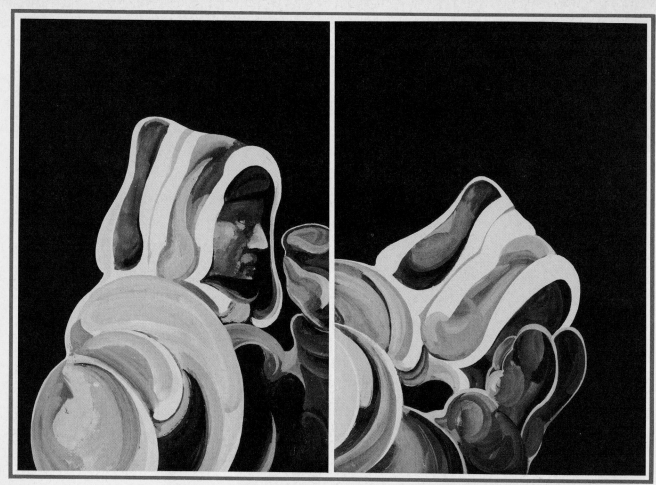

"... the wind whipped at the right side of his face, and iced him up, and he had to thaw himself, and the pain between his eyes was horrible."

DAVID WALKER

Sometimes the winds came stealthily. Sometimes they came full strength out of calm. This was such a wind. It rolled down on Simon Kepple Skafe as fast as a southbound express.

No sound of wind—time to check that the pressure ridge ran unbroken east and west as far as he could see—a rumour of wind—time to see that the team were going strong, swinging southwest from the pressure ridge. Already they had ceased to be eleven dogs and a lifeless sled, and had become a black corporate caterpillar moving on the white—a rushing

of wind, a curtain billowing at him from the north—time to put up both hoods, to put on his wolfskin mitts, to miss his dark glasses. Then the wind was here.

The parallel tracks were not hard to see, although the wind whipped at the right side of his face, and iced him up, and he had to thaw himself, and the pain between his eyes was horrible. But he kept on. Sometimes the tracks were two or three inches deep in the changing immutable skin of the snow; sometimes they were the faintest indentations; but he

38

could follow them, and now, any minute now, he would come in the loud wind upon the chaos of his dogs, dead dogs, murdering dogs and upset sled.

But he did not come upon them. He blundered into a crack in the ice and bruised his shin, and cursed about that, and saw ahead for the fifteen or twenty feet that he could see, ahead and to either side, and all he could see was bare dark ice through the wrack of snow. He went a little farther to see bare dark ice, no square-cut trail of a sled that ran on steel.

Now he faced the wind. It was a killer. It cut his face with knives and then it froze him up. It froze his cheeks and nose. It froze his eyelids shut. He turned his back to it, and thawed his face again, bowing his head to meet his mitts.

The cold was seeping into him. He knew what would be the first thing to go—his feet. If your hands went, there was something you could do—put them inside your bosom, rub them—and he did that now. But your feet—could you take off your socks to rub them? Could you put them in your bosom? You could jump about and run about and waste more body heat to keep your feet alive a little longer.

Where The High Winds Blow, London, 1960

THOMAS H. RADDALL

When you put on the phones it was as if your inner self stepped out of the bored and weary flesh and left it sitting in the chair in that barren room. For a space you were part of another world, the real, the actual living world of men and ships and ports, in which Marina was nothing but a sandbar and a trio of call letters in the signal books. Whistling, growling, squealing, moaning, here were the voices of men transmitted through their finger tips, issuing in dots and dashes, speaking twenty languages in one clear universal code, flinging what they had to say across the enormous spaces of the sea.

Here were the Americans with their quenched-spark sets, their high flute notes; and British tramps with their synchronous-rotaries, their hoarse baritone whose tune was halfway down the scale; the Canadians and their high wailing rotaries; the curious musical pop-pop-popping of the Germans with their Telefunkens; the French tramps and trawlers bleating like small sheep lost in the green wet pastures of the sea, and their liners crying out in quick precise tenor to the shore; the harsh scream of the occasional Japs, whose names were all something-*Maru*, jamming the six-hundred-metre wave with their infernal five-kilowatt sparks for an hour at a time, oblivious of international regulations; the quick, jerky piping of the Italians; the ringing manly bosuntones of the Norwegians, the Swedes and Danes.

All these sparks bellowed, cried, muttered or whispered together on the six-hundred-metre wave, the main channel for ship traffic. At night when the darkness increased their range by three, four or five times the uproar was terrific, the sound of a vast swamp on a spring night filled with vociferous frogs. By day the range and the Babel subsided; but there was seldom quiet. Ships talked to each other, or they demanded notice from the shore, crying the attention of New York or Boston or Cape Race or Marina, that outpost which could pluck messages far out of the ocean air and fling them on to the landline at Halifax. To wireless operators on the North Atlantic run these stations, known indifferently by name but intimately by their call signals—NAH, WBF, VCE, VCT—these were the tongues and ears of North America, the listening posts, the speaking trumpets of the continent.

The great liners with their tall masts and powerful transmitters bestrode the ocean, hurling messages now to one side, now the other. These were the prima donnas of the show, with strong clear voices sheering through the boom and trill of the chorus, uttering a few clipped notes here and there, and then bursting forth in long arias addressed to London, Paris or New York. Their voices rang about the wide sea spaces and all the others shrank to a murmur. But when the last cadenza died in a final dot or dash the chorus rose once more, the vast tramp-navy, the rabble of the sea, insistent and tumultuous, demanding the notice of each other or of some distant station on the land.

In all this medley there were certain sounds that had special meaning. Your own call signal first; but that was burned into your mind with letters of fire so that, waking or dozing in a dull watch, or reading or writing or pottering with the dials, its merest whisper brought you erect and alert in the chair, reaching out for pencil and message pad. There was CQ, the anonymous call that might mean anybody, the constant "Hey, Mac!" of the groping tramps. There was QST, the general call to all stations, ship and shore, which usually had to do with navigation warnings, icebergs or derelicts in the lanes, and suchlike matters. But most significant was a simple group of dots and dashes that for convenience were written SOS, although it could have been VTB or any combination of letters involving three dots, three dashes and three dots, all run together without pause. This was the magic symbol by which all the frogs in the great sea-swamp could be hushed in a minute. For every operator, even for cynics like Skane and old hands like Carney, that sound never lost its thrill, its quick clutch at the heart.

Usually the cry came from some foundering tramp, one still small voice in the uproar, barely heard by one or two ships on the edge of its range. But those ships spoke quickly, urgently, and were heard by the nearest shore station, the traffic policeman whose voice was law. Then a lonely man at the key of some outpost like Marina sent a trumpet call ringing through Babel like the voice of God, calling QST—"All Stations"—and demanding silence, adding a swift flicker of dots and dashes "STD BI FOR SOS." Silence fell within his range, and on the edge of it other shore stations took up the cry, and it went up and down the coast. Here and there a small ship-voice, uncomprehending, uttered a call or went on with some petty business; but then a shore station or a nearby ship cut in with a savage QRT—"Shut up!"

When this took place at night, with its enlarged range, the great silence spread like an infection all the way from Labrador to Florida, and you felt in that enormous emptiness hundreds of alert men on the coast and in the ships, listening, waiting, straining to catch the voice of distress. It was magnificent—all the traffic, all the urgent business of that vast stretch of sea and seaboard held up and silenced because, somewhere in the darkness, a few men were in peril.

The Nymph and the Lamp, Toronto, 1950

Jerome put his hand on the knob of the bedroom door and pulled it open. He saw the Engineer bent double clutching his groin and he knew where his mother had hit him that last time. Beyond the Engineer's hunched body he saw his mother's legs and thighs naked in the moonlight, but the hunched man was between the boy and her face.

It was the dog who betrayed Jerome's presence. Whining into the room, the spaniel rubbed against the man's legs and made him turn. The Engineer gasped, his face came around distorted with his sick pain and was horrible with the knowledge of what he himself had just done. But he saw Jerome and recognized him, and the moment he saw him he plunged. The boy dodged back and the Engineer stumbled and hit the floor with a crash, his spanner rattling away from his right hand. Jerome saw that his pants were down about his lower legs and that it was these which had tripped him. On the floor the Engineer looked up, his mouth shut, his violence as silent as that of a fish in the sea. Jerome turned to run, escaped from the room, reached the kitchen door, felt the dog against his legs and had the presence of mind to push him back before he himself went out. He closed the door behind him and with his nightshirt fluttering and his feet bare he ran across the moonlit, chip-strewn clearing into the darkness of the forest. When he was in the trees the undergrowth began cutting his bare feet, he stopped, turned and lay flat.

Nothing moved in the clearing. The long cookhouse with the two metal pipes that served as chimneys stood silent, its sloping roof whitened by the moon, its walls dark, its windows glittering like gun metal. He heard the sigh and gurgle of the river as it poured among the tree trunks along the flooded banks, but there was no sound of men and no light in any of the bunkhouses. He could not see the bunkhouse which was still occupied, but if there had been lights in it he would have seen their glimmer through the trees.

With the instinct of an animal Jerome got up and changed his position, slinking through the shadows among the stumps at the edge of the forest-fringe to a place he knew about thirty feet away. He found it, a depression in the ground about ten feet from the edge of the moonlight, and lay down and scooped pine needles over himself to conceal the whiteness of his shirt and skin. Lying flat with his chin in his hands and his elbows in the needles, he stared at the kitchen door and listened to the pounding of his heart.

The Engineer was only ten feet away when Jerome first saw him. He was skirting the forest-fringe with the spanner in his hand, staring into the darkness of the trees and stopping to take quick looks behind him. He wore no cap, his mackinaw shirt was open and in the moonlight Jerome saw the splash of dark hair rising out of his shirt to his throat. The man stopped directly in front of him and Jerome kept his head down, pressing his face into the needles, the needles itching in his hair. Once he lifted his eyes and saw the man's feet and noticed they were small feet even in those high leather boots. There was a crunch of bracken as the man entered the woods, one of his boots came down within a yard of Jerome's head, but the engineer was staring into the total darkness of the forest and did not look down at his feet. In the cool air of the night Jerome could hear the man

pant and thought he could feel the heat of his body. The boots turned and went back out of the forest into the clearing and as they crunched farther away Jerome looked up and saw the man's shoulders go around the corner of the cookhouse and down the path to the bunkhouses.

"I knew for certain that he was after me. He was putting himself between me and the men asleep in the bunkhouse. He knew I couldn't get around through the woods without making a noise. He knew the path was the only way I could hope to go."

Jerome wondered if he ought to call out, but he knew how hard the men slept and he knew who would be the first to hear him. In any case he was too frightened to call. Except for that single jeering laugh of his mother and the man's single outburst of obscenity, what had been done that night had been done with the silence of animals killing each other in the dark.

Jerome lay still until he began to shiver and when the shivering came it was so violent it seemed to shake the ground. It was like being tied up in the cords of his own muscles shaking the earth so that everyone living on it must know where to find him.

Getting to his feet, he beat the pine needles off his nightshirt and scraped some more of them out of his hair. Others chafed the tender skin between his thighs, but these he disregarded as he stepped slowly out of the forest into the moonlight. He stopped, waiting for the man to appear and give chase, but the only sound he heard was the pounding of his own heart and the only man he saw was the man in the moon. He believed there was a man in the moon who saw everything and didn't care, who sat up there seeing and not caring and laughing to himself, and he thought he was laughing now. With his nightshirt fluttering, the boy ran across the clearing, opened the kitchen door and went in. This time he forgot about the dog, who jumped outside and ran away before Jerome could close the door.

Inside the bedroom the blind was drawn and the darkness was total. Jerome found the match box, lit the lamp and turned to look. His mother's body lay like a sack under the blankets because the engineer had covered her and pulled the blind before going out. Jerome lifted the blanket, put his hands to her face and felt the fingers of his right hand sink into a warm stickiness. He jerked them back as though he had put them into fire and stood frozen.

"The bad wound was on the left side of her head and her left eye was bruised by his fist. Her mouth was open and her clear eye was open and angry. She looked far angrier than frightened. My mother died in a rage."

Her body was not yet cold, but it had lost some of its warmth and the blood barely oozed now that the heart had ceased to pump it. Blood was dark and wet all over the pillow and wetly thick in her hair; her breasts were like chalk-white balloons when he tried to shift her body. It was only then that he knew absolutely that she was dead. He cried out to her, he beat her naked breasts with his palms to wake her and all the time he did this he understood she was dead. Knowing she was dead he called to her to come alive again and take care of him, yet all this while he was glad the Engineer had not been like the other men whom she had humiliated.

Then he froze once more, for a step creaked outside. He blew out the lamp and turned to run into the darkness of the cookhouse where there were tables to hide under, but he was too late. The kitchen door creaked open and he crawled under the bed and crouched there against the wall with the sag of the spring just over his head.

The man entered and when Jerome heard him sniff, he knew he was smelling the snuffed wick of the lamp. When the man lit a match it was like an explosion of sound and light simultaneously, but the man did not carry the match to the lamp. Jerome saw his boots standing by the bed as the light slowly died. Then darkness again. Then the Engineer let out a slow, choking sob and went away. Jerome heard his feet go away noisily, heard him bump into a chair in the kitchen, open the door and leave.

He crouched shivering with cold and fright, and he might have stayed there for hours if the dog had not returned to the room. The dog came under the bed whining and nuzzling, and Jerome felt his long, wet tongue licking his feet. The feeling of the dog's tongue horrified him and he rolled over and pushed the animal away, pressing his hands against its muzzle. The beast whined appreciatively and Jerome's hair bristled when he knew the dog was licking his mother's blood off his fingers. He hit the dog and heard him whine. He hit him as hard as he could on the muzzle and the dog let out a yelp and left him alone. Then Jerome came out from under the bed and stood up.

Years afterwards he told Catherine that this was the first of many occasions when a sudden, clear-headed coolness came to him after moments of paralyzing terror. He was only ten years old, but he knew exactly what had happened and what else would happen if his mother's murderer caught him. He knew the murderer had left the bedroom because he was in terror of what he had done there, but he also knew he would be on the watch outside. The Engineer would almost certainly be watching by the kitchen door, for that was the natural way for Jerome to get out and it would also be the shortest route to the bunkhouse where the rest of the men were sleeping.

Jerome had to escape from the horror of that room where his mother lay dead. He took his clothes from the hooks where they hung: his shirt, stockings, pants, sweater and cap, and the heelless larrigans of cowhide he wore all year round. He took them out to the kitchen and dressed beside the stove which still was warm, with the dog nuzzling and whining, and he had to push the dog away several times as he pulled on his stockings. After he was dressed he washed the remaining blood from his hands under the pump and dried them on a roller towel. Very clear in the head now, he opened the big ice chest where the food was and took out the first thing he found. It was a garland of blood sausage much too clumsy and big to carry, so he cut it into lengths and stuffed a length of sausage into each of the side pockets of his pants. He left the kitchen and entered the long eating barn where the benches and trestle tables were, heading for the door at the far end, a door rarely used, and when he reached it he found it unbarred. He guessed that the Engineer had used this door when he had first gone into the clearing to search for him.

"It must have been the dog that saved me that first time. When I ran out into the clearing, the dog must have gone into the eating barn and when the Engineer heard him moving there, he must have mistaken him for me. That was the mistake that gave me time to hide."

The dog was with Jerome now and this time Jerome made no error; he caught him by the long hairs at the back of his neck, held him while he stepped out, then pushed him inside and closed the door on him.

From this corner of the cookhouse the distance to the edge of the forest was no more than twenty yards and nobody was in sight as Jerome ran across it and disappeared into the trees. He worked his way silently through trees and deadfalls until a quick coolness touched his cheeks and he knew he was near the water on the edge of the northwest branch where his canoe was beached. In flood time the branch invaded the forest a distance of thirty yards or so, and now it was pouring through the trunks of the trees, gurgling and sighing as it strained through the scrub and deadfalls, and Jerome saw quick flashes of light as the moon struck here and there against the living water.

He worked his way along, his oiled larrigans keeping the moisture off his soles, but once his foot sank into a hole and the icy wetness poured in through the laceholes and his foot felt cold and soon went numb. After a few minutes he reached the place where the canoes and rowboats were beached, his own little canoe among them. The camp motorboat was moored to a jetty about a hundred yards downstream in the main river, but the canoes and rowboats were moored where the current was weak, and now he saw their snouts projecting out of the blackness of the woods into the moonlight. He stepped out, looked up to see the sky a wide open dome with a moon in the middle of it and a vast circle of light shining around it.

"I knew I was going to make it. Every time afterwards when I was older, every time when I've been in danger and everything seemed hopeless, some moment like this always came. Suddenly I'd hear myself saying, 'You're going to make it. You're going to make it after all.'"

The short birch bark canoe with the air cans under the thwarts was easy to lift, he turned it over and ran it out into the water. He found his own paddle made to fit his height, and with a single movement he pushed the canoe off and swung himself over into the stern seat, then crept forward and settled down just about midships, got the paddle working and guided the canoe past a tree trunk and clear of some fallen branches. The movement of the current kept pressing him inshore, but he paddled hard on the left into a backwash that took the canoe gently out, he changed sides and gave two hard thrusts on the right, and then the canoe floated silently out into the great wash of moonlight where the branch widened into the main course of the river. The current of the branch carried him far out from the shore and when he felt himself making leeway he knew he was in the central stream at last. He gave two more thrusts and pointed the bow downstream, and at once he began to move fast on a river wide, firm, silver and alive bearing him down past the silent camp, utterly alone for the first time in his life, bearing him down under that wide open sky through the forest to the open sea which he knew was at its end.

Jerome paddled as he had been taught to paddle in a current, slowly and evenly, making long, steady sweeps of the paddle and after each stroke taking a short rest with the blade trailing behind like a steering oar. The river at this season and place was flowing at more than five miles an hour, breaking and gurgling in the shallows and sparkling in the moon, but out in the central current the flow was so satin-smooth the eddies were like whorls of polished glass. A thin mist lay patchily over water colder than the air, and the moon was enormous in the wide greenly-shining sky.

"When I grew older and learned how human organisms behave," he said, "I knew I was in that queer state of euphoria that often comes after shock. The response of the adrenal glands to danger. But that's a mechanic's way of looking at it. It's just as real for a man to say, after he's escaped a danger to his life, that he feels twice as alive as he ever felt before. All that night I never thought of my mother. I just thought about the canoe and the river and I was so alert that everything I saw and did—everything—I still remember."

Steadily the tiny canoe went down the river between the trees, following the curves almost by itself in the current. Now that he was secure in the canoe, Jerome eased further back against the air-can lodged under the stern seat and got the head up and sank the stern to give more purchase for the current to take him along. Often he passed floating logs and once he came up with a raft of them lodged on a hidden rock and damming the current, the water washing over and making the whole raft pitch and heave as though things were alive under it. He paddled around, touched logs once or twice and when he was clear he found himself in a flotilla of individual logs that had shredded out from the raft and were going down by themselves. He kept on paddling down, occasionally rubbing against a travelling log and sometimes afraid of holing his canoe, but as the logs were going in the same direction there was little danger of this. There were no lights on the shore, no cabins or houses, there was nothing but the forest, the sky, the moon, the river, the canoe and the logs floating down to the sea.

"I had no sense of time that night, but I'd guess it was about one in the morning when I first heard the motorboat. I can still hear it. It was a primitive boat, nothing but an old high-bowed fishing boat with an engine installed. Its motor was always getting out of order and the Engineer was the only man in the camp who could do anything with it. When I first heard it, the boat was still around the bend I had just rounded, and its sound came to me muffled by trees."

Jerome was abnormally strong for his age, his shoulders powerful even then, and now fear gave him its added energy. He paddled hard toward the shore, but at this point the current was so swift that when he tried to move athwart it the canoe was swept hard a-lee, he knew it would take him minutes to reach the shore and that even if he did, the back-washes would sweep him into the current again. A hundred yards ahead was a small wooded island in the middle of the stream and he brought the bow about and paddled for his life making the featherweight birch bark craft jump to his strokes. The drub-drub-drub of the motorboat struck his ears solidly and looking back he saw its dark shape with the hunched outline of the Engineer sitting at the hand-wheel in the starboard forequarter. As Jerome drew in toward the island he saw that many logs had got there first. Instead of a beach there was a mat of logs bobbing in the press of the stream and he was panic-stricken, for the log mat spread in clear moonlight about twenty yards out from the shore, and he knew he could never get through it to hide in the trees. There were all kinds of logs there, long ones and pit-props mixed, some of them piled on top of others and the whole mat creaking in the current. "I had never seen this island before but in a vague way I knew about it. There were several islands like that in the river and they caught tons of logs every year. Once the drives had gone down, work gangs used to follow to clear the islands one by one. That was one reason why men were still left in the camp."

The canoe lifted, slid smoothly up onto some half-sunken logs, stopped dead, and there was nothing for Jerome to do but lie in the bottom and wait. He peered over the side smelling the wet logs and hearing the gurgle and lap of the stream, the canoe bobbing gently with the logs while the motorboat came straight on growing larger all the time, its drub-drub-drub filling the river and the man at the wheel looming up. Jerome was sure the man was staring straight at him, but when the boat was about twenty-five yards off the island the Engineer moved and Jerome saw the bows swing sharply off and an instant later the dark length of the boat went out of sight around the left side of the island.

"Then I knew what he was doing. He was running away. All the men knew about the railway track that crossed the river at the town just inside the estuary. It was the railway a man made for when he got into trouble or just wanted to get away. Sometimes a man left after a fight and sometimes he just left. Looking back on it, I know the Engineer was numb with his own fear. He may have been drinking and that may have been why he didn't see me. Or maybe he was just exhausted by what he had done and in the state of mind when a man can't think or see anything because he can't stand thinking or seeing anything and does one thing automatically after the other. I don't know. But he was certainly getting away as fast as he could and in the only way he knew. There was no telegraph or telephone and it would be morning by the time any of the men would find my mother and a good time would pass before they missed the Engineer and put two and two together. He'd have lots of start. He'd reach the railway long before any of the men could reach it, and once he was at the tracks he'd have his choice of trains moving east or west. I knew nothing about east or west so far as the railway was concerned, not then. I didn't know that east was down to Moncton and Halifax and a dead-end, and that west was up to Quebec and Montreal, and that he'd certainly go west. But I did know he'd be able to catch a train, for all the trains stopped in that town for water."

For a long time Jerome lay in the canoe listening to the diminishing throb of the engine. Such wind as there was came up the river and it must have been twenty minutes before the throbbing ceased. It would die away and return, die and throb up again, but at last there was no sound but the lap of the river and the slow, water-softened creak of the shifting logs.

With the passing of the motorboat Jerome's euphoria left him and he began to shiver and cry. He was chilled because at dawn the cold increased and his left foot, which he had soaked while moving through the trees, began to ache. He reached into his pocket and felt the stickiness of the blood sausage he had stored there, he took it out, washed it in the river, bit off a mouthful and ate it. The taste of blood made him feel sick but he went on eating until his shivering stopped and he felt new strength grow inside of him. He scooped water out of the river in his cupped hands and sucked it in through his teeth though it was so cold it made them ache. Meanwhile more logs from upstream were floating down and kept looming at him out of the dark water, hunching at him silently, pressing at him out of the dark as though they were the river's muscles forcing him out. The log mat was loose enough for him to get his paddle into the water and he changed position and pushed and paddled until at last the canoe gave a quick slip sideways, swerved

"When the man lit a match it was like an explosion of sound and light simultaneously."

broadside on to the stream and began to list against the mat of logs as he paddled hard to get clear toward the left-hand channel. A new log loomed at him about to ram but he fended it off, struck hard with the paddle as the canoe's bow yawed against the pressure of the stream, then the unseen hand of the current caught him, he struck with the paddle on the left, the bow shot around and again he was in the flow, passing the island so effortlessly that he was by before he knew it and now in a widening river he went on with the current pouring down through the forest to the sea.

After a time—how long he did not know for he had lost all sense of time—he became conscious that the world was lighter and opening up. Instead of seeing the forest as a dark mass on either side of him, he saw it clear and close with individual trees standing out. Now the western sky where the moon was had become darker than the east, soon there was more light in the east than there had been in the dome of moonlight under which he had sailed since leaving the camp, and looking over his shoulder he saw the moon low over the forest, its light a pallid copper-coloured lane along a river that had become steel grey. Colours appeared, a flush of pink in the east broke apart until it looked like the parallel bars of a gate across the pathway of the dawn, the bars merged, the colours grew stronger, they swelled into a cool conflagration that flushed up into the wide and real sky as the entire world opened up.

Now Jerome became aware of life all around him as birds called in the forest on either side of the river, he saw the white trunks of a stand of birch, and as the current at this point swerved in toward the shore, the carolling ring of bird calls was loud and near. A crow flew out from a pine top and its cawing racketed back and forth across the river echoing from shore to shore. The hammer of a hungry woodpecker whacked against a dead trunk while a larger bird, one of the blue herons called cranes in the Maritime Provinces, flew slantwise across the rising dawn and turned slowly, its long legs folded in under its body and trailing behind, its snaky head hanging down as it quested for fish with slow flaps of its wings heading upstream along the right bank. Jerome heard a snick and saw the flash of a trout's belly. He paddled on through clear water with hardly a log in sight and within ten minutes there were snicking flashes all around him as trout broke the surface to feed on early flies, the first run of the season in from the sea, quick, slim fish with bellies as bright as silver coins, firm and fierce from a winter of cold salt water as they drove up against the current to the beds where they had been spawned. Jerome saw the lazy roll of a salmon about ten feet from the canoe, the little humping of water as the fish turned and went down; he heard a splash behind him but when he looked over his shoulder there was only a ruffle of broken water; he paddled a few minutes more, the trout still snicking, and then directly in front of the canoe the river broke open and a huge salmon slashed out shining, paused in the air with its hard muscles bending its body like a sickle and dropped with a drenching splash, the canoe crossed the broken water, and Jerome looking over the side saw the last twisting tail-thrust as the big fish went down.

Still the tiny canoe throbbed down the stream, the boy in the stern, and around the next bend he saw a shack but no smoke from its chimney pipe. Now he was sleepy and tired and stopped paddling; he sat with the paddles across his knees and his head sunk forward.

"I must have slept like that for half an hour, when I woke the canoe was drifting slantwise and light was hurting my eyes."

It was the rising sun, a turmoil of gold like a tremendous excitement in heaven pouring its arrows into the forest and flashing them off the stream. His limbs dead and cold, Jerome straightened the bow of the canoe and let it drift in a current much slower now because here the river was deep and he felt the huge unseen pressure of the tide lower down. Close to the shore he passed a deer drinking on a sandspit and after a while he was afraid that if he fell asleep again he would lose his paddle. A small cape stood out with a sentinel pine, the canoe struck it with a soft crunch and Jerome crawled ashore and dragged half of it clear of the stream. Then he got back in and slept.

When he woke the sun was almost directly overhead, his nostrils were dry with heat and his body felt tired, hot, heavy and stiff. It was a May morning without a cloud in the sky and already the heat had made the balsam forest pungent.

"The time must have been somewhere between eight o'clock and nine. At that season of the year the sun rises about five, so I must have been asleep nearly three hours. If it hadn't been for the glare I suppose I'd have gone on sleeping all day. I was in the aftermath of shock. Even now I can't tell you how far I had come down the river, but I had been paddling with a fast current for at least four hours before I fell asleep.

"But I didn't think about distances when I woke up. I didn't even know what distances were. What I remember is how I felt. I felt black. I felt the way I felt that morning after I first killed a man in the war. I saw my mother's dead face hard and angry in front of mine. God, she was an angry woman, that mother of mine. I saw the Engineer with his spanner and when I tried to eat some of my sausage I nearly vomited it up. I had to get out of that forest and get off that river. Far away was where I wanted to go, and then I thought about the trains."

Though he did not know it, Jerome was now close to the sea and was paddling in a new kind of river. As it nears salt water that river becomes wide and is tidal for several miles. The town lies a distance inland and Jerome could not see the open water of the Gulf, but he could smell it and his cheeks felt a new, salty moisture in the air. He became conscious of settlement along the shores—not a town, but a scattering of frame houses and large breaks in the forest where there were fields and cattle. He also became aware that paddling had turned into heavy, leaden work, for the river was much wider here than it had been at the camp, and its current was stopped by the pressure of an incoming tide from the sea. Jerome ached all over his body as he forced the canoe forward, he sobbed with exhaustion and shock and was drowned in his own sweat, he was on the point of giving up when he rounded a final bend and there, right in front of him, was the black iron bridge that carried the main railway line between Halifax and Montreal. Beyond it was a small wooden bridge for road traffic and beyond that the river seemed enormously wide. There was a town on Jerome's left, a small, drab town built almost entirely of wood, and through his sweat he remembered having been in it before, last fall when he came down in the steamboat with his mother and some men, the time she bought him his first ice cream. As his canoe drifted in toward the bridge he backed water and tried to ease toward the shore. He was so tired he cried. Then he almost dropped his paddle in terror, for a train appeared out of nowhere almost on top of him as it crossed the bridge.

"It was only a small work-train—an old-fashioned engine with two olive-grey cars and a caboose on the end. It made an awful racket though, for it crossed that iron bridge with me almost underneath it. Its exhausts were crashing as it got up speed and it belched smoke from the soft Cape Breton coal all the engines burned in those days. The whole river seemed to shake as it crossed the bridge, but by the time I passed under it the roaring had stopped and I heard the singing drone that rails make when a train goes away down a track. I looked up and saw a man on the platform of the caboose looking down at me and his face was shiny black. He was the first Negro I ever saw and I wondered if all the people in the world outside the camp were black like him."

Jerome forced himself into a last spurt of action and paddled the canoe across the current, making heavy leeway, toward a jetty on the left bank between the two bridges. He remembered it from the time when the steamboat had landed him there. The sight of the jetty also reminded him of the motorboat and he became terrified, for what if the Engineer were waiting for him on the wharf? But there was no sign of the motorboat either at the wharf or along the shore.

"He had either beached it above town or sank it in the river. He'd have wanted to walk quietly into town at dawn before the people were up and hide somewhere near the tracks till a train stopped."

Two men in dungarees and peaked caps were sitting on the curb of the jetty watching Jerome as he paddled in, but neither of them moved as he swung against the landing stage. He climbed out and hung onto the canoe with no plan whatever. He was just doing one thing after another and the next thing he did was to take the painter and secure it to a mooring post.

"Wheer'd yew git thet canoe from, son?"

A lean, unshaven face with a chicken throat was staring down at him from the curb of the wharf.

"It's mine."

"Littlest goddam canoe I ever seen," the man said and spat into the water.

Jerome climbed the ladder stiffly and as he reached the wharf the man made a lazy half-turn in his direction.

"Wheer'd yew come from, son?"

"I bin paddlin'."

The man spat again but did not answer and continued sitting with his legs dangling and his unshaven lantern jaws working steadily on his cud of tobacco. Jerome, afraid of everything and everyone and tired in every bone, walked shakily off the dock onto a dirt track that ran along the riverside of the little town. He reached the railway, bent down and touched one of the shiny rails and found it so hot it burned. When he reached the station he saw men unloading freight out of a solitary box car and was surprised that none of them were Negroes. Jerome sat on a bench under the overhang of the station roof and ate one whole length of his blood sausage, and there he continued to sit an unknown length of time half-asleep and half-awake like the town itself, but feeling a little stronger now there was food in his stomach.

The Watch that Ends the Night, Toronto, 1959

RALPH CONNOR (CHARLES WILLIAM GORDON)

Once more the campus is cleared. Battered and bloody as to features, torn and dishevelled as to attire, but all eager and resolved, the teams again line up, knowing well that they have before them a half-hour such as they have never yet faced in all their football career.

It is 'Varsity's kick. Campbell takes it carefully, and places it in touch well within the McGill twenty-five. After the throw-in, the teams settle down to scrimmage as steady as at the first, with this difference, however, that 'Varsity shows perceptibly weaker. Back step by step their scrimmage is forced toward the centre, the retreat counterbalanced somewhat by the splendid individual boring of Campbell and Shock. But both teams are alert and swift at the quarters, fierce in tackle and playing with amazing steadiness.

Suddenly Carroll nips up the ball and passes hard and swift to the half back immediately behind him, who in turn passes far out to Bunch on the left wing. With a beautiful catch Bunch, never slacking speed, runs around the crowd, dodges the quarters, knocks off Martin, and with a crowd of men of both teams close upon his heels, makes for the line.

Before him stands Bate alone. From his tall, lank make one might easily think him none too secure on his legs. Bunch determines to charge, and like a little bull rushes full at him.

But Bate's whole football life has been one long series of deceptions, and so he is quite prepared for this kind of attack. As Bunch comes at him he steps lightly aside, catches the half back about the neck, swings him round and lands him prone with such terrific impact that the ball flies out of his grasp.

Immediately little Brown has it, passes to Martin, who on being tackled passes to The Don. The field before him is full of the enemy, but The Don never hesitates. Doubling, twisting, knocking off, he eludes man after man, while the crowds on the line grow more and more frantic, and at length, clearing the main body, he sets off across the field to more open country on the 'Varsity left. Behind him come Campbell, Shock, Martin and others, following hard; before him stand three of the McGill defence: Dorion, McDonnell and Mooney. He has already made a great run, and it looks as if he cannot possibly make through.

First Dorion springs at him, but The Don's open hand at the end of a rigid arm catches him full in the neck, and Dorion goes down like a stick.

Big McDonnell bears swiftly down upon him and leaps high at him, but The Don lowers his shoulder, catches McDonnell below the wind and slides him over his back; but before he can get up speed again little Carroll is clutching at his hips, and Mooney, the McGill full back, comes rushing at him. Swinging round, The Don shakes Carroll partly off, and with that fierce downward cut of his arm which is his special trick, sends the little quarter flying, and just as Mooney tackles, passes the ball over his shoulder to Shock, who is immediately pounced upon by half a dozen McGill men, but who, ere he is held, passes to Campbell, who in turn works forward a few yards, and again on being tackled, passes to The Don. It is a magnificent bit of play.

The spectators have long since passed all bounds of control, and are pouring on the field, yelling like mad people.

Even the imperturbable old lady loses her calm for a moment, and gripping Helen's arm exclaims, "Look at that now! Man, man, yon is a grand laddie."

There is no chance for The Don to run, for a swarm of the McGill men stand between him and the line only a few yards off. Then he does the only possible thing. Putting his head down, he plunges into the crowd in front of him.

"Come on, Shock," yells Campbell. Instantly a dozen 'Varsity men respond to the cry and fall in behind Campbell and Shock, who, locking arms about The Don, are shoving him through for dear life.

There are two minutes of fierce struggle. Twenty men in a mass, kicking, scragging, fighting, but slowly moving toward the McGill line, while behind them and around them the excited spectators wildly, madly yelling, leaping, imploring, adjuring by all kinds of weird oaths to "shove" or to "hold." In vain the McGill men throw themselves in the way of the advancing mass. Steadily, irresistibly the movement goes on. They are being beaten and they know it.

"Down! down!" yells big Huntingdon, dropping on his knees on the line in front of the tramping, kicking 'Varsity phalanx.

A moment's pause, and there is a mass of mingling arms, legs, heads and bodies, piled on the goal line.

"Held! held!" yell the McGill men and their supporters.

But before the referee can respond Shock seizes The Don below the waist, lifts him clear of the mob, and trampling on friend and foe alike, projects him over the struggling mass beyond the enemy's line, where he is immediately buried beneath a swarm of McGill men, who savagely jump upon him and jam his head and body into the turf.

"He's in! he's in!" shrieks Betty, wildly waving her hand.

"Will it be a win, think ye?" anxiously inquires Shock's mother. "It will hardly be that, I doubt. But, eh—h, yon's the lad."

"Down! down!" cries the 'Varsity captain. "Get off the man! Let him up, there!"

But the McGill men are slow to move.

"Get up!" roars Shock, picking them off and hurling them aside.

"Get up, men! Get up! The ball is down," yells the referee through the din, into the ears of those who are holding The Don in a death grip.

With difficulty they are persuaded to allow him to rise. When he stands up, breathless, bleeding at the mouth, but otherwise sound, the crowd of 'Varsity admirers go into a riot of rapture, throwing up caps, hugging each other in ecstatic war dances, while the team walk quietly about recovering their wind, and resisting the efforts of their friends to elevate them.

The Prospector, New York, 1904

". . . the widening huddle, fists swinging, gloves and sticks littering the ice."

MORLEY CALLAGHAN

In the corner to the left of the Canadian goal a Ranger forward was blocked out and held against the boards by a Canadian defenceman, who cleared the puck up the ice. The Ranger forward, skating past the defenceman, turned and slashed at him, breaking the stick across his shoulder. The official didn't see it. The play was at the other end of the ice. The defenceman who had been slashed spun around crazily on his skates, dropped to his knees, and circled around holding his neck. The crowd screamed. The other Canadian defenceman, dropping his stick and gloves, charged at the Ranger forward and started swinging. The Ranger forward backed away, his stick up, trying to protect himself. The official, stopping the play, made frantic motions at the fist-swinging defenceman, waving him off the ice. Another Ranger forward came out of nowhere and dived at the defenceman and tackled him; then all the players converged on one another, each one picking an opponent in the widening huddle, fists swinging, gloves and sticks littering the ice. Some of the players fenced with their sticks. The crowd howled in glee. The referee finally separated the players and handed out penalties. He gave a major penalty to the Canadian defenceman who had first dropped his stick to attack the Ranger forward who had really precipitated the brawl; he gave a minor to the Ranger forward who had dived at this defenceman and tackled him. And the forward who had broken his stick over the defenceman's shoulder, the instigator, the real culprit, was permitted to escape. He skated around lazily, an indifferent innocent.

"What about him?" the priest asked Catherine as he pointed at the Ranger. "Yes, what about him? Look at the fake innocent," Catherine cried. She thrust out her arm accusingly. Ten thousand others stood up, pointed and screamed indignantly, "Hey, what about him? Why don't you give *him* a penalty?" The Ranger skated nonchalantly to the bench to get a new stick. His air of innocence was infuriating, yet the referee, the blind fool, was deceived by it. The players on the Canadian bench, all standing up, slapped their sticks on the boards, screamed at the referee, and pointed. The referee, his hands on his hips, went right on ignoring the angry booing. He proposed to face off the puck.

"Boo-boo-boo!" Catherine yelled, her handsome face twisted, her eyes glazed with indignation. "He's letting him go scot-free. The one who started the whole thing."

The stout French Canadian, who had been standing up shouting imprecations in bewilderingly rapid French, suddenly broke into English. Twelve thousand people were also screaming, but by shifting to English he imagined he would get the referee to listen to him. His jaw trembled, his eyes rolled back in their sockets, he was ready to weep; then his face became red and swollen, and he cried out passionately, "Blind man! Idiot! All night you are a blind man! A thief, a cheat! You're despicable–go on back home, go out and die! I spit on you!" He cupped his hands around his mouth and let out a gigantic moan.

The ice was now a small white space at the bottom of a great black pit where sacrificial figures writhed, and on the vast slopes of the pit a maniacal white-faced mob shrieked at the one with the innocent air who had broken the rules, and the one who tolerated the offence. It was a yapping frenzied roaring. Short and choppy above the sound of horns, whistles, and bells, the stout French Canadian pounded McAlpine's shoulder; he jumped up on his own seat, he reached down and tore off his rubbers and hurled them at the ice. A shower of rubbers came from all sections of the arena and littered the ice as the players ducked and backed away. Hats sailed in wide arcs above the ice and floated down.

"They've all gone crazy," McAlpine muttered to Catherine. "Just a crazy howling mob."

The Loved and the Lost, Toronto, 1951

SIR WILLIAM VAN HORNE

All the manliness of the civilized world is due to wars or the need of being prepared for wars. All the highest qualities of mankind have been developed by wars or the dangers of wars. Our whole civilization is the outgrowth of wars. Without wars, religion would disappear. All the enterprise of the world has grown out of the aggressive, adventurous, and warlike spirit engendered by centuries of wars.

Letter to S. S. McClure, 1910

EARLE BIRNEY

Turvey was a little dashed when he found that he was in a different platoon from Busby and the Icelanders, a group which the tall youth on his right described as the Goon Squad. They were standing easy, in a corner of the square, waiting for their first drill.

"It's for morons, brother; you gotta low O-score, I bet. Watcha make, you know?"

"Eighty-nine."

"Mine's seventy-six," said the tall one, who had responded at rollcall to the name of Roach. There was a hint of superiority in his voice. "They dont take em much lower." He cocked his jaw confidentially. "It's all horse-feathers though. Aint none a these crystal-ball bastards can drill a gopher at a hunerd yards with a twenty-two like I can, I bet yah. Trouble is though, they gointa make us do extra drill. Ten weeks we gointa be in this dump, brother; mosta them oney goin to be here eight. And they got the collich boys and brainstorms separated off and I heard they gointa let them out in six. It's the joes like us gointa do the fightin though, you watch. Can yah wrassle?"

The platoon was "shunned" before Turvey could reply, harried around the parade square for a while and then led off by a stumpy morose sergeant over a windy field and halted near a row of dwarf gibbets from each of which hung stuffed gunnysacks. Another group of trainees was already in action here, bayonets fixed, making involved twisting rushes at the bloated brown torsos and inflicting bright straw wounds as they passed. The sergeant in charge of the stabbing operations broke off and went into a huddle with their own sergeant. Roach, who seemed to have everything taped beforehand, whispered delightedly:

"They's a ballup somers; rookies dont have no baynit drill

"He found his mudcased plate and filed it in his battleblouse for cleaning later."

for a month yet, I heard; we gotta letcher on the parts of a rifle cordin to what our corp said; by geez they oughta have some of these officers right here in the Goon Squad."

A young lieutenant appeared, bony-kneed in undersized shorts. He joined the sergeants fretfully; there was a great fluttering of training schedules among them. The lieutenant's treble, indistinct in the fitful wind, rose higher with impatience.

"Do anything you like with them, sergeant, until the next period but get them out of here. Take them over to the assault course and–ah–show them around."

Turvey's sergeant looked more depressed than ever, and surprised as well. He stood at attention for a moment; the natural sag of his thin lips deepened, his eyebrows rose over round eyes. Then evidently he made a decision. He clamped his long jaw firmly and said, "Very good, sir," with that curious combination of astonishment, submission, and contempt which practised sergeants use in addressing foolish subalterns. Then he saluted with slightly exaggerated precision and led his charges over to a series of earthworks and entanglements at the far end of the camp.

He stood them easy on the top of a high earth bank and warned them to pay attention, but for a long time he just stared at the slouching group. His round bulbous eyes regarded them in a way that reminded Turvey of his father when he was about to climb into the pigpen at Skookum Falls and stab a favourite hog. His father always got attached to his pigs. There was certainly pity in the sergeant's eyes, but when his voice came it was carefully tough; in fact it was like gristle.

"All right, men. This here's the assault course. It starts with this here ramp. When I give the word of command, the three leadin men will walk up the ramp, jump down onto the platform, then crawl *under* the barb wire, *acrost* the water hazard, *over* that there wall, and back *through* them sewer pipes. Now I'll repeat that and remember you gunna do this as fast as you can and no holdin up."

Thirty uneasy men stood and regarded the ramp. From the edge of the earth bank in front of them, three parallel planks, spaced about two feet apart, sloped steeply up to a cross beam. The beam was supported by log pillars whose bases, together with the platform to which the sergeant had referred, were hidden by the crest of the bank. Beyond the ramp the terrain dropped; they could see a confusion of trampled mud crossed with spiny coils of wire and spotted with hollow concrete pipe. Beyond these again was a reedy swamp and, on its far side, a kind of billboard at least ten feet high and apparently naked of ledge or handhold.

The sergeant had repeated his instructions exactly, except that his voice had sunk lower and lower until at the end, when he asked for questions, Turvey was almost sure he had said, "Any last requests?"

"How high's the ramp, sarge?" It was Ball, a potbellied chap with a little sunburned face. His steel helmet, issued that morning, seemed about to come down like a snuffer and extinguish the orange glow of his nose.

The sergeant gazed at him grimly. "This here ramp is regalation height." There was silence.

"We keep our helmets on?" It was Ball again.

The sergeant moved his thin lips soundlessly like a man at prayer. The surprised arch of his eyebrows seemed to have become permanently fixed and his pop eyes rolled up and down the front row.

"This here is an assault course, see. You supposed to be attackin over broken ground. Theys enemy in the woods beyond that there swamp. So, you gunna keep your helmets on your heads and carry your rifles atta *trail* and"—he surveyed the lot of them desperately—"any bastard gets his barrel muddy—" He left the threat unfinished as if he already despaired of its effectiveness. There were no more questions.

They were brought to attention, right-turned, and steered in column of three upon the ramp. Turvey was in the second triad of shufflers to tackle the swaying planks; in front of him was Roach; they were on the outside right. Halfway up his plank, Turvey heard the first yell. It came from Mc-Guigan, the broad-beamed Irishman who had been the first to poise at the top of the middle plank and been precipitated out into space as much by the prancing board as by the watchful bark of the sergeant standing on the bank behind them. The yell, which had a pained animal quality about it, was followed at split-second intervals by remarkably similar cries from the lead man on the left and from Roach.

Pressing to the crosslog Turvey could see, a dizzying distance below him, the three who had jumped. Roach was already barging on towards the barbed wire, cursing ornately in rhythm with his agonised limp. The lefthand leader was belly down and gasping in the mud like a stranded fish, his helmet several yards off. The Irishman, after his first howl, was now quietly staring at the sky, one arm draped over a corner of the landing platform. As Turvey gazed, the voice of the sergeant, devoid now of anything but blind relentless command, came pelting up at him from the rear:

"Keep movin, keep movin. Next three over. Get the lead outa your arse. This aint no sight-seein tour."

Turvey tried to balance himself on the rim until he could find the likeliest spot to aim his leaden feet. At least fifteen—was it twenty?—feet below him there lay in wait a rectangle of heel-gouged, sunbaked clay, rimmed with knotty logs and raised about two feet above the surrounding bog. The whole little contrivance seemed scarcely roomy enough for one man to land on accurately, let alone three, abreast, helmeted, and carrying rifles. At least they hadnt been asked to fix bayonets beforehand. He was trying to decide whether he would be more likely to survive if he aimed at the end of the raised sacrificial altar or if he tried to overleap it and hit the mud (there was a risk of crashing on the prone Irishman, either way), when the rifle of the man behind, lurching up the ramp under the impetus of the sergeant's insults, connected neatly with the centre of Turvey's rump. Turvey leapt without further calculation.

His left foot landed exactly in one of the ramp's fossilized foot-prints; after the rest of his body pitched forward, Turvey's army boot was retained in the clay's grip and Turvey's solid one hundred and sixty pounds pivoted on his ankle before dragging it clear. Still clutching his rifle in one hand and reaching for his ankle with the other, he executed a complicated forward somersault and came to rest sitting in the mud.

Between shoots of pain and while groping for his false teeth, which had shot out, he heard the sergeant urging the third trio over the top, and the fourth, and the fifth. He found his mudcased plate and filed it in his battleblouse for cleaning later. Then he hopped over and sank beside the Irishman, who had revived sufficiently to drag himself clear of the growing human waterfall. They regarded the fate of this stream which the sergeant was too busy initiating above to observe in its full spate below.

Roach somehow had cleared the first hurdle of wire and had even remembered to hold his rifle clear of the mud, but preoccupied with this soldierly trick, and still limping, he had tried to go over instead of under the second row of concertina. Caught in its intricate fangs he was engaged at the moment mainly in weaving together most of the rather ingenious obscenities at his command.

The bog-fish whom Turvey had glimpsed from the ramp's top had recovered his breath and, sitting up, was now totally absorbed in the job of getting mud out of the interstices of his face.

More victims were flung down to them as they watched. Ball, the sunburned soldier who had starred at question time, came flapping down like a shot grouse, shedding his rifle in mid-air; he ricocheted from the platform and landed on his head by Turvey's feet. Turvey was able to pry Ball's oversized helmet up to his forehead before it could smother him, and boosted him to his feet, whereupon the newest victim, who seemed to have lost his sense of direction, if indeed he had yet got his eyes open, ran straight back into one of the ramp posts, banging his helmet over his ears once more. He slumped gently under the striped shadow of the ramp and took no further interest in the action.

By this time about thirty had cascaded over the little cliff. Of these a dozen, by some mystery of hardihood, had picked themselves up and reached the barbed wire. Five were in fitful rest among its briary coils; the remainder were bogged down at various levels in the water hazard. Except Roach. That hero of the hour had recovered from his limp, and the wire, struggled through the swamp and, still clutching a muddy object that had been his rifle, was leaping galvanically at the billboard in a futile attempt to clutch its top with his free hand. Suddenly a new voice shrieked above the sergeant's:

"Halt!" it cried hysterically. "Call your men back, sergeant." The spindly legs of the young lieutenant they had seen at the bayonet ground were dancing on the bank. "My God, what's going on here? Who told you to put these men over this course?"

The sergeant advanced stiffly until he was the regulation two paces from the lieutenant, saluted beautifully and froze to attention. "Beggin your pardon, sir, you did. Your orders waš for me to take this here platoon over the assault course."

"You imbecile!" screeched the officer, forgetting to return the salute, "I said take them over TO the assault course, *TO* the assault course! I just wanted them out of the road until we found out what the hell we're supposed to do with them. Dont you know the Engineers condemned this ramp yesterday?"

"Yes, sir, but your orders wa—"

"Didnt you read the sign over there?" The lieutenant's voice went into a squeak with rage and he thrust a wavering swagger stick at a notice tacked on one of the ramp's posts, OUT OF BOUNDS TO ALL TROOPS. "Didnt you read your Part One Orders this morning? Where's your bloody hea—" But the lieutenant at last remembered that his audience was too large and unselect for the occasion. He gazed at the little Dantean circle below him, the still faintly writhing field of battle, and made a soldierly effort to sound nonchalant.

"As you were, lads. No, ah, serious casualties, I take it?"

When the various grunting figures had been unhooked from the wire, pried from the mud, and assisted to the bank it was found that twelve of the thirty were indeed intact. Of the remainder all but one were, like Turvey, suffering from nothing worse than a sprained or broken ankle; the exceptions were Joey Deerfoot, the Huron, who had broken a heel and bitten a tooth off on his own knee, and McGuigan, whose back had unaccountably splintered.

Turvey, Toronto, 1949

PHILIP CHILD

But with the grey daylight they found themselves in a morass utterly devoid of any homely landmarks. The shell-pocked terrain had been chewed and spat forth by a Cyclops. The landscape lacked relevance to humanity or to anything growing. It was simply *empty*. True a captured "pill-box" and a few rotting tanks were visible, on the crest of the ridge ahead paleolithic rubble marked what had been a village, and here and there splintered tree trunks cut off short bristled like the beard on a corpse. But all these things had long since died; men had gone to earth there, earth to mud, and trees to splintered stumps. The only living things visible were the guns scattered everywhere, barely discernible in the conquering monotony, and inhabiting the waste like lost spirits in hell. The landscape was significant of nothing and the significance of mere emptiness was appalling. To see so vast a tract of fruitful earth pulped into a cancerous girdle made one feel uneasy in that part of one deep down that never feels secure because it belongs to the earth and fears to be reduced to the primitive element of mud into which human clay and man's machines have been absorbed. It was a landscape. It was a raped landscape, naked, raw, and expiring. . . . A cockney dispatch rider came chugging up the road (almost deserted in day-time), whistling cheerfully. His appearance in that place and in that mood was ridiculous and inappropriate—and reassuringly human.

On the 7th of June, 1917, the British Army took Messines and began the Third Battle of Ypres; on November 6th they took Passchendaele and, looking down for the first time since 1914 on the Plain of Flanders, ended the battle having advanced through fourteen thousand three hundred yards of hell at a cost of three hundred thousand casualties. Pilckem, Langemarck, Menin Road, Polygon Wood, Brookseinde, Poelcappelle, Passchendaele, and again Passchendaele—these are the battles of 1917 fought in the Salient, and in these battles at some time or another the majority of the divisions of the British Army in France went through the "blood bath"—often twice or thrice: grim names for Britain to remember, and sacred.

Men advanced through porridge-like mud in which they sometimes sank to their waists, wearing sandbags about their boots to keep them from sinking deeper, using a sandbag filled with mud for a pillow when they infrequently slept; slipping, stumbling, gliddering, struggling, pulling one another out of that slough. In broad daylight flights of wasps with black crosses on their wings flew low and stung them with machine guns as if they were crawling grubs. At night the roads and duckboards were continuously swinged with steel, yet over them men, mules, and ammunition had to go. Blazing shell dumps lit their purgatorial passage. They fought incessantly, gaining a rod here, often pushed back in a counter-attack there, struggling in gas masks, holding rifles in numbed hands. Frequently they suffered many barrages in a single day. The stretcher bearers—eight men to a stretcher in that mud—wandered in No Man's Land; sometimes their bullets found them and they fell and, sinking into the mud, were not. Often men sat down and cursed and sobbed and then got up and stumbled on. Rarely they hummed a song or whistled *Instead of hugging a saucy wench I cuddle a sandbag in a trench*—only there were few sandbags and fewer trenches. Somehow many of them existed and survived; but they were not the same men afterwards, for they had seen more than death, they had faced corruption of the soul, and despair.

A spray of multi-coloured lights had soared from the section of shell-holes and pill-boxes marked red in the trench maps, bursting into a shivering cluster. This beautiful firework, worthy of its task, had slipped the leash from a straining pack of upthrust, sleek steel muzzles and the barrage charged down upon them. It swooped down the air on steel wings. It gored the earth with self-destroying roars, blasting it and tossing it upwards in great fistfuls. . . . Dan looked behind him: spouts of smoke and mud were dancing a hornpipe there too; and to their flanks; and in front of them. . . . It was what gunners called a box barrage; its purpose was to isolate them within walls of steel and sound. You had the illusion that the earth was slipping about you, and it was no mere illusion. Beside Dan, a boy threw himself flat, then jumped up–to go where? A gout of wet mud plastered him across the shoulders and sent him squattering into the unsumped scum at the bottom of the enlarged shell-hole. Officers and men had tensed themselves instantly, adopting to their sudden need their several tried soul-attitudes with the speed of habit, as one braces oneself to physical pain after a short surcease. One felt like a cork in a hurricane. What terrified was the rhythm of the sound to which one's nerves danced a jangled accompaniment. Each shell swinged the distant air, increased to a full-throated roar that promised completion this time, and burst its sides in triumphant self-immolation. . . . Time ceased to have meaning. . . . A long time. A long time.

The barrage had lifted and dropped behind them. The subaltern straightened himself as well as he could without showing all of his head above the shell crater, and threw away his cigarette. "Well, lads, here they come!"

They came in little uneven knots of men, lightly weighted with equipment, but none the less stumbling and sliding down into scummy shell-holes, struggling through the mud that sucked at the legs like glue. In driblets they came, but there were a lot of them. . . . They withered to the chatter of rifles and Lewis guns like a house of cards when you flip your finger. Then our own barrage came down like a breaking comber and simply blotted them from sight in smoke.

The infantry officer scurried past him not bothering to stoop any longer and shouted over his shoulder. "They're in on the left. Bring your bombs, gunner. Now's your chance!" Dan got Loversedge and they scuttled down the shallow ditches that were ditches no longer but a tossed-up runnel of stinking mud vaguely conforming to the trench line: as if a shaking finger had been run through a bowl of porridge. Action lifted his spirit and cleared his mind of the poisoning thoughts that formed like a cesspool while you were waiting to be blown to fragments. As he ran he marvelled that anyone could have stayed alive in these crazy ditches while the earth round about and beneath was being pummelled into new shapes. The answer was that not many had; all that remained of most of the defenders lay beneath him and before him and had to be tripped over and trodden under as he ran. But those few, those devoted few, who were left alive were firing, cursing or singing, or simply firing as coolly as if they were at the butts.

A black object on a short stick came hurtling towards them end over end. It was not well aimed and exploded short. Coal-scuttle helmets were visible bobbing and weaving to the left. "While my bombs last," Dan thought. He threw at the helmets. Arms splayed out centrifugally above the rim of a shell crater. He heard groans. He felt neither fear, nor rage, nor pity, only the release of power.

"Here she comes!" he shouted suddenly. "Four minutes short and sharp, and over we go."

A big gun fired behind them and in an instant rushing and roaring sound battened upon the terrain and the German trenches blossomed in smoke and tumbling dirt. As far north and south as they could see, columns of white and brown and greenish smoke spouted, curled, intertwined into a fluctuating wall through which scarlet fangs of flame darted where shells burst. The German artillery answered the challenge. Back of the British front line and in front of it, on the parapet, on the parados, coronets of earth shot up and curled over, spattering steel helmets.

The bark of guns, the cough of howitzers merged into a full-throated, throbbing roar that split the sky in two and held it open. And yet still the sound mounted to a climax. The chaos of noise, the twining of taut nerves brought nausea to many of the waiting men, the nausea changed to insufferable rage and battle lust, straining to be slaked by the release of power held in tension.

Jobey's voice shouting in his ear: "Makes up for the Salient, sir . . . blasted shells . . . can't get me!"

Quentin. . . . He liked to quote Homer. "Antilochus, wail thou for me rather than for the dead–for me who live." . . . Damn glad I'm alive though. *Three minutes.* Here's Quentin thrown on the dustheap for his principles and who's the better for it? . . . Maybe not, though. . . . *Two minutes.* Mustn't guard my groin. What's coming, is coming. . . . If I come through I'll try to see men's souls. *Forty seconds.* God Almighty and Jesus Christ forgive me if I take a life, I'm a different sort of man from Quentin.

Twenty seconds. "Fix bayonets! First wave–over we go, men. Keep up close to the barrage." Boots, in toe holds on the front side of the trench, scrambled and hoisted an irregular line of men over the parapet. They went up, over, and disappeared to eyes below the parapet level. . . . Behind the flickering, rocking line of shell bursts seventy yards in front of them the line of men advanced, then knelt to wait for the barrage to jump forward, then broke up as men darted into trenches and shell-holes to clear out the Germans at bayonet point, then sped on again to the line of the barrage.

"Now us," shouted Dan. "Come on Loversedge, let's see if you're really immortal."

The copse of trees toward which they moved seemed quite near–yet far away. Machine guns chattered steadily through the barrage and the bullets zipped and cracked through the air making the still weeds at their feet jump suddenly. Shells, bursting round them in such numbers, confused Dan's shell-sense. They advanced in short bounds, taking whatever cover there was to take, between rushes. A last rush swept them into the wood, bayonets levelled to kill, teeth set and bared, breath whistling, nerves taut and burning with blood lust.

In the wood there were live Germans, some still with fight in them; field grey figures grappling with men in khaki. A wounded German cowered behind a tree, too frightened to put up his hands. Two others knelt with their hands high above their blanched faces. In the mêlée the wounded German who had not made up his mind got bayoneted. So did the two kneeling figures, since in a scrap where Death himself was dancing about among panting figures thrusting a bayonet–*in, out*–there was neither time nor inclination for fine distinction of conduct. . . . The fight was sharp and soon ended.

Gasping for breath, Dan relaxed and glanced about him. His fury died down. He was in a narrow trench just within the boundary of the wood. British infantry were about him. Of his own men, two had fallen somewhere. Jobey stood beside him.

"Well, Loversedge, here we are."

"What did I tell you, sir? Shells never do me no harm."

"Boots, in toe holds on the front side of the trench, scrambled and hoisted an irregular line of men over the parapet."

Lying on the trench bottom a few yards from them was a wounded Bavarian of the Leibregiment who had fallen with a stick bomb clenched in his hand. Stealthily this man raised himself with one hand; then, holding the bomb under his armpit, he pulled the cord and tossed it at them, willing that they should all go to heaven together. The handle struck Jobey's chest, the bomb bounced back into the mud and stuck there, handle down, sizzling. Moved by some impulse —Dan never knew for certain what it was—Jobey threw himself upon the bomb and covered it with his body.

The bomb exploded with a sharp crack. The German slumped down with a bullet through his brain. The war was over for Jobey Loversedge. . . .

Dan stooped over him. *You won't need your new boots now, Jobey. . . . You saved my life, and lost yours. . . . You had no dealings with time, Jobey. . . . All my life I have believed in death, but you saved my life and lost yours. Why did you? Why?*

The Germans had given up the copse and now they turned their guns on it. Dan climbed out of the trench. "Must see about the Lucas lamp." Shells were crashing into the trees, sending splinters of wood and steel flying. A sudden conviction flashed upon him: "I'm going to be hit. Beatrice. . . ."

A splinter needled through the foliage with a whine that dropped half a note in the scale as it came. He heard the whine. Then the splinter hurtled against his helmet; he fell and knew no more of that battle.

God's Sparrows, London, 1937

COLIN McDOUGALL

The mortar concentration lasted three minutes. Behind came the German tanks and infantry: waves of infantry, rolling through the forest and out on to the open killing-ground. They were following closely, perhaps only fifty yards, behind their mortar barrage. The men of the Rifles saw this, and despite the interdicting fire they stayed at the top of their slit trenches or their windows, and they kept on firing.

The first attack was beaten off. Lumbering in blind the German Mark 4s were easily picked off by the hull-down British tanks. The infantry were cut down by machine-guns and the blasts of 25-pounders, far in the rear, firing their concentrated DFs. But after such a show of force it was plain the enemy would come again: this had been a full battalion attack launched against each flank of the Rifles' position.

When the lull came the men of Ten Platoon looked out of the windows of the two stone houses they occupied and saw the battle litter they had helped create. Five German tanks were burning; the dead were spread, in lumps and bundles, over the ground. At the sunken roadbed Twelve Platoon had suffered most. Wounded men lay on the banks of the road, crying out terribly for help. Among them the furthest-advanced German tank wore the body of its dead commander draped like a pennant round its turret.

Corporal DiCicco stirred angrily at Sergeant Mitchell's side. "Can't we help those guys?" he said, pointing to the wounded.

Mitchell's own face was an ugly scowl. "Wait," he said.

And a moment later they saw Captain Adam out on the ground directing stretcher-bearers. The unwounded men of Twelve Platoon came walking back to the houses, their faces white, carrying extra weapons and bandoliers of ammunition. Sergeant Mitchell moved about assigning them new fire positions at the windows.

Then the artillery concentration hit the village. The men held to the quaking floors of their houses as though there was danger they might fall off. When the mortaring began again they knew the infantry were coming, so they stood up and went back to their windows.

Sergeant Mitchell directed the platoon's fire from an upstairs window. Kneeling beside him, firing his Bren gun, was Simpson. Unbelievably, the front edge of Simpson's helmet had been smashed flat. His hands, caked with dried blood, ministered expertly to his gun. The barrel was overheated and Simpson had to fire in very short bursts. As he fired he sang his song. "Maybe it itches," his voice croaked. Then a short burst. "But—" Another burst of three rounds— "It kills the sons of the bitches!" Final burst, magazine off, new magazine flicked on; finger gentling on the trigger again, and the fire and the song continued. It would continue, Mitchell knew, as long as there were men to fire at, or until the barrel burst.

Mitchell's thoughts were grim as he fired his own rifle. There simply were not enough Simpsons, not enough Bren guns, to stop this kind of attack. The tanks were firing high-explosive shells in their windows; the houses were slowly collapsing. Two British tanks were burning. And some of the German infantry had got beyond the sunken roadbed.

Simpson rolled from his window and fell to the floor. "Stopped!" he bellowed. "Can't get another round through the bloody barrel."

He lay on the floor swearing. A moment later Mitchell dropped himself as a burst ripped the woodwork and lodged a jagged splinter in his cheek. He lay within inches of Simpson's sweat-caked face. The two men regarded one another solemnly; their lips blasphemed in slow unison. Suddenly Simpson started to laugh. "Yeah," he said. "Things are sure tough all over. Give me a rifle and let's get the show back on the road."

But Mitchell was already on his feet. At one window he saw Corporal DiCicco lobbing grenades as fast as he could pull the pins. That meant that the infantry were all around them.

"Back to the windows!" Mitchell roared.

He seized a tommy-gun, raced to DiCicco's window, poked his head and shoulders through, aimed, and started to fire.

"The Padre stood on his feet and faced them. . . . Only his eyes were alive: two coal-black eyes burned in the white mask of rubble."

At first the silence was not quite believable. Before there had been a torrent of thought-devouring noise but now there was nothing: no mortaring, no shelling—nothing but silence. At first men spoke in the loud, half-shouting tone they had used to pierce the previous volume of sound, but once the silence was accepted their voices dropped to a whisper, as though they hoped by this means to avert the onset of invading noise again.

It was ten o'clock in the morning; the sun was well up, the day was hot. Adam and Sergeant Mitchell stood together looking out of a window. From the field, with its dead bodies and burning tanks, vapours of heat steamed from the ground. There was only one question in everyone's mind.

"Will they come again?" Mitchell asked, in the low voice all had adopted.

"Maybe not," said Adam.

In reality he was sure the enemy would attack again, but there were reasons why they might not and it did good to speak them aloud. "After all," he said, "they've lost all their tanks, what amounts to two battalions of infantry. Unless they have more tanks, and more men—"

"Good," declared Simpson, speaking from the floor. "The bugger will fire now." He clicked the retaining catch on the barrel of his Bren, and looked up at Adam. "What about ammunition, sir?" he asked. "I've only got one magazine left."

"It's coming up from BHQ," Adam replied. "Whatever there is left."

He turned to Sergeant Mitchell. "Everyone might as well stand down. We'll know soon enough if they're coming again."

Adam set out to tour his defensive position. His whole force, including British troopers from the burned-out tanks, now occupied only three houses. In the street, sheltered between the houses, NCOs were doling out the last precious rounds of ammunition. Stretcher-bearers lifted their burdens with painful care over the rubble and debris. Some of the men sat cleaning their weapons; others picked at opened tins of bully beef, or simply sprawled in the sun.

Every man Adam spoke to replied in the same quiet voice which had become the universal speech of Caielli. And everywhere, with no orders given, men were working: moving bricks to strengthen fire positions, or helping to carry the dead and wounded. When orders were necessary these were mere gestures or soft-spoken words. There was no voice of command, and certainly no voice of anger heard in Caielli.

There was a gentleness about every soldier in Caielli. Each man was considerate toward his fellows. Faults and meannesses which at other times would have drawn quick anger were overlooked, or even ceased to exist. Even little Ewart, Adam now noted with surprise, cigarette dangling from his lip, was helping to lift a body over the rubble, although he could have been taking his ease alone somewhere. In times of extremity Adam had seen this same thing before. There was tenderness in the streets of Caielli.

At the sunken road Adam found the British tank major. His body lay half out of his tank turret. Adam looked, and he thought with a pang of sorrow: We'll never drink that bottle of whisky now. . . . It must have been an AP shell because the major had no head: there was only the red, meaty stump of his neck. Adam closed his eyes. The sunlight burned his eyelids; the smell of charred flesh was stifling, choking. Quickly he turned away.

Adam called his platoon commanders together, although there was little to deliver in the way of orders. They sat on the brick floor of a cellar: Sergeant Mitchell from Ten Platoon, a corporal representing Twelve Platoon, and Lieutenant Venner, an experienced officer, commanding Eleven Platoon. At one end of the cellar a ramped door had been ripped off. Sunlight and rubble dust filtered through.

Their small affairs of business were soon concluded, but long after there was reason to do so they continued to sit together on the brick floor. It was cool and restful here. For a moment Adam's thoughts drifted back to that other cellar, the first cellar—at the Castello Donato in Sicily. He looked at Mitchell and he started to grin.

But suddenly every glance darted to the beamed ceiling of the cellar. An immense whoosh of sound possessed the sky; each one of them knew at once that some huge projectile was hurtling toward them.

Instinctively each man rolled flat on the bricks and started to count. Adam peered in Mitchell's face, which lay within inches of his own. "Twelve seconds!" he said in a voice of awe.

The sky was strangling in a noose of noise, then the shell struck upon the south slope of the village. Every brick and stone in Caielli was loosened; the brick floor they lay on trembled with concussion.

Lieutenant Venner was the first to speak. "Big enough to be 280-millimetre," he said, in a tone of objective appraisal.

"May be a good sign," Adam remarked. "It could be a hate stonk if they're not going to attack again."

The bombardment continued. With each explosion the cellar shook; masonry tumbled outside. Adam found the brick pleasantly cool on his cheek. Around him his men held to the quaking floor, smoking cigarettes, listening and waiting. In the doorway a swirling cloud of rubble dust almost obscured the sun.

Then, for an instant, this dim light was blotted from view. A gaunt figure loomed in the opening, crashed through, and rolled on the floor before them. The figure was enveloped in a loose, hampering garment; there was a thrashing struggle until it was launched to its feet. The garment turned out to be a trench coat. The figure was Padre Philip Doorn.

The Padre stood on his feet and faced them. As he moved flakes of debris snowed from his head and shoulders; his face was pasty-white. Only his eyes were alive: two coal-black eyes burned in the white mask of rubble. One arm of the trench coat lifted. His mouth was a black gash.

"Back to your posts, men—" cried the Padre, in a voice of sternest doom. "The enemy has overrun your position."

The men on the floor stared at the accusing figure. They could read battle noises like a musical score; they knew there was no enemy attack; yet here came this alien creature flopping among them, reviling, accusing. He brought with him a new and ugly passion, quite foreign to the spirit of Caielli which they had all earned and shared between them this day. The men on the floor looked and felt anger flare inside them.

Adam came to his feet; he made a noise in his throat and he started forward. But Sergeant Mitchell caught him from behind. "The man's demented!" Mitchell hissed in his ear.

Adam stopped and looked at Sergeant Mitchell with surprise—not at what Mitchell said, but at the word he chose to use. Adam's arms dropped to his side. He moved out of the way.

Mitchell and Lieutenant Venner exchanged a glance. Then they started to advance, shoulder to shoulder. On their faces they wore broad, reassuring smiles. Together they moved upon the erect, monumental figure. Slowly, carefully, they closed in on Padre Doorn.

Execution, Toronto, 1958

"They were no longer villages, but only heaps of broken masonry and dust."

EDWARD MEADE

Six or seven kilometres from Caen, on a rise of land dominating the river Orne and the city itself, three little villages formed a triangle–Buron, Gruchie and Authie. Their apex pointed northward toward the sea.

It was here, on the night and morning of June 7th and 8th, that the Canadian assault battalions caught the full savage force of the first German counter-attack upon the Normandy plain. Suffering heavy casualties, the Canadians fell back to their support lines. There they dug in grimly and held their positions against the almost continuous hammer blows of the Germans. They dug in and held, until the counter-attack had spent itself. Then they brought in their dead from the field–all that they could reach, and buried them, then set about strengthening their positions.

They held there for thirty days, within sight of the three little towns. In time they gave the place the name of Hell's Corner, and even back on the beaches, among men who had never been there, the name inspired a reverence and awe for those who lived in that savage inferno.

For thirty days they waited, giving no ground. Not a day passed when they weren't shelled. Their foxholes became as familiar to them as the houses on their home-town streets, and when a bomb knocked out a foxhole they viewed it as a Londoner viewed the bomb devastation in the middle of his street. Through rain and mud and blistering sun they held on and could not be broken. Their strength dwindled and was reinforced. Night after night their patrols went out into No-Man's-Land under the artillery fire. Often the patrols had to lie doggo while a German patrol passed, and sometimes the patrols fought it out to the grim end. In time they came to know more about the Germans who faced them than they knew about their own comrades on their flanks.

But there was no fraternizing with the enemy, in spite of the bulletin board which one wiseacre erected by his foxhole, which proclaimed the daily market-price which the

Germans were prepared to pay for commodities such as bully-beef, cigarettes and wool socks. On this list, three Iron Crosses were worth a tin of sardines, and a trenchful of Jerries was worth one grenade. No, there was no fraternizing, for the Canadians in Hell's Corner faced the 12th ss Panzers—the most fanatical of all Hitler's hoodlums.

The plain before the three villages was dotted with the burnt-out wrecks of tanks—Shermans mostly, but there were Tigers and Panthers there, too. The three villages gradually crumbled. Tons of artillery shells crashed into them and through them. They were no longer villages, but only heaps of broken masonry and dust. Here and there a wall stood to mark where a house had once been, and even these had neat shellholes through them. The orchard trees were blackened, splintered ghosts that brooded over the desolation and the dead lying in the ruins.

Then, exactly one month from the morning when they had rolled up against the terrific onslaught of the fast German counter-attack, the Canadians rose from their positions and attacked across the fields. Their long wait was over: now their revenge came for that month of hell and fury.

It was the hardest fought battle since D-Day. The attack opened with a terrific artillery bombardment from the Canadian twenty-five pounders and mediums. The infantry went in under it, fanning out across the fields. The Germans opened up with a heavy mortar barrage which met and overlapped the Canadian barrage. The Canadians went in without protection, standing up. The Germans kept in their weapon pits and allowed their positions to be infiltrated. Then they opened up with their small arms, firing through the curtain of their own mortar barrage into the backs of the Canadians.

It was small arms and grenade fighting all the way. Every trench, every foxhole, had to be cleared, one by one. It was man against man, hand to hand, in the fields and amid the ruined houses, under the overlapping artillery barrages. The Panzers knew how to fight and how to die a fanatical death. Their positions were strong.

One by one the trenches and foxholes fell, filled with German dead. Across the fields the Canadians advanced. By noon they owned the three villages and opened up the country to the south as far as Franqueville. What was left of the 12th ss Panzers were prisoners and there were not many. The rest lay on the battlefield.

The Canucks owned Hell's Corner for good, though what it had cost none could then say. They did not stop to count their dead. The next morning they pushed on across the plain to the heart of Caen.

A few days previous to this action men of an eastern Canadian regiment on the immediate right flank of Hell's Corner had staged an attack of their own. Their neighbours on either flank knew little about it for some time. The commands knew, and word of it filtered to the rear and then came forward again, spreading from foxhole to foxhole, from one gun position to another. It was spoken of as "an advance of a mile or two," and "tough going," but for the time being it meant very little to the individual soldier sitting in his weapon-slip looking out across the front. Somebody had done something, and in a stalemated period of war that was good news, but not such good news that it would make anyone uncork the last bottle of looted, frenzy-fixin' Calvados.

In reality, this attack was of considerable importance when, in a few days, it became linked to the grand offensive for the city of Caen. For the attack was against the village and airfield of Carpiquet. When it fell it unlocked the enemy's defence ring around the city—that ring of steel which had come to be regarded as almost impenetrable. Caen was the enemy's right flank; it was also the Allied left. If the enemy could gain control of the plain north of Caen, by turning the Allied flank, he could command the beaches. Disaster to the entire campaign would be the result. Caen had to be taken.

Carpiquet was the first wedge that the Allies drove into that ring. The village, three miles due west from Caen, was the centre of a great German airfield. True, the airfield had been almost completely destroyed long ago both by aircraft and artillery. But the Germans had built the remains into a solid defensive position. Day after day, night after night, the Allies had poured a withering barrage of artillery into it. Patrols probed it nightly. Tanks and self-propelled guns covered it from close range. The village held, even when there was no village left, but only a ghostly mass of ruins rising from the plain. The fight for Carpiquet had been long and grim. The Germans held out in their concrete encasements that had walls of reinforced concrete six feet thick and steel armour plating that could withstand any reasonable siege. Behind them they had reinforcements, and supplies that poured in over the network of roads leading to Caen.

The Canadians advanced like an inexorable tide. They had tanks, tank busters, flame-throwing tanks, sappers and heavy assault equipment to back them up. It was more than an attack; it was an all-out assault upon a defensive position so strongly fortified that it had stood continuous artillery bombardment for weeks. The infantry cleared the open country, mopped up the trenches and machine-gun nests. The flame throwers scorched the enemy out of his concrete emplacements and the infantry mopped up. Sappers cleared pathways for the tanks, laid charges that literally blew pillboxes into the air, demolished whole buildings upon the nests of snipers in hiding. Tank fought tank to the death. They cut the enemy lines to pieces.

The Germans counter-attacked with strong armour. The attack was beaten off, and blazing Panthers littered the land —funeral pyres for their crews. Yard by yard, foxhole to trench to concrete pillbox, the infantry advanced. The enemy put up a terrific artillery and mortar fire that carpeted the battlefield. Casualties soared, the ranks thinned. But the attack swept on.

They took Carpiquet and consolidated on the south side of the village, across the east-west road through it. They held there for five days in that small bulge in the battlefront which they had created, until the attack from Hell's Corner began, and closed their exposed flank to the east.

Those five days and nights seemed an eternity. Every position they dug into was shelled and mortared by the enemy, who still held firmly on the great airport beyond the village within hailing distance.

Carpiquet was to be remembered as one of the hardest, bloodiest battles of the war. It was also something more. It was the first wedge driven into the Nazis' strongest front in Normandy. The small bulge which the eastern Canadians had made in the battle line was like a finger protruding from a clenched hand—a finger pointing the way out of France.

Five days later the Canadians broke out of Hell's Corner and swept down across the plain to Caen, the city of the dead.

Remember Me, London, 1946

PEOPLE 3

JOHN D. ROBINS

I can approach a solitary tree with pleasure, a cluster of trees with joy, and a forest with rapture; I must approach a solitary man with caution, a group of men with trepidation, and a nation of men with terror.

The Incomplete Angler, Toronto, 1943

CANADA FRANCHISE ACT 1885

[A Person is] a male person, including an Indian and excluding a person of Mongolian or Chinese race.

SIR WILLIAM VAN HORNE

I have been too busy all my life to cast a thought so far back as my grandfather.

Attributed to Van Horne in
Canadian Quotations and Phrases, compiled by
Robert H. Hamilton, Toronto, 1952

SIR JOHN A. MACDONALD

Bishop Taché has been here and has left for the Red River . . . He is strongly opposed to the idea of an Imperial Commission, believing, as indeed, we all do, that to send out an overwashed Englishman, utterly ignorant of the country and full of crochets, as all Englishmen are, would be a mistake.

Letter to Sir John Rose, 1870

PETER McARTHUR

An Englishman's social standing seems to depend on the number of people he can afford to despise. The average Englishman has so deep a reverance for antiquity that he would rather be wrong than recent.

To Be Taken with Salt, London, 1903

Robins   Van Horne
Macdonald   McArthur

EDWARD MEADE

The village was not far from the company camp. It stood on the northern slope of a gradual hill and looked down over a broad, sweeping valley, patchworked with tiny hedged farms. On the south side of the hill was a deep forest. Through this forest wandered a lane that led to the unit's lines. On the brow of the hill, facing each other across a road, stood two tiny churches.

It was Christmas Eve. There was a dance in the church hall. The girls of the village were already there, waiting for the soldiers to arrive. Old women bustled about the hall with refreshments they had brought. From the centre of the ceiling a great Christmas bell hung suspended by paper ribbons. The three-piece orchestra tuned their instruments. The flat, broken music of their tuning carried out on the still night air and mingled with the thin, delicate sound of the bell from the Catholic church.

As the soldiers came along the path through the forest they heard the church bell, muffled and delicate in the distance, like music from an old-fashioned music-box. Overhead, through the naked, silent trees, some stars twinkled in the north. The air was crisp and exhilarating, and the men walked briskly in little groups, talking and laughing.

And then, suddenly, in a shimmer of magic silver out of the night, snow began to fall. A faint whisper crept through the forest and a soft confining weight seemed to press down upon the earth. The men stopped still and, unbelieving, looked up into the fine swirling mantle. Across the mind of every man swept the ecstatic memory of the snowlands of his beloved Canada. With a wild quickening blood-beat they shouted for joy.

"Yi-pee! Yi-pee!"

"Snow! Snow! Look! Feel it!"

They danced in the roadway; they turned their faces to the sky to catch the soft melting crystals on their faces; they even stuck out their tongues and tasted it. Mad, like drunken men, they continued on their way, reeling, singing, shouting, and their uproar rolled through the night. Villagers standing at the crossroads heard them and watched them approach, and, frightened, drew back from them.

"Canadians!" a woman snorted, and turned her child away from them. But the child, wild-eyed with curiosity, peeked around at the men.

In the dance hall the girls and old women heard their shouting and singing as they approached.

"The Canadians are coming!" someone shrieked.

"They're drunk. Hear them!"

Titters and faint shrieks mingled in the suddenly tense air of the hall. Everyone stood with caught breath waiting for the "drunken Canadians" to appear.

The men burst into the hall in a wild clamour. They stormed the timid orchestra. One soldier dragged the pianist from his instrument, stool and all, and standing over the keyboard, thumped out the opening bars of a wild reel. Another took the violin from the bald man's hand with a "Thank you, daddy," and began to fiddle the reel. The soldiers on the floor found breathless but willing girls, and in a moment the hall rocked to the wild, happy surge of the old-time reel.

The night was half gone before the people realized that the Canadians were not drunk at all, but simply full of wild soaring spirit. Impossible for the English, with their utter lack of emotionalism, to understand the wildness of the soldiers. Had anyone explained to them that there were on earth people to whom the miracle of falling snow brought a wild, unutterable happiness, they would have shaken their heads in complete mystification.

Remember Me, London, 1946

BRIAN MOORE

At the back of the theatre, penned two by two behind a velvet rope, a line of people waited. The usherette, a girl not much older than Paulie, came up to him. "Single, sir? We have seats in the first six rows."

There was something about her: her accent was not Canadian. He smiled at her, drawn by that immigrant bond, and followed her from the lighted area into the darkness of the theatre. Poor kid. Her scapula bone stuck out at right angles against the maroon stuff of her uniform. New Canadians: thousands like her came here each year; thousands started all over again in humble circs. You heard such stories: lawyers forced to take work as checkers, doctors as lab assistants, professors driving trucks. And still they came, from every country in Europe, riding in old railroad colonist cars to the remote provinces of this cold, faraway land. Why did they do it? For their children's sake, it was said. Well, and wasn't he driving a truck now for his daughter's sake? Wasn't he one of them? Wasn't he, too, a man who would always be a stranger here, never at home in this land where he had not grown up? Yes: he, too.

The girl's flashlight showed him an almost empty row, lowering its beam as she waited for him to enter his seat. He wanted to stop, take her by the arm, lead her back up the aisle into the light again. To say: "I too am an immigrant," to compare impressions, reminisce, to tell the things that immigrants tell. But the flashlight beam snapped off. He could no longer see her. He sat down, purblinded by the coloured images on the huge screen above. He looked around. Here were the solitaries. Some slept, some slumped in morose contemplation of the film giantess kicking yard-long legs, while some, like him, ignored her and peered about them in the shadows, hoping for a glance, a promise of company.

How long was it since he'd sat down here? Years, years. But he remembered: mitching away long school afternoons in the picture houses off O'Connell Street, huddled down in his seat for fear someone might see him and tell his parents. And later, as a university student, the lonely Saturday nights in cheap front seats, hoping that some American daydream would banish the private misery of having no girl, no place to go. Well, and was he going back to all that? For if he lost Veronica now, who would have him, a man nearly forty with a grown-up daughter on his hands? Wouldn't he end his days here among the solitaries?

Enough of that. He tried watching the film, but somehow the filmed America no longer seemed true. He could not believe in this America, this land that half the world dreams of in dark front seats in cities and villages half a world away. What had it in common with his true America? For Canada was America; the difference a geographer's line. What had these Hollywood revels to do with the facts of life in a cold New World?

The Luck of Ginger Coffey, Boston, 1960

MORDECAI RICHLER

Proud they were. They had come to conquer. Instead they were being picked off one by one by the cold, drink, and indifference. They abjured taking part in the communal life. They mocked the local customs from the school tie to queueing, and were for the most part free of them by dint of their square, classless accents. Unlike their forebears, they were punk imperialists. They didn't marry and settle down among the natives. They had brought their own women and electric shavers with them. They had through the years evolved from communists to fellow-travellers to tourists. Tourists. For even those who had lived in London for years only knew the true life of the city as a rumour. Around and around them the natives, it seemed, were stirred by Diana Dors, a rise in bus fares, Test matches, automation, and Princess Margaret. The aliens knew only other aliens. It was reported occasionally that the men in bowler hats had children and points of view, that, just like in the movies, there were settlers in Surrey, miners in Yorkshire, and workers who—aside from being something you were for like central heating or more gin cheaper—were bored with their wives, suspicious of advertisements, and, just like you, inclined to wonder at three-thirty in the afternoon what it would be like to come home to Sophia Loren.

Norman felt stupid.

Around and around him men clocked in every morning at 7:30, girls sat down after an eight-hour shift at Forte's to write letters to Mary Grant. Clocks, cars, pyjamas, and railway ties were produced. Around him the real £. s. d. world existed. The only sons of white fathers went out to Malaya to murder the only sons of yellow fathers in the interests of national prestige. At eleven every morning pimpled boys went from office to office with lukewarm tea in tall chipped white cups for girls who took letters from their bosses beginning, "In reply to yours of the 23rd inst." Middle-aged couples failed to see the latest Martin and Lewis at the local Gaumont because they couldn't afford it. High-strung boys from Wapping failed their eleven-pluses. Old age pensioners were admitted free to the public baths. Around and around him people had already realised that they would never be able to sleep in until eight on a Monday morning or go for a walk in the park on a Wednesday afternoon or see Paris. Around him moved a real city where Sally's choice of a lover, Charlie's script, Winkleman's chance of a production, and his own loneliness were of no bloody account.

Norman's thoughts turned to Thomas Hale in Canada and he wondered how it looked to him. Hale came over every year like a kafka with office to mark you down either in the book of sales or the book of rejection slips. Again and again he discovered the would-be author of the Great Canadian Novel and shipped him off to London, often at his own expense, only to discover that his hopeful had taken to gin or television writing by the time he got round to him again. But Hale was indefatigable. He didn't know that the British didn't care a damn about Canada. That, as far as they were concerned, somewhere out there between lost India and them lay the loyal Dominion of Canada, where Lord Beaverbrook came from. He also didn't know what it was like to live in London.

The Canadians had come to conquer. They were the prodigal offspring of a stern father. Coming home again, however, they had not counted on the old man having grown feeble while they had prospered overseas. They were surprised that the island was great only in terms of memory or sentiment. The choice of coming to England, where the streets were paved with poets, rather than to the United States bespoke of a certain spiritual superiority, so they were appalled to discover that this country was infinitely more materialistic than their own, where possessions were functional, naturally yours, and not the prize of single-minded labour. They were surprised to discover that they had arrived too late.

A Choice of Enemies, London, 1957

ETHEL WILSON

Mrs. Emblem's three husbands have each contributed a little, financially, to her present state. She is a good manager, born to be a wife and a mistress; and to each of her three husbands she has been honest wife and true mistress. From time to time she works because she likes the extra money, and because although she is Mrs. Emblem and therefore a happy woman, she sometimes feels a certain vacuity which is not filled by cleaning and polishing her room, shopping (which usually means walking through the shops with one of her friends), going to a show, and playing whist or bridge with Mr. Thorsteinsen, Mr. Jacobs, and Maybelle. She is hardly aware of the poignant communications of sky, of birds, of ocean, forest, and mountain, although she thinks Vancouver is a nice place. She does not see around or beyond the tangible male or female human form and its appearance and peculiar requirements. I think, in order to be perfectly happy, she still needs to look after someone. You cannot help liking Mrs. Emblem. She is so nice; she is perhaps too fat, now, to be beautiful; but she is –to Mr. Thorsteinsen, to Maybelle, to Mortimer Johnson and to me–alluring, and so she had been to the two sod cases and the divorce.

She and Maybelle can talk indefinitely, over a cup of coffee at Mrs. Emblem's place, or over a cup of tea at Scott's (where they will have their fortunes read) about themselves, their pasts and their futures, and what they counsel each other to do. Mrs. Emblem is not lonely–exactly. But she has enjoyed long and varied male companionship; that is what she is formed for, and that is what she –less ardently now–sometimes craves. And yet something holds her back. Perhaps she is growing indolent; perhaps she does not wish at her age to submit herself to a new elderly marriage whose intimacy youth no longer sanctions and makes charming; perhaps she has discovered the joys of privacy and does not wish to lose them, for at least she now owns herself.

She discusses endlessly with Maybelle the advantages and disadvantages of a further marriage, the feelings that she has about Mr. Thorsteinsen, and the opportunity she has for becoming an investigator–or what her niece Myrtle calls a snoop–in one of the large department stores. She would not

---

"It was reported occasionally that the men in bowler hats had children and points of view . . . and, just like you, [were] inclined to wonder at three-thirty in the afternoon what it would be like to come home to Sophia Loren."

"Mrs. Emblem . . . looked idly at the least important page, that is to say the front page, of the newspaper, which necessitates no turning."

be a good snoop; she is too memorable, and her golden quality draws, usually, geniality and attention from those who serve her. She knows that she can always get a job at a certain downtown millinery store where she worked steady for two years but they would want her all day, and she does not like that. Then Maybelle and she discuss Maybelle's problems, which are similar and are also capable of being extended indefinitely over the tea-leaves. In theory she goes to church. But she does not go to church. Her son is married and lives in Lethbridge and she promises to go and visit there some day. The only relative that she has in Vancouver is her niece Myrtle Hopwood who married that nice no-good fellow Mort Johnson, and she likes Myrtle as little as anyone she knows. But she keeps in touch with her, because Myrtle is of her family, child of her own sister. She has watched Myrtle throughout her curious unsatisfactory years without being able "to do anything about it". She is more kind to Myrtle than Myrtle knows, and is ready to befriend her.

After Mrs. Emblem came in from Myrtle's on Tuesday night she took her time and, moving ponderously, gracefully, and slowly, she went to bed, drawing her curtains apart and allowing some fresh air, and noise, to come in from Burrard Street. She did not take off her make-up the way it says to do in the paper, because there might be a fire, or a burglar, or she might die, or might be ill or have to have the doctor, and she would not like to be discovered without her make-up. She just reduces it and freshens it a little. But in the morning she can, and will, take it all off, and, later, put it all on again.

Mrs. Emblem made some cocoa, and this she sipped at leisure as she looked idly at the least important page, that is to say the front page, of the newspaper, which necessitates no turning. You cannot turn the pages of a newspaper in bed and drink cocoa at the same time with complete comfort and safety. But she has some cookies and she will nibble these when she gets to the real page-turning part. The front page has sometimes a good murder which develops on see page two. Apart from that it is very uninteresting, as it deals in long words or in meaningless initials such as OPA, UNO, TUC, FBI (everyone's gone mad), and with countries who do not seem to be able to get on together and have no particular bearing on her life (or so she really seems to think), and with elderly men who have no news value for Mrs. Emblem. The same applies to the editorial page but that is worse. It is a dead loss, except occasionally for the correspondence. The same applies also to the sports pages and to those pages devoted sometimes to church and to music and the drama.

First of all (have a cookie) she turns to the Society page. She does not regard the Society page with the feeling, which must surely be suspicion by the way it works in her, of Myrtle. She likes the people who figure there for her entertainment. She wishes she knew far far more about them and the interesting congenial lives which they lead. She likes them to get married. How they rush about (little she knows) to meetings, to luncheons, to teas, to cocktail parties, to dinners, to more meetings, to Harrison Hot Springs, and to California. More power to them. She has no snobbish admiration for these people who so industriously and sometimes vainly spend themselves, and are so prodigal of their smiles, and rush about so much; but they give her vicarious pleasure and are part of the same show which includes the movie advertisements and the funnies. Mrs. Emblem has one or two favourites among those people who rush about; she likes to see their pictures. She says to Maybelle, "I didn't think that picture of Mrs. H. Y. Dunkerley did her justice, did you?" She really is a darling.

She then turns to the funnies. She has her favourites there also, which seem to touch obscurely on something in her own long experience or in her imagination. Sometimes her eyes crinkle and vanish in a smile (have a cookie). Little Orphan Annie, the eternal little girl who never grows up, is profoundly identified with herself. Annie is the normal person, always right in motive and performance and endearingly young, the little monster. Who would not be Annie? Things are not made too difficult for those who read about Annie. Look at the new character who makes his abrupt appearance in the picture. The lines of his jaw, his brow, at once disclose good or evil. You know exactly where you are: would that one's own acquaintance were so marked. The line of his jaw invites your apprehension or your confidence; but beneath it all, you do not worry. Annie will be all right. Mrs. Emblem passes on down the page, slowly perusing all the funnies, including those funnies which exhibit life in its more debasing forms and are anything but funny. And then she turns to the Personal Column and this is the newspaper's climax (have a cookie).

Sometimes the Personal Column disappoints. There may only be the working man who wishes to meet a respectable woman of between 30 and 40, no objection to one child, object matrimony. Mrs. Emblem dwells but idly on this working man; he does not tempt her, even in thought; his youth forbids. Her interest kindles at the sight of the Scandinavian gentleman well fixed, desires to meet widow fond of dancing and shows, object companionship and matrimony no triflers. She puts the Scandinavian gentleman through his paces and thinks there is no doubt something wrong with him. What Scandinavian gentleman well fixed could not find plenty of companions for shows and matrimony without advertising for them? He must have bad habits. She considers the retired business man who would like to meet up with a single widow, and here she laughs. What does he mean by a single widow? Well, I am not a single widow so that won't do. She is not too sure about the Canadian Catholic non-smoker, or about the English gentleman age sixty-five with means, Protestant, desires to meet sincere widow, although they sound the safest. She lives through each of these mysterious romances each night, weighs them and sometimes makes her selection. They are real life. But she would never dare. She will no more write to the English gentleman than Mort will slug Myrtle although he often declares that he will; these things happen in the mind alone; and Mrs. Emblem will never write to the English gentleman.

The Equations of Love, Toronto, 1952

STEPHEN LEACOCK

The Reverend Edward Fareforth Furlong of St. Asaph's was a man who threw his whole energy into his parish work. The subtleties of theological controversy he left to minds less active than his own. His creed was one of works rather than of words, and whatever he was doing he did it with his whole heart. Whether he was lunching at the Mausoleum Club with one of his churchwardens, or playing the flute—which he played as only the episcopal clergy can play it—accompanied on the harp by one of the fairest of the ladies of his choir, or whether he was dancing the new episcopal tango with the younger daughters of the elder parishioners, he threw himself into it with all his might. He could drink tea more gracefully and play tennis better than any clergyman on this side of the Atlantic. He could stand beside the white stone font of St. Asaph's in his long white surplice holding a white-robed infant, worth half a million dollars, looking as beautifully innocent as the child itself, and drawing from every matron of the congregation with unmarried daughters the despairing cry, "What a pity that he has no children of his own!"

Equally sound was his theology. No man was known to preach shorter sermons or to explain away the book of Genesis more agreeably than the rector of St. Asaph's; and if he found it necessary to refer to the Deity he did so under the name of Jehovah or Jah, or even Yaweh, in a manner calculated not to hurt the sensitiveness of any of the parish-

ioners. People who would shudder at brutal talk of the older fashion about the wrath of God listened with well-bred interest to a sermon on the personal characteristics of Jah. In the same way Mr. Furlong always referred to the devil not as Satan but as Sû or Swâ, which took all the sting out of him. Beelzebub he spoke of as Behel-Zawbab, which rendered him perfectly harmless. The Garden of Eden he spoke of as the Paradeisos, which explained it entirely; the flood as the Diluvium, which cleared it up completely; and Jonah he named, after the correct fashion, Jon Nah, which put the whole situation (his being swallowed by Baloo, or the Great Lizard) on a perfectly satisfactory footing. Hell itself was spoken of as She-ol, and it appeared that it was not a place of burning, but rather of what one might describe as moral torment. This settled She-ol once and for all: nobody minds moral torment. In short, there was nothing in the theological system of Mr. Furlong that need have occasioned in any of his congregation a moment's discomfort.

There could be no greater contrast with Mr. Fareforth Furlong than the minister of St. Osoph's, the Rev. Dr. McTeague, who was also honorary professor of philosophy at the university. The one was young, the other was old; the one could dance, the other could not; the one moved about at church picnics and lawn teas among a bevy of disciples in pink and blue sashes; the other moped around under the trees of the university campus, with blinking eyes that saw nothing and an abstracted mind that had spent fifty years in trying to reconcile Hegel with St. Paul, and was still busy with it. Mr. Furlong went forward with the times; Dr. McTeague slid quietly backwards with the centuries.

Dr. McTeague was a failure, and all his congregation knew it. "He is not up to date," they said. That was his crowning sin. "He don't go forward any," said the business members of the congregation. "That old man believes just exactly the same sort of stuff now that he did forty years ago. What's more, he *preaches* it. You can't run a church that way, can you?"

His trustees had done their best to meet the difficulty. They had offered Dr. McTeague a two-years' vacation to go and see the Holy Land. He refused; he said he could picture it. They reduced his salary by fifty per cent; he never noticed it. They offered him an assistant; but he shook his head, saying that he didn't know where he could find a man to do just the work that he was doing. Meantime he mooned about among the trees concocting a mixture of St. Paul with Hegel, three parts to one, for his Sunday sermon, and one part to three for his Monday lecture.

Arcadian Adventures with the Idle Rich, London, 1914

JAMES SINCLAIR ROSS

We had callers today from Randolph, the next town, fifteen miles from here. The Reverend and Mrs. Albert Downie, to extend a word of brotherly encouragement and cheer. A quaint, serene little pair—piety and its rib in a Ford more battle-scarred even than ours—the parson and his wife in caricature.

He is bald and thin, confident and kindly. Like a just-awakened Rip Van Winkle who was an earnest little Boy

*"Perhaps they expected hymns.
I played two Chopin waltzes
and they exclaimed politely
that all music was sacred."*

Scout when he fell asleep, a lecture still ringing in his ears on *The Abundant Life*. You couldn't imagine him ever racked by a doubt or conflict. He said a word of prayer for us, and finished radiant. I glanced at Philip, and for a minute wished that I were the artist, with a pad and pencil at my hand.

Mrs. Downie has white hair and blue eyes, and a voice like a teaspoon tinkling in a china cup. A frail, tiny woman, with a fussy, beribboned hat too big for her that she has likely salvaged from a mission barrel, and that makes mine in contrast seem quite modish. And supporting it so bravely, with such stalwart, meek assurance. Over the tea and sponge cake I had a few gaunt moments, looking down a corridor of years and Horizons, at the end of which was a mirror and my own reflection. They had heard I was a musician, and wondered would I render something. Perhaps they expected hymns. I played two Chopin waltzes, and they exclaimed politely that all music was sacred.

As For Me and My House, New York, 1941

ROBERTSON DAVIES

The funeral tea was even more of an ordeal than Solly had foreseen. Such a function is not easily managed, and his mother's two old servants had been quick to declare that they were unable to attempt it. They were too broken up, they said. They were not so broken up, however, that they were incapable of giving a lot of trouble to the caterer who had been engaged for the work. They thought poorly of his suggestion that three kinds of sandwiches and three kinds of little cakes, supplemented by fruitcake, would be enough. The relatives from Montreal, the Hansens, would expect cold meat, they said; and as it was so near Christmas ordinary fruitcake would not suffice; Christmas cake would be looked for. Madam had never been one to skimp. When old Ethel, the cook, remembered that Thursday had always been Madam's At Home day, she had a fresh bout of grief, and declared that she would, after all, prepare the funeral tea herself, if it killed her. Solly had been unable to meet this situation and it was Veronica who, at last, made an uneasy peace between Ethel the cook, Doris the housemaid, and the caterer.

The caterer had his own, highly professional attitude toward funeral teas. What about drinks? he said. Sherry would be wanted for the women who never drank anything except at funerals, and there were always a few Old Country people who expected port — especially if there was cold meat. But most of the mourners would want hard liquor, and they would want it as soon as they got into the house. These winter funerals were murder; everybody was half perished by the time they got back from the graveyard. Solly would have to get the liquor himself; the caterer's banquet licence did not cover funerals. He would, of course, supply all the glasses and mixings. He advised Solly to get a good friend to act as barman; it wouldn't do to have a professional barman at such an affair. Looked too calculated. Similarly, the icing which said Merry Christmas would have to be removed from the tops of the fruitcakes. Looked too cheerful.

Obediently, Solly procured and hauled a hundred and fifty dollars' worth of assorted liquors from the Government purveyor on the day before the funeral. But his acquaintance among skilled mixers of drinks was small, and in the end he had to ask the Cathedral organist, Humphrey Cobbler, to help him.

Was Solly grieving for his mother, when he wept during the singing of *My Task*? Yes, he was. But he was also grieving because Veronica had had such a rotten time of it during the past three days. He was worrying that there would not be enough to eat at the funeral tea. He was worrying for fear there would be too much to eat, and that the funeral baked-meats would coldly furnish forth his own table for days to come. He was worrying that Cobbler, triumphant behind the drinks-table, would fail to behave himself. He was worrying for fear the Hansen relatives would hang around all evening, discussing family affairs, as is the custom of families at funerals, instead of decently taking the seven o'clock train back to Montreal. He was hoping that he could live through the next few hours, get one decent drink for himself, and go to bed.

Solly and Veronica rode to the graveyard in an undertaker's limousine with Uncle George Hansen, Mrs. Bridgetower's brother, and Uncle George's American wife. But as soon as the burial was over they hurried to where Solly had left their small car earlier in the day, and rushed with irreverent haste back to the house, to be on hand to greet the mourners when they came ravening for liquor, food and warm fires.

"Do you think they'll all come?" said Veronica, as they rounded the graveyard gate.

"Very likely. Did you ever see such a mob? I didn't think more than a hundred would go to the cemetery, but it looks as if they all went. Have we got enough stuff, do you suppose?"

"I can't tell. I've never had anything to do with one of these things before."

"Nor have I. Ronny, in case I go out of my head before this tea thing is over, I want to tell you now that you've been wonderful about it all. In a week or so we'll go for a holiday, and forget about it."

When they entered the house it looked cheerful, even festive. Fires burned in the drawing-room, dining-room and in the library, where Cobbler stood ready behind an improvised bar. There was some giggling and scurrying as Solly and his wife came in, and Ethel and Doris were seen making for the kitchen.

"Just been putting the girls right with a strong sherry-and-gin," said Cobbler. "They're badly shaken up. Needed bracing. Now, what can I give you?"

"Small ryes," said Solly. "And for heaven's sake use discretion, Humphrey."

"You know me," said Cobbler, slopping out the rye with a generous hand.

"I do," said Solly. "That's why I'm worried. Don't play the fool for the next couple of hours. That's all I ask."

"You wound me," said the organist, and made an attempt to look dignified. But his blue suit was too small, his collar was frayed, and his tie was working toward his left ear. His curly black hair stood out from his head in a mop,

and his black eyes gleamed unnervingly. "You suggest that I lack a sense of propriety. I make no protest; I desire only to be left to My Task." He winked raffishly at Veronica.

He's our oldest friend as a married couple, thought she, and a heart of gold. If only he were not so utterly impossible! She smiled at him.

"Please, Humphrey," said she.

He winked again, tossed a lump of sugar in the air and caught it in his mouth. "Trust me," he said.

What else can we do? thought Veronica.

The mourners had begun to arrive, and Solly went to greet them. There was congestion at the door, for most of the guests paused to take off their overshoes and rubbers, and those who had none were scraping the graveyard clay from their feet. It was half an hour before the last had climbed the stairs, left wraps, taken a turn at the water-closet, descended the stairs and received a drink from Cobbler.

They had the air, festive but subdued, which is common to funeral teas. The grim business at the graveside done, they were prepared to make new, tentative contact with life. They greeted Solly with half-smiles, inviting him to smile in return. Beyond his orbit conversation buzzed, and there was a little subdued laughter. They had all, in some measure, admired or even liked his mother, but her death at seventy-one had surprised nobody, and such grief as they felt for her had already been satisfied at the funeral. Dean Jevon Knapp, of St. Nicholas', bustled up to Solly; he had left his cassock and surplice upstairs, and had put on the warm dry shoes which Mrs. Knapp always took to funerals for him, in a special bag; he had his gaiters on, and was holding a large Scotch and soda.

"I have always thought this one of the loveliest rooms in Salterton," said he.

But Solly was not allowed to answer. Miss Puss Pottinger, great friend and unappeased mourner of the deceased, popped up beside him.

"It is as dear Louisa would have wished it to be," she said, in an aggressive but unsteady voice. "Thursday was always her At Home day, you know, Mr. Dean."

"First Thursdays, I thought," said the Dean; "this is a third Thursday."

"Be it what it may," said Miss Puss, losing control of face and voice, "I shall think of this as dear Louisa's – last – At Home."

"I'm very sorry," said the Dean. "I had not meant to distress you. Will you accept a sip – ?" He held out his glass.

Miss Pottinger wrestled with herself, and spoke in a whisper. "No," said she. "Sherry. I think I could take a little sherry."

The Dean bore her away, and she was shortly seen sipping a glass of dark brown sherry in which Cobbler, unseen, had put a generous dollop of brandy.

Solly was at once engaged in conversation by his Uncle George Hansen and Uncle George's wife. The lady was an American, and as she had lived in Canada a mere thirty-five years, still found the local customs curious, and never failed to say so.

"This seems to me more like England than at home," she said now.

"Mother was very conservative," said Solly.

"The whole of Salterton is very conservative," said Uncle George; "I just met old Puss Pottinger mumbling about At Homes; thought she was dead years ago. This must be one of the last places in the British Empire where anybody has an At Home day."

"Mother was certainly one of the last in Salterton to have one," said Solly.

"Aha? Well, this is a nice old house. You and your wife going to keep it up?"

"I haven't had time to think about that yet."

"No, I suppose not. But of course you'll be pretty well fixed, now?"

"I really don't know, sir."

"Sure to be. Your mother was a rich woman. You'll get everything. She certainly won't leave anything to me; I know that. Ha ha! She was a wonder with money, even as a girl. 'Louie, you're tighter than the bark to a tree,' I used to say to her. Did your father leave much?"

"He died very suddenly, you know, sir. His will was an old one, made before I was born. Everything went to Mother, of course."

"Aha? Well, it all comes to the same thing now, eh?"

"Solly, do you realize I'd never met your wife until this afternoon?" said Uncle George's wife. "Louisa never breathed a word about your marriage until she wrote to us weeks afterward. The girl was a Catholic, wasn't she?"

"No, Aunt Gussie. Her mother was a Catholic, but Veronica was brought up a freethinker by her father. Mother and her father had never agreed, and I'm afraid my marriage was rather a shock to her. I'll get Veronica now."

"Why do you keep calling her Veronica?" said Uncle George. "Louie wrote that her name was Pearl."

"It still is," said Solly. "But it is also Veronica, and that is what she likes me to call her. Her father is Professor Vambrace, you know."

"Oh God, that old bastard," said Uncle George, and was kicked on the ankle by his wife. "Gussie, what are you kicking me for?"

At this moment a Hansen cousin, leaning on a stick, approached and interrupted.

"Let's see, George, now Louisa's gone you're the oldest Hansen stock, aren't you?"

"I'm sixty-nine," said Uncle George; "you're older than that, surely, Jim?"

"Sixty-eight," said Jim, with a smirk.

"You look older," said Uncle George, unpleasantly.

"You would, too, if you'd been where I was on the Somme," said Cousin Jim, with the conscious virture of one who has earned the right to be nasty on the field of battle.

"You people certainly like it hot in Canada," said Aunt Gussie. And she was justified, for the steam heat and three open fires had made the crowded rooms oppressive.

"I'll see what I can do," said Solly and crept away. He ran upstairs and sought refuge in the one place he could think of which might be inviolable by his mother's relatives. As he entered his bathroom from his dressingroom his wife slipped furtively in from the bedroom. They locked both doors and sat down to rest on the edge of the tub.

"They're beginning to fight about who's the oldest stock," said Solly.

"I've met rather too many people who've hinted that our marriage killed your mother," said Veronica. "I thought a breather would do me good."

"Mother must have written fifty letters about that."

"Don't worry about it now, Solly."

"How is Humphrey doing?"

"I haven't heard any complaints. Do people always soak like this at funerals?"

"How should I know? I've never given a funeral tea before."

A Mixture of Frailties
Toronto, 1958

GABRIELLE ROY

Florentine was struck dumb. Her first reaction to the sight of Rose-Anna was to heave a sigh of relief that she had not turned up sooner, when Jean and Emmanuel had been at the restaurant. But the next moment she reproached herself for this. Leaning far over the counter, she greeted Rose-Anna with forced gaiety.

"See who's here!" she cried. "My mother!"

This was not the first time Rose-Anna had dropped in to say hello to Florentine when passing the store, but for many months she had left the house so seldom that this visit was totally unexpected.

Florentine looked at her mother in wonder. As often happens to members of a family who see each other every day, she had been blind to the changes that had come over her mother's face. There were wrinkles at the corners of her eyes that Florentine had never seen, there were lines of fatigue she had never even dimly perceived, and yet at one glance the girl beheld all the suffering, all the courage in that face. So after a long absence or some violent emotional experience, one sees in a flash what the years have done to a remembered image.

For a long time she had not seen her mother anywhere but at home, bent over the stove, or mending, and for the most part in the dim light of early morning or evening. Rose-Anna had only to appear in the bright glare of the store, dressed in her street clothes, she had only to emerge from the twilit obscurity in which she had buried herself so many years for Florentine to see her as she really was. Her pathetic smile, that gave the effect of trying to escape notice or at least of diverting it from herself, made Florentine heartsick. Up to then she had helped her mother out of a sense of fair play. She was proud to do her part, but to tell the truth she was far from meek about it and sometimes she felt as if she were being imposed upon. Now for the first time in her life she knew a moment of pure joy at the thought that she had not been ungenerous to her family. But that was not enough. She was filled with a sudden desire to be good to her mother today, to be gentler and more attentive and more generous than she had ever been, to mark the day with some special act of kindness, the memory of which would be sweet no matter what happened. And in the same breath she understood why this strange wish had come to her: it was that her mother's life appeared to be like a long dreary voyage under leaden skies that she, Florentine, would never make. It was as if today they were in a sense saying farewell. Perhaps this very moment marked the point of separation. In any case Florentine foresaw an inevitable parting of the ways. The threat of separation is needed to make some people aware of their own feelings:

thus Florentine realized only now that she loved her mother.

"Mamma," she said in a transport, "come and sit down!"

A little breathless, Rose-Anna sat down on one of the revolving chairs.

"I thought I'd stop in as long as I was passing by," she explained. "Your father is home, as you know. Out of a job!"

It was just like her mother, thought Florentine, to speak of their private troubles without a moment's delay. Once she was out of the house she looked about her with a shy smile that seemed to be seeking warmth from the youthful faces about her, but however she strove to be gay, the language of tribulation came to her lips as soon as she opened her mouth. Those were her words of greeting. And perhaps those were the ones most likely to touch a member of her family, for what held them all together if not their common troubles? Over a period of ten or twenty years, could not their family life be summed up by the troubles they had shared?

She continued, but in a lower voice, as if she were abashed to speak of such things in strange surroundings:

"And so I went out early to look for a house, Florentine."

She had said all this in the morning. Florentine frowned, and hated herself as she felt her good resolution weakening. Then she rebounded to her gentler mood.

"You were right to stop in," she said. "It just happens that we have chicken at forty cents today. I'm going to treat you."

"But Florentine, I only wanted a cup of coffee to perk me up a little."

And her lips seemed to be muttering with terror: "Forty cents, how expensive!" Knowing the price of food so well, knowing how to prepare filling meals at small cost, she had always felt a peasant's reluctance to go to a restaurant and pay for food that she could have cooked—she could not help estimating the difference—for so much less money. But all her life too, she had had a suppressed desire to indulge herself just once in the extravagance.

"Oh well," she said, her stern self-control breaking down with fatigue, "a little piece of pie, Florentine, if you insist, or a couple of doughnuts. I might try that."

"No, no," cried Florentine.

In contrast with her mother's dread of spending money she suddenly recalled Jean's lordly gesture when he gave her a tip. That may have been what she admired most in him, his careless way of tossing a coin on the counter, his look of indifference as it fell from his hands. She and her family on the other hand hated to let money out of their sight even to pay for what they needed. They followed it in their minds, clinging to it as it left them, as if it were part of them, as if it were torn from their flesh. When Rose-Anna was low in her spirits, her children often heard her for no apparent reason bemoaning the fact that she had not got her money's worth out of a tiny expenditure made long ago.

Florentine lifted her chin, nettled by her own thoughts, which seemed to set Jean so much above the rest of them.

"No, no," she repeated impatiently. "You're going to eat a big meal, Mother. You don't visit your daughter for dinner often enough!"

"That's true," said Rose-Anna, rising to Florentine's high spirits. "It's the first time, I think. But just give me a cup of coffee. Really, Florentine, that's all I want."

Her eyes dogged the waitresses as they bustled about, dazed by their youth and energy. She glanced furtively at Florentine, because here amid the shining mirrors and the bright colours her daughter seemed to have climbed high above her family, and for a moment she felt as much diffidence as pride. In a confused way she felt too that it was unwise to badger Florentine with their domestic problems, that it was cruel to cast a cloud over her youth, and she made up her mind to assume a happier expression, however awkwardly it sat upon her face.

Smiling, but ill at ease, she said: "I mustn't form the habit of going out, or you'll have me on your hands more often than you like. It's nice and warm here. And it smells so good. And you look quite fetching yourself, I assure you!"

These simple words were like balm to Florentine's heart.

"I'm going to order the chicken for you, you'll see how good it is," she cried.

She wiped the table where her mother sat, brought her a napkin, a glass of water, offering her all those little attentions that she paid to strangers day after day without any pleasure, but which today filled her with real joy. It seemed to her that it was the first time she had gone through the motions of cleaning the table and setting a place, and a song rang through her head as she moved to and fro, making the work effortless.

"You have a fine job. This is a good place," commented Rose-Anna, misunderstanding the reason for Florentine's good cheer.

"That's what you think!" cried the girl, with a quick shrug of the shoulders.

Then she burst out laughing.

"I've had good tips today, I must admit," she confided.

A picture of Jean and Emmanuel came to her mind. Unable to perceive that their liberality indicated that her position in regard to them was almost like a servant's, she nodded her head complacently, recalling with delight the large coins each of them had left for her.

"I always get more tips than any of the other girls, you know," she said.

Then she brought Rose-Anna a full plate, and, since the rush hour was over, took a few minutes off to watch her mother eat.

"Is it good? D'you like it?" she asked repeatedly.

"First-rate," said Rose-Anna.

But again and again some deep-seated conviction that spoiled the slightest extravagance for her would make her add:

"But it's too dear, you know. Forty cents! I don't think it's worth all of that. You must admit it's quite dear!"

When she finished the chicken, Florentine cut her a piece of pie.

"Oh, I can't," said Rose-Anna. "I've eaten too much as it is."

"It's all included in the price," insisted Florentine. "It doesn't cost extra."

"All right then, I'll try it," said Rose-Anna. "But I'm not hungry any more."

"Taste it all the same," said Florentine. "Is it good? Not as good as yours, is it?"

"Much better," said Rose-Anna.

Then Florentine, seeing her mother relaxed, almost happy, felt a deep, overwhelming compulsion to add to the happiness she had conferred. She slipped her hand into her blouse and brought out two crisp new bills, which she had been saving for some new stockings. And as her fingers touched the stiff paper, she saw in her mind's eye the sheer silk stockings she might have bought, and a sigh escaped her.

LUNCHEONETTE

LAZARE

"Should I buy the flute, the pretty little toy flute, or should I buy stockings, underwear, food?"

"Here," she said, "take this. Take it, Mother."

"But you've already given me your money for the week," objected Rose-Anna, slow to understand.

Florentine smiled and said:

"This is extra. Take it."

And she thought to herself: I'm good to Mamma. I'll be repaid for this; it will be counted in my favour. She still felt a twinge of regret for the loss of her silk stockings, but this only gave her renewed assurance that she would be happy presently. She pictured the party the next evening and in her incredibly childish way supposed that by reason of this single generous act she would cut an even more brilliant figure there, that she would receive deep and touching confirmation of Jean's regard for her.

A flush had spread over Rose-Anna's cheeks.

Brushing the crumbs from her coat, she mumbled, "I didn't come here for that, Florentine. I didn't come here to ask for money. I know that you don't have much left over from your pay."

Yet she took the two bills, put them in her change purse, and the change purse in her handbag for greater safety. Carefully folded, hidden away, they seemed already to have embarked on their mysterious career, their battle against so many wants.

"To tell the truth," confessed Rose-Anna, "I happen to need it right now."

"Oh!" exclaimed Florentine, losing some of her pleasure at these words, "and you wouldn't have told me!"

She saw her mother's piteous, beaten look, full of gratitude and admiration. She saw her mother rise painfully and leave, skirting the counters and stopping here and there to touch an object or feel a piece of material.

Her mother! Rose-Anna seemed very old to her. She moved slowly and her tight coat made her stomach bulge out. With two extra dollars hidden deep in her bag, the bag held close to her side, she was less sure of herself than before. Pots and pans, bolts of material, all the things she had long denied herself the privilege of looking at, fascinated her. Countless yearnings swelled within her, but she went steadily on her way, the money that had given rise to them buried in her pocketbook. Certainly she was poorer now than when she had entered the store.

As she watched this silent drama, all Florentine's joy was turned to bitterness. The rapture she had felt in being generous and unselfish gave way to a sense of aching frustration. It had been a total loss, completely useless. It was a drop of water in the desert of their lives.

At the other end of the store, Rose-Anna had stopped at the toy counter, and picked up a little tin flute. As a salesgirl approached, however, she put it down hastily, and Florentine knew that Daniel's desire for the flute would never be any closer to realization than this. Her mother's good intention was quickly suppressed. Likewise between her desire to help Rose-Anna and the peace of mind her mother would probably never have, nothing would be left but the aching memory of a good intention. If she alone could escape from their narrow life, that would be a great achievement, but even for her it was very hard. She would have been happy to take her family with her and raise them also to a position of ease and comfort, but she knew that it was useless to think of it.

She forced herself to smile at her mother, who seemed to be asking her advice: "Should I buy the flute, the pretty little toy flute, or should I buy stockings, underwear, food? Which is more important? A flute like a ray of sunshine for a sick child, a happy flute to make sounds of joy, or food on the table? Tell me which is more important, Florentine?"

Florentine brought herself to smile once more as Rose-Anna, deciding at length to leave the store, waved goodbye, but by that time she was ready to rip all her good intentions to shreds, like a useless rag.

The Tin Flute, Toronto, 1947
Translated from the French by Hannah Josephson

*"The notion of dying
had made her afraid.
She loved her husband
and wanted to die
loving him,
but she was afraid...."*

MORLEY CALLAGHAN

Sometimes Father Macdowell mumbled out loud and took a deep wheezy breath as he walked up and down the room and read his office. He was a huge old priest, white-headed except for a shiny baby-pink bald spot on the top of his head, and he was a bit deaf in one ear. His florid face had many fine red interlacing vein lines. For hours he had been hearing confessions and he was tired, for he always had to hear more confessions than any other priest at the cathedral; young girls who were in trouble, and wild but at times repentant young men, always wanted to tell their confessions to Father Macdowell, because nothing seemed to

shock or excite him, or make him really angry, and he was even tender with those who thought they were most guilty.

While he was mumbling and reading and trying to keep his glasses on his nose, the house girl knocked on the door and said, "There's a young lady here to see, father. I think it's about a sick call."

"Did she ask for me especially?" he said in a deep but slightly cracked voice.

"Indeed she did, father. She wanted Father Macdowell and nobody else."

So he went out to the waiting-room, where a girl about thirty years of age, with fine brown eyes, fine cheekbones, and rather square shoulders, was sitting daubing her eyes with a handkerchief. She was wearing a dark coat with a grey wolf collar. "Good evening, father," she said. "My sister is sick. I wanted you to come and see her. We think she's dying."

"Be easy, child; what's the matter with her? Speak louder. I can hardly hear you."

"My sister's had pneumonia. The doctor's coming back to see her in an hour. I wanted you to anoint her, father."

"I see, I see. But she's not lost yet. I'll not give her extreme unction now. That may not be necessary. I'll go with you and hear her confession."

"Father, I ought to let you know, maybe. Her husband won't want to let you see her. He's not a Catholic, and my sister hasn't been to church in a long time."

"Oh, don't mind that. He'll let me see her," Father Macdowell said, and he left the room to put on his hat and coat.

When he returned, the girl explained that her name was Jane Stanhope, and her sister lived only a few blocks away. "We'll walk and you tell me about your sister," he said. He put his black hat square on the top of his head, and pieces of white hair stuck out awkwardly at the sides. They went to the avenue together.

The night was mild and clear. Miss Stanhope began to walk slowly, because Father Macdowell's rolling gait didn't get him along the street very quickly. He walked as if his feet hurt, though he wore a pair of large, soft, specially constructed shapeless shoes. "Now, my child, you go ahead and tell me about your sister," he said, breathing with difficulty, yet giving the impression that nothing could have happened to the sister which would make him feel indignant.

There wasn't much to say, Miss Stanhope replied. Her sister had married John Williams two years ago, and he was a good, hard-working fellow, only he was very bigoted and hated all church people. "My family wouldn't have anything to do with Elsa after she married him, though I kept going to see her," she said. She was talking in a loud voice to Father Macdowell so that he could hear her.

"Is she happy with her husband?"

"She's been very happy, father. I must say that."

"Where is he now?"

"He was sitting beside her bed. I ran out because I thought he was going to cry. He said if I brought a priest near the place he'd break the priest's head."

"My goodness. Never mind, though. Does your sister want to see me?"

"She asked me to go and get a priest, but she doesn't want John to know she did it."

Turning into a side street, they stopped at the first apartment house, and the old priest followed Miss Stanhope up the stairs. His breath came with great difficulty. "Oh dear, I'm not getting any younger, not one day younger. It's a caution how a man's legs go back on him," he said. As Miss Stanhope rapped on the door, she looked pleadingly at the old priest, trying to ask him not to be offended at anything that might happen, but he was smiling and looking huge in the narrow hallway. He wiped his head with his handkerchief.

The door was opened by a young man in a white shirt with no collar, with a head of thick, black, wavy hair. At first he looked dazed, then his eyes got bright with excitement when he saw the priest, as though he were glad to see someone he could destroy with pent-up energy. "What do you mean, Jane?" he said. "I told you not to bring a priest around here. My wife doesn't want to see a priest."

"What's that you're saying, young man?"

"No one wants you here."

"Speak up. Don't be afraid. I'm a bit hard of hearing," Father Macdowell smiled rosily. John Williams was con-

fused by the unexpected deafness in the priest, but he stood there, blocking the door with sullen resolution as if waiting for the priest to try to launch a curse at him.

"Speak to him, father," Miss Stanhope said, but the priest didn't seem to hear her; he was still smiling as he pushed past the young man, saying, "I'll go in and sit down, if you don't mind, son. I'm here on God's errand, but I don't mind saying I'm all out of breath from climbing those stairs."

John was dreadfully uneasy to see he had been brushed aside, and he followed the priest into the apartment and said loudly, "I don't want you here."

Father Macdowell said, "Eh, eh?" Then he smiled sadly. "Don't be angry with me, son," he said. "I'm too old to try and be fierce and threatening." Looking around, he said, "Where's your wife?" and he started to walk along the hall, looking for the bedroom.

John followed him and took hold of his arm. "There's no sense in your wasting your time talking to my wife, do you hear?" he said angrily.

Miss Stanhope called out suddenly, "Don't be rude, John."

"It's he that's being rude. You mind your business," John said.

"For the love of God let me sit down a moment with her, anyway. I'm tired," the priest said.

"What do you want to say to her? Say it to me, why don't you?"

Then they both heard someone moan softly in the adjoining room, as if the sick woman had heard them. Father Macdowell, forgetting that the young man had hold of his arm, said, "I'll go in and see her for a moment, if you don't mind," and he began to open the door.

"You're not going to be alone with her, that's all," John said, following him into the bedroom.

Lying on the bed was a white-faced, fair girl, whose skin was so delicate that her cheekbones stood out sharply. She was feverish, but her eyes rolled toward the door, and she watched them coming in. Father Macdowell took off his coat, and as he mumbled to himself he looked around the room, at the mauve-silk bed-light and the light wallpaper with the tiny birds in flight. It looked like a little girl's room. "Good evening, father," Mrs. Williams whispered. She looked scared. She didn't glance at her husband. The notion of dying had made her afraid. She loved her husband and wanted to die loving him, but she was afraid, and she looked up at the priest.

"You're going to get well, child," Father Macdowell said, smiling and patting her hand gently.

John, who was standing stiffly by the door, suddenly moved around the big priest, and he bent down over the bed and took his wife's hand and began to caress her forehead.

"Now, if you don't mind, my son, I'll hear your wife's confession," the priest said.

"No, you won't," John said abruptly. "Her people didn't want her, and they left us together, and they're not going to separate us now. She's satisfied with me." He kept looking down at her face as if he could not bear to turn away.

Father Macdowell nodded his head up and down and sighed. "Poor boy," he said. "God bless you." Then he looked at Mrs. Williams, who had closed her eyes, and he saw a faint tear on her cheek. "Be sensible, my boy," he said. "You'll have to let me hear your wife's confession. Leave us alone a while."

"I'm going to stay right here," John said, and he sat down on the end of the bed. He was working himself up and staring savagely at the priest. All of a sudden he noticed the tears on his wife's cheeks, and he muttered as though bewildered, "What's the matter, Elsa? What's the matter, darling? Are we bothering you? Just open your eyes and we'll go out of the room and leave you alone till the doctor comes." Then he turned and said to the priest, "I'm not going to leave you here with her, can't you see that? Why don't you go?"

"I could revile you, my son. I could threaten you; but I ask you, for the peace of your wife's soul, leave us alone." Father Macdowell spoke with patient tenderness. He looked very big and solid and immovable as he stood by the bed. "I liked your face as soon as I saw you," he said to John. "You're a good fellow."

John still held his wife's wrist, but he rubbed one hand through his thick hair and said angrily, "You don't get the point, sir. My wife and I were always left alone, and we merely want to be left alone now. Nothing is going to separate us. She's been content with me. I'm sorry, sir; you'll have to speak to her with me here, or you'll have to go."

"No; you'll have to go for a while," the priest said patiently.

Then Mrs. Williams moved her head on the pillow and said jerkily, "Pray for me, father."

So the old priest knelt down by the bed, and with a sweet unruffled expression on his florid face he began to pray. At times his breath came with a whistling noise as though a rumbling were inside him, and at other times he sighed and was full of sorrow. He was praying that young Mrs. Williams might get better, and while he prayed he knew that her husband was more afraid of losing her to the Church than losing her to death.

All the time Father Macdowell was on his knees, with his heavy prayer book in his two hands, John kept staring at him. John couldn't understand the old priest's patience and tolerance. He wanted to quarrel with him, but he kept on watching the light from overhead shining on the one baby-pink bald spot on the smooth, white head, and at last he burst out, "You don't understand, sir! We've been very happy together. Neither you nor her people came near her when she was in good health, so why should you bother her now? I don't want anything to separate us now; neither does she. She came with me. You see you'd be separating us, don't you?" He was trying to talk like a reasonable man who had no prejudices.

Father Macdowell got up clumsily. His knees hurt him, for the floor was hard. He said to Mrs. Williams in quite a loud voice, "Did you really intend to give up everything for this young fellow?" and he bent down close to her so he could hear.

"Yes, father," she whispered.

"In Heaven's name, child, you couldn't have known what you were doing."

"We loved each other, father. We've been very happy."

"All right. Supposing you were. What now? What about all eternity, child?"

"Oh, father, I'm very sick and I'm afraid." She looked up to try to show him how scared she was, and how much she wanted him to give her peace.

He sighed and seemed distressed, and at last he said to John, "Were you married in the church?"

"No, we weren't. Look here, we're talking pretty loud and it upsets her."

"Ah, it's a crime that I'm hard of hearing, I know. Never mind, I'll go." Picking up his coat, he put it over his arm;

then he sighed as if he were very tired, and he said, "I wonder if you'd just fetch me a glass of water. I'd thank you for it."

John hesitated, glancing at the tired old priest, who looked so pink and white and almost cherubic in his utter lack of guile.

"What's the matter?" Father Macdowell said.

John was ashamed of himself for appearing so sullen, so he said hastily, "Nothing's the matter. Just a moment. I won't be a moment." He hurried out of the room.

The old priest looked down at the floor and shook his head; and then, sighing and feeling uneasy, he bent over Mrs. Williams, with his good ear down to her, and he said, "I'll just ask you a few questions in a hurry, my child. You answer them quickly and I'll give you absolution." He made the sign of the cross over her and asked if she repented for having strayed from the Church, and if she had often been angry, and whether she had always been faithful, and if she had ever lied or stolen—all so casually and quickly as if it hadn't occurred to him that such a young woman could have serious sins. In the same breath he muttered, "Say a good act of contrition to yourself and that will be all, my dear." He had hardly taken a minute.

When John returned to the room with the glass of water in his hand, he saw the old priest making the sign of the cross. Father Macdowell went on praying without even looking up at John. When he had finished, he turned and said, "Oh, there you are. Thanks for the water. I needed it. Well, my boy, I'm sorry if I worried you."

John hardly said anything. He looked at his wife, who had closed her eyes, and he sat down on the end of the bed. He was too disappointed to speak.

Father Macdowell, who was expecting trouble, said, "Don't be harsh, lad."

"I'm not harsh," he said mildly, looking up at the priest. "But you weren't quite fair. And it's as though she turned away from me at the last moment. I didn't think she needed you."

"God bless you, bless the both of you. She'll get better," Father Macdowell said. But he felt ill at ease as he put on his coat, and he couldn't look directly at John.

Going along the hall, he spoke to Miss Stanhope, who wanted to apologize for her brother-in-law's attitude. "I'm sorry if it was unpleasant for you, father," she said.

"It wasn't unpleasant," he said. "I was glad to meet John. He's a fine fellow. It's a great pity he isn't a Catholic. I don't know as I played fair with him."

As he went down the stairs, puffing and sighing, he pondered the question of whether he had played fair with the young man. But by the time he reached the street he was rejoicing amiably to think he had so successfully ministered to one who had strayed from the faith and had called out to him at the last moment. Walking along with the rolling motion as if his feet hurt him, he muttered, "Of course they were happy as they were . . . in a worldly way. I wonder if I did come between them?"

He shuffled along, feeling very tired, but he couldn't help thinking, "What beauty there was to his staunch love for her!" Then he added quickly, "But it was just a pagan beauty, of course."

As he began to wonder about the nature of this beauty, for some reason he felt inexpressibly sad.

"A Sick Call" in *Morley Callaghan's Stories*, Toronto, 1959

"... a disturbing conflict was going on inside him. Just what demon had urged him to choose this painter?"

ROGER LEMELIN

It all began one June evening in the main hall of the Provincial Museum.

"Monsieur le curé Ledoux! What a surprise! I did not know that modern painting interested you!"

"Perhaps, perhaps," the old priest stammered, smiling mysteriously.

The speaker, an eminent ecclesiastic and a discriminating connoisseur of art, looked in perplexity after curé Ledoux, who, like a waggish spy, was threading his way through the groups of guests. This particular evening happened to be the first night of an exhibition of the works of a young painter, Paul Lafrance. He had just arrived back from Paris, where, for three years, he had busied himself in imitating Picasso. Paul Lafrance was almost six feet tall and did not weigh more than one hundred and thirty pounds. His long, mouse-coloured hair, his pale blue eyes, the Parisian's skeptical smile on his lips, his check suit and the short, fat women surrounding him, all contributed to making him appear more scrawny and more dejected. The weird designs and the violent colours of the canvases gave the walls an air of ludicrous astonishment. Some so-called connoisseurs, Provincial Government officials, were scrutinizing, criticizing, and appraising each work with pretentious gestures and glances. They had no money. The other guests, holding Martinis, were chatting about fishing and politics and glancing absent-mindedly at the paintings. These dilettantes, these business men flocking to an opening night through a taste for fashionable gatherings, behaved like gapers invading a circus famous for its five-footed giraffes. They are very extraordinary giraffes but the gapers don't buy them. Paul Lafrance had not yet sold one canvas.

"Monsieur Ledoux, you here?"

The old priest nodded, smiling artfully, his eyes almost closing. His cassock, greenish from being worn too long, was a trifle short and revealed his dusty boots, topped by thick, black, woollen socks. Now and then he rubbed a nervous hand through his tousled grey hair, and with the other crumpled a large chequered handkerchief into a ball in the opening of his roomy pocket.

Apparently unaware of the astonished murmurs that followed in his wake, he reached the first canvases and began to examine them one by one with an outstanding gravity, as if he had to condemn them to heaven or hell. Whatever was he doing at this exhibition? Those who knew him had reason to be astonished.

Monsieur Ledoux was rector-founder of St. X parish in the poorest district of Quebec. For some time there had been a great deal of talk about him all over the city. After fifteen years of untiring apostleship he was seeing his parishioners of early days (swearers, drunkards, thieves) become exemplary citizens. But it was through his new church that old curé Ledoux had become famous. This temple was costing three hundred thousand dollars. Very good. His parishioners must be workingmen of heroic calibre to have consented to such a sum. Again very good. But all that would not be enough to have Monsieur Ledoux talked about at every social gathering. Monsieur Ledoux's famous church was not like the others! That was why! Gothic in style, it was the only one in the city without pillars! The high-altar was visible from every seat. That isn't all. Monsieur Ledoux had had air-conditioning installed. It was probably the first innovation of its kind in all the churches in America! It had been said for a long time that curé Ledoux, son of peasants, was an uncouth and uncultured man. But what about this air-conditioning, this absence of pillars?

Monsieur Ledoux glided from one canvas to another with a concentrated air that one would not have expected of him. Someone offered him a Martini, which he refused with a gesture of annoyance. After some twenty minutes' examination he buried his large nose in his chequered handkerchief and glanced furtively around him.

"Make up your mind, Thomas, make up your mind!"

Monsieur Ledoux was talking to himself. He often did that. Everybody called him "Monsieur le curé", so Monsieur Ledoux often said to himself: "Thomas! Eh! Thomas!" The priest walked towards the painter, Paul Lafrance, whose back was turned, and pulled discreetly at his sleeve.

"Monsieur l'abbé?"

"Curé Thomas Ledoux. Your work interests me. It's modern. Give me your address."

The pale blue eyes gazed at the old priest as Paul Lafrance mechanically recited his address. Monsieur Ledoux, having moistened his pencil with saliva, wrote down the number in a little notebook. He closed it, smiling like an accomplice.

"Perhaps you will hear from me."

He shuffled off towards the cloakroom. The painter and the guests, piqued with curiosity, gazed after him.

Monsieur Ledoux boarded a streetcar. With his chin sunk in the fleshy cushion that prosperity had placed round his neck since the erection of his famous church, he appeared to doze in heavenly bliss. His head swayed from left to right with the jerks of the streetcar and in rhythm with the rolling wheels on the rails. All at once the old priest sat bolt upright and opened his eyes watchfully. By an intuition peculiar to clergy, he had sensed the nearby presence of a church.

It was the Basilica of Quebec. Monsieur Ledoux stared at it intently with an affectionate expression that gave way to one of triumph. The celebrated Basilica, the Cardinal's chapel, was filled with unfortunate pillars and had no air-conditioning system. Not like Monsieur Ledoux's church! His chin disappeared once more into its cushion and Monsieur Ledoux, having made sure of Paul Lafrance's address, began to doze again.

Monsieur Ledoux got off the streetcar in his parish and walked toward the presbytery. It was ten o'clock at night. Like a proud landowner he sniffed the air of his domain and glanced fondly at the humble homes of his flock. All at once he found himself in front of the unusual temple that crowned his saintly ambitions and filled him with pride. He stopped and, swaying with his hands behind his back, eyes half-closed as though in ecstasy, he gazed at it. His lips curled into a blissful smile: "Thomas, Thomas, it's really true, it is your church, your church, you old Thomas, you!"

His rapture was suddenly interrupted. Two devout women, faithful parish workers, were standing beside him and admiring the temple with him.

"What a fine church, eh, Monsieur le curé! The electric organ has been bought. All we need is the Stations of the Cross."

Monsieur Ledoux turned round abruptly to them and said with puerile haste:

"We'll have them in a month. They'll be unique, these Stations of the Cross. The first of their kind in America, even in the whole world, perhaps. Thomas says so."

Open-mouthed, the two housewives, delighted by this news and slightly shocked by the unexpected "Thomas" of Monsieur Ledoux, watched him go away. Monsieur le curé, less repentant for having said too much than annoyed by this familiar use of Thomas that he had not been able to restrain before these good women, went into the presbytery furiously sniffing up a pinch of snuff. He went up to his office and on his way was addressed by the youngest of his curates, abbé Constant, the door of whose room was open. Comfortably seated in a leather armchair, he was busy reading James Joyce's novel *Ulysses*. Abbé Constant, who had been ordained two years before, put himself in the category of the young clergy with advanced ideas who clamour for a youthful Church, suited to the needs of the time. He often smiled at certain of Monsieur Ledoux's old-fashioned preferences but he was very fond of him all the same.

"Are you beginning to sleep away from home, Monsieur le curé?"

"I've just come back from the Museum, from the first night of an exhibition of modern painting," Monsieur Ledoux replied, blushing.

Wide-eyed with astonishment, abbé Constant gazed at his superior without saying a word.

Monsieur Ledoux, annoyed at having blushed, added defiantly: "Yes, I have decided that our Stations of the Cross will be modern art. The first in America. And I think I'm going to choose this artist, Paul Lafrance."

"But . . . Monsieur le curé," ventured abbé Constant, who was beginning to collect his wits, "don't you think our parishioners are scarcely prepared for . . . for Stations of the Cross like that?"

Then Monsieur le curé stiffened haughtily and said with triumphant solemnity:

"And it's you, young man, who reproached me for being old-fashioned! I have eliminated pillars, have had air-conditioning installed, and now it's the turn of modern art. Well, good night. Don't go to bed too late. You say five o'clock mass tomorrow morning."

Abbé Constant was too astonished to go on with *Ulysses*. He went to bed.

The young curate's objection hastened the execution of the project because the curé could not tolerate anyone to doubt the worth of his ideas. Monsieur Ledoux rarely consulted his churchwardens where the financial affairs of his parish were concerned. He made his decision and, as a matter of form, called them together in order to tell them about it. As Monsieur Ledoux was cunning enough to make them believe that he had acted under their influence, these gentlemen (a fruit merchant, a grocer, and a streetcar conductor) nodded their heads gravely in approval. In the matter of the Stations of the Cross, Monsieur Ledoux presented them with the accomplished fact.

The artist Paul Lafrance set the price of his work at twenty-five hundred dollars for fourteen pictures representing the different stages in the Passion of Christ, according to the rules of modern art. Moreover, the surrealist painter promised to visit all the churches in the city, in order to make sure that his Stations of the Cross would be completely different from the others. Monsieur le curé promised to pay for the cost of the canvas, the paint, the frames, and to board the artist while he was doing his work. The brightest room in the presbytery was turned into a studio by the painter and the curé. The latter was anxious to keep up a daily inspection of his Stations and to become acquainted with the mysterious caprices of Modern Art.

The sight of the long-haired artist and the fabulous price of twenty-five hundred dollars made the churchwardens open their eyes wide, but Monsieur Ledoux remarked with a knowing smile:

"Churchwardens like you are blessed by God, who allows you to buy something more rare and beautiful for a church already unique." These gentlemen puffed out their chests, looking at one another. What a curé!

It was an extraordinary experience for Paul Lafrance. Newly arrived from Paris where, many a time in front of his artist friends he had made fun of the French Canadian's lack of taste for painting and where, before anti-clerical dilettantes, he had slandered the Canadian clergy, he now found himself with an order for fourteen surrealist paintings from the priest of a parish of workingmen, when as yet he had not sold a single canvas during his exhibition. This was a great piece of news in all the artistic circles of Quebec

and many of the painter's friends insisted on visiting his studio and meeting Monsieur le curé Ledoux. For a whole week the rumour circulated about St. X Parish that Monsieur le curé had had a celebrated artist brought by aeroplane from Paris. But Monsieur Ledoux remained impervious to questions. "Wait until Sunday at high mass."

The Sunday arrived. The church was packed to the doors. The absence of pillars and the air-conditioning were never so appreciated as on that day. All the flock were craning their necks in order to get a better look at the artist, Paul Lafrance, seated among the altar boys on a kind of throne usually reserved for visiting bishops. Lafrance, who had acquired pagan ways in Paris and given up his religion, was thinking that Art leads everywhere, even to Rome. He compared himself to Michelangelo and with some satisfaction imagined himself becoming a prince of the Church. All these glances raised towards him, the proximity of the altar and the religious propriety which surrounded him, prompted him to recall his prayers. He smiled imperceptibly at the thought that he was paid twenty-five hundred dollars to rediscover his faith. Monsieur le curé climbed into the pulpit.

"My very dear brethren:

"Heaven sends us a messenger of beauty from Europe. It is quite in keeping that Providence should direct his steps to our temple which, without doubt, is one of the dwellings on earth preferred by the Almighty. This church has been built in the most modern style and it would be illogical if the Stations of the Cross which will decorate it should be in the style of past centuries. If the art of building has been perfected to such a degree as to result in a work of art like ours, the art of painting has also evolved, and we must make it a duty to require as much of painting as of building. Thus, in honouring progress, we honour the Lord who is kind enough to bestow it upon man. My very dear brethren, you have before you, in the chancel, the celebrated painter, Paul Lafrance, who, tomorrow, will begin your Stations of the Cross, a work of which your grandchildren's children will be proud and which will make our church even more famous."

During the days that followed, the presbytery became, in the parishioners' eyes, a mysterious laboratory where a magician armed with brushes devoted himself to all kinds of artistic alchemy. Many curious ones tried to obtain the favour of casting a glance at Lafrance's work, but Monsieur le curé kept this privilege for himself. Out of consideration, Monsieur Ledoux did not visit the studio for the first two days. Paul Lafrance took his meals at the same table as the curé and his curates and long discussions on cubism, impressionism and surrealism took place between the abbé Constant and the artist, who seemed to get along with each other very well. In the course of these conversations, which he did not understand in the least, Monsieur Ledoux often blew his nose, pretending he had a cold in order to excuse himself for having nothing to say.

However, at the fourth meal, tired of blowing his nose, the curé became impatient and determined to find some books which would deal with these mysteries. But he dared not ask the painter in front of abbé Constant. He rose from the table briskly, during the dessert, and, very politely, asked:

"Is your work progressing, Monsieur Lafrance?"

"Yes. The first picture is finished. Some last touches and it will be perfect."

Monsieur Ledoux, warped by fifteen years of financial administration, gave himself up to a rapid calculation. One picture in two days, fourteen in twenty-eight days, ninety dollars per day. He was a little disappointed. It had seemed to him that, because of the importance he attached to this work, it should take some months to complete.

"Do you wish to see it?" asked the painter.

The two men went off to the studio and Monsieur Ledoux, on catching sight of the picture, cried out in stupefaction.

"Don't you like it?" the painter ejaculated, distressed.

Monsieur Ledoux shook his head and frowned.

"I think the feet and the arms of the Christ are unusually long. It gives an odd effect. Don't you think so?"

The painter, already inflamed by the fervour of the artist defending his work, opened his mouth to make a declaration of his principles, but a second's reflection and a brief glance at Monsieur Ledoux persuaded him to change his tactics.

"It's because it's new that it takes you by surprise. You'll become accustomed to it and then you'll like this style. Painting has changed a great deal. It's no longer photography. Moreover, you insisted that my Stations of the Cross should be an innovation."

"I don't deny it."

Monsieur le curé, chin in hand, was reflecting. To tell the truth, a disturbing conflict was going on inside him. Just what demon had urged him to choose this painter? Moreover, from the first glimpse on the opening night at the Museum he ought to have foreseen the dangers with which modern art threatened his Stations of the Cross! The word "modern" and the success of his church had blinded him. Obviously, he had not acted with his customary prudence in paying a thousand dollars in advance to the painter. It was now too late to retreat. He could not dismiss the painter after the enthusiastic recommendation he had given him. Monsieur Ledoux abruptly put an end to his reflections.

"Monsieur Lafrance, I'm not disputing the beauty of your work and I think that in the long run I shall understand it. But I do not forget that I have eighteen thousand parishioners who are not so well prepared as I to appreciate your work. And they are the ones who pay for it. So please shorten those arms and feet a little. Anyhow, you know what I mean."

The painter seemed highly shocked but the curé had already left. With clenched fists, Monsieur Ledoux went to his room muttering: "Thomas, you're nothing but a proud old peacock. You've got yourself into a fine mess. Because you have a new church without pillars and with air-conditioning you think you're the hub of the universe. You old fool, go and pray a little while and ask God to get you out of this tight corner. Above all, thank Him for the blow to your pride."

He met abbé Constant in the hall.

"Well, now, Monsieur le curé, what do you think of Monsieur Lafrance's work?"

"Stupendous! Stupendous!"

Monsieur Ledoux did not add anything further but went up into his room and knelt down. His prayer lasted an hour and, apparently, the Lord advised him to persevere in his project in order to punish him.

Regular torture then began for Monsieur Ledoux. He made an effort to show a great enthusiasm for the Stations of the Cross but his common sense told him: "Thomas, you know very well that these paintings are dreadful. You're courting disaster." In order to be convinced of the beauties of modern art he consulted a clergyman renowned for his artistic knowledge. Monsieur Ledoux even obtained some large books on the subject. All to no purpose. The frequent visits he paid to the artist's studio only succeeded in adding to his despair. Artists like Paul Lafrance are as uncompromising as the Ten Commandments. The painter went on with the work in his own way and the further it progressed the longer, it seemed to Monsieur Ledoux, the feet and arms of the Christ became. Those violently coloured paintings with monstrously grotesque figures appeared to Monsieur Ledoux like a Mardi Gras masquerade. The good curé lost his appetite and the fleshy cushion around his neck decreased considerably. He never mentioned the Stations of the Cross in the pulpit and his parishioners, who were waiting impatiently for the unveiling, were astonished. What was happening to him?

Then something most unfortunate occurred. The verger, who was a very inquisitive man, succeeded in getting into the studio while the curé was away, and glanced at the pictures. Immediately word went round the parish that the People of the Passion were all crippled and walking in paths of blood. Alarmed, the housewives called on the curé and confessed their anxiety. He smiled, closing his eyes.

"Ladies, I suspect you of inventing rumours in order to force me to satisfy your curiosity. They're all untrue. In the meantime, if it will give you any pleasure, I can tell you that the Holy Women in our Stations of the Cross are the portraits of the most devout ladies in the parish."

Delighted and flattered, the ladies left the presbytery quite content. Monsieur le curé, overwhelmed, did not know what to do. While feeling so downcast, he came face to face with abbé Constant. Forgetting his pride, he confessed hesitantly to him:

"Monsieur l'abbé, I think you were right. I have made a mistake. Our parishioners are not ready to appreciate our Stations of the Cross. What am I going to do?"

Abbé Constant, who for some days had known his curé's state of mind, behaved himself as befits a good priest. He did not laugh at him but cheered him up and offered to help him. The two priests set to work and prepared a ten-page circular in which the symbolic beauty of modern art was praised with forceful adjectives. The circular was printed and distributed to the parishioners by the altar boys. In the face of this incomprehensible action, the parishioners began to be seriously alarmed.

The work was finished one Saturday afternoon and the painter's satisfaction equalled the curé's distress. The artist received the balance of his payment, thanked the curé, and left like a great lord. To put an end to the great martyrdom he was enduring the good curé announced that the exhibition of the work would be on Sunday morning, a quarter of an hour before high mass. Certain remarks of dissatisfied parishioners about the circular on modern art had reached the curé's ears and he fearfully visualized the moment of the ceremony. He passed a dreadful night and every time he woke up he implored Heaven to calm his anguish and to see to it that his parishioners would bow down in admiration before the Stations of the Cross.

At half-past nine, the verger, whose rising indignation was mingled with fits of laughter, hung the pictures in the empty church. Monsieur le curé, hidden behind the altar, perspired profusely while waiting for the doors to be opened.

A crowd of parishioners interested in the fate of their church stamped and jostled outside the entrances. Finally the doors opened and there was a rush into the temple. There was not a single sound from the thousand gaping mouths, so great was the stupefaction. Then there burst out fourteen rounds of horrified cries which were relayed from picture to picture in a kind of chain of explosions. The women protested the most violently.

"They're frightful. Look at the Christ! The arms are longer than the legs, the feet longer than the thighs and the hair does not curl. Horrible! Just look at the face! The chin is pointed, the eyes are all wrong."

Among the group of good ladies who thought themselves represented by the Holy Women of the Passion were some white with anger and others who were crying, for the Holy Women of the Stations of the Cross looked like enormous frogs. The churchwardens seemed to be in a bad humour and were whispering: "Twenty-five hundred dollars for these daubs! A child could do them!"

Other men threw up their hands, expostulating: "The cross is much too small and it's snowing flowers into the bargain! Just look, will you! The hands are pierced with nails and don't even bleed!"

A rebellious atmosphere reigned in the church. The parishioners were all coming to the same conclusion: Had Monsieur le curé gone crazy? Every eye searched for him.

Behind the altar, Monsieur le curé Ledoux, face white as his surplice, mopped his brow. To cap everything, the air-conditioning system had gone out of order the day before. It was July and the heat was tropical.

Ten o'clock mass began and no one paid any attention to the service. The church was full of whispers and ripples of muted laughter. How shameful! Such a shocking thing in such a beautiful church! Monsieur le curé went up into the pulpit more dead than alive. He would have preferred to be at Rome, prostrate at the Pope's feet and thinking only of the beauties of Christianity. "Face the music, Thomas!" His voice was weak and his hands trembled.

"My very dear brethren:

"I am only an old man whose dearest wish, as you know, is to give you a church finer than all the others. For a long time I had dreamed of acquiring a magnificent Stations of the Cross for you. At last, it is in front of you, but instead of the admiration that I expected, you show dissatisfaction. I do not hide the fact that I am broken-hearted by your attitude. But I pray heaven that your eyes will become accustomed to this work and recognize its beauties in the end. My very dear brethren..."

Monsieur Ledoux felt himself grow faint and made no effort to resist swooning. The churchwardens, while carrying him to the vestry, remarked: "Not surprising that you fainted! Throwing twenty-five hundred dollars to the devil like that!"

Monsieur Ledoux's fainting had sown consternation in the hearts of his flock, but not to the point of changing their opinion of his famous Stations of the Cross. These events filled the parishioners' conversation for several days and Monsieur le curé deemed it wiser to keep to his bed. As long as there was anxiety about his condition no one complained about the Stations of the Cross. But although Monsieur le curé kept out of sight he was, nevertheless, most active. From various sources of information he learned that his faithful flock were attending church less and less frequently and those who came to the religious services spent their time laughing at the ridiculous paintings. On the other hand, the temple was invaded by a curious crowd from neighbouring parishes attracted by the peculiar Stations of the Cross.

Monsieur Ledoux's celebrated church had become a kind of museum where one forgot to kneel and took the liberty of talking and laughing boisterously. Monsieur Ledoux endured many bitter moments. After having enjoyed too briefly the importance of his church, he was already suffering from its decline. Then it was that Providence deemed him to have been punished enough and inspired him with an ingenious idea. Why hadn't he thought sooner of the Mother Superior of the Convent?

She had some talent for painting and Monsieur le curé had often gone, on Sunday afternoons, to see her paint saints, ships, rivers, and roses in delicate colours with a dainty brush. He had her roused at ten o'clock at night and the good Mother Superior, all of a tremble, ran to the presbytery. When she left Monsieur Ledoux, she said these words: "I can paint these fourteen pictures in two weeks, I promise you. But I repeat that I am not equal to the task. Pray God I may succeed."

The Mother Superior's work was kept a great secret. Monsieur le curé went to the convent three times a day and all those who met him wondered why he wore such a cheerful expression when the church continued to be profaned by inquisitive folk who came from all over. Ten days after the Mother Superior's visit, Monsieur Ledoux telephoned to a very important person who nearly fainted after hearing the curé's words. But that is another story. Two days after his telephone call, on Saturday night, about eleven o'clock, a Government truck stopped at the side door of the church and two workmen, under Monsieur Ledoux's direction, carefully carried fourteen packages from the church to the truck.

The next morning, at ten o'clock mass, the church witnessed the finest sight imaginable. The frightful Stations of the Cross had disappeared and were replaced by fourteen beautiful paintings in delicate colours, with handsome men, beautiful women and a Christ that resembled Clark Gable.

The flock were filled with rapture that was soon transformed into deep piety. Many good ladies shed tears of joy and all the deeply affected parishioners raised grateful glances towards the altar. The church was exorcised and restored again to the bosom of the Lord. Monsieur Ledoux went up into the pulpit in triumph.

"My very dear brethren:

"Your joy moves me to the highest degree. The magnificent Stations of the Cross that you see before you are due to the brush of the Convent Mother Superior who deserves all our gratitude. As for the other Stations of the Cross, I thought those pictures were meant, after all, for experts. So I gave them to the Provincial Museum. My very dear brethren, let us rejoice in the Lord. Our church has resumed its march toward celebrity; it is the first in the city without pillars; the only one in America to possess an air-conditioning system and the first in the world to make a gift of the Stations of the Cross to the Museum."

"The Stations of the Cross" in *Canadian Short Stories* (edited by Robert Weaver and Helen James), Toronto, 1962. Translated by Mary Finch

4

❧ POLITICS ❧

THE OLD FLAG.
THE OLD POLICY.
THE OLD LEADER.

SIR JOHN A. MACDONALD

Those who dislike the colonial connection speak of it as a chain, but it is a golden chain, and I, for one, am glad to wear the fetters.

House of Commons Debates, March 30, 1875

❀

I am greatly disappointed at the course taken by the British Commissioners. They seem to have only one thing in their minds—that is, to go to England with a Treaty in their pockets—no matter at what cost to Canada.

Letter to Charles Tupper, April 1, 1871

❀

EDWARD BLAKE

The history of the diplomatic service of England, as far as Canada is concerned, has been a history of error, blunder, wrong, and concession.

House of Commons Debates, 1882

❀

VINCENT MASSEY

He raised the subject of future relations between the U.S.A. and Canada and spoke apprehensively of the process of disentanglement which must follow the war when the Americans must withdraw and leave us in full control of our own bases and their wartime installations. The P.M. showed that he had grave doubts as to whether international agreements on this which Canada had secured from the United States provide any practical guarantee against the United States' claims and pretensions. When I suggested that the Americans, although undoubtedly friendly, did not take us seriously enough as a nation, King said that Canadians were looked upon by Americans as a lot of Eskimos. This was a striking observation made by a man who had been so often accused of being subservient to American policy. When I suggested that a spirited attitude towards Washington was essential he warmly concurred.

What's Past is Prologue, Toronto, 1963

❀

Vincent Massey by Gitano   Maclean's, *1933*

We were always quite prepared to accept membership on important committees, but Canadian delegations, under the instructions they received before leaving home, were almost morbidly anxious to avoid 'commitments'—wicked word—and the effect we had on the deliberations of the League was paltry, even negligible. I cannot help quoting some reflections recorded in 1937 by Hume Wrong of the Department of External Affairs, referring to an international conference at which he represented Canada:

We should not be here at all, as our instructions should be summarized as: say nothing and do nothing unless you can undo something of what was done at Geneva. . . . Dining alone this evening I developed a plan for the perfect representation of Canada at Conferences. Our delegate would have a name, even a photograph; a distinguished record, even an actual secretary—but he would have no corporeal existence and no one would ever notice that he was not there.

What's Past is Prologue, Toronto, 1963

JOHN CONWAY

Official oratory about the undefended frontier is misleading. The frontier has been undefended in large part because it is undefendable, not because of any profound similarity between the two peoples, who are, in fact, different in their historical experience, their political philosophy, and their view of the world outside North America. They are complementary to each other, but they are not identical. Both may legitimately claim to be the legatees of British notions of free government, but the legacy is not a unified one. The American people entered into their legacy by a revolutionary act in 1776. By that act they defined their identity and released the energies that would during the next century and a half create a great nation and a great literature, a new vision of the nature and destiny of man.

We Canadians have so far failed to enter fully into our legacy, and this is our one great, overreaching problem as our centennial approaches. On its solution everything else depends. We have failed to vest sovereignty where it properly belongs–in the Canadian people. Instead, we have allowed it to remain in the British monarchy, and in doing so we have divided our country and inhibited our emotional and creative development as a people. A nation, like an individual, can achieve integrity and identity only out of its own experience and not derivatively from a parent. This, and not French-Canadian particularism, is at the root of our present difficulties. Our internal dissensions are intrinsically less serious than those that plagued the thirteen colonies when their leaders were labouring to create the American Union, but because of our failure to recognize a national identity distinct from that of Great Britain, they have been allowed to assume proportions that have come close to paralyzing our parliamentary machinery. Our identity cannot emerge clear and dominant until sovereignty, both real and symbolic, is brought to rest in ourselves.

As it is now, the Crown as a symbol of sovereignty encourages British Canadians to ignore their own failure to build a united nation by allowing them an illusory participation in a history and a greatness not properly theirs. They feel free therefore to indulge in that xenophobia toward the French which is one of the most unpleasant and uncivilized traits of the English middle class. Because of this the French can avoid responsibility for their own intellectual stultification and their unreasonable contentiousness by pointing out, correctly enough, that the British have an overriding loyalty outside Canada and that they, the French, are the only true Canadians. And the 20 per cent of our population which are of neither British nor French ancestry are left in a patriotic vacuum, ready only too often, particularly if they are greatly gifted, to leave the country in search of an environment charged with affirmative rather than negative concerns. When we take the long-overdue step and transfer sovereignty to where it properly belongs, it will become clear that Canadians–British, French, and European alike–have been and are engaged in a common enterprise which is of far greater concern than the separate concerns of each group; and just as the United States has given classic expression in literature, philosophy, and political theory to its interpretation of the New World, so will we begin to give classic expression to ours.

"What Is Canada?" *Atlantic Monthly* (November, 1964)

DONALD CREIGHTON

In 1867, the last day of June was a Sunday; and in Christian British North America Sunday was a day of quiet, and rest and reflection, and churchgoing. It was also a day of visits and family parties and discreet jollification; and since Monday, Dominion Day, was to be a holiday, the Canadians had been granted that rare gift of their generation, a long weekend. Tomorrow there would be picnics, parades, and sports; and today farmers and their wives and children were driving down dusty country roads to pay calls, have dinner, or stay the night with friends or relatives in the next concession, or the nearby village, or the neighbouring township. The big table in the spacious winter-kitchen–all culinary arrangements had, of course, been transferred to the summer-kitchen late in May–was crowded with six or eight extra places; and there had been a piece of fresh beef, and a ham from the smokehouse, and new potatoes and new peas. In the afternoon they all went to church, the women and girls in their best summer crinolines, the men in rather rusty top hats. It was so bright and hot that the women had worried a little about their dresses sticking to the varnished oak pews. And the minister preached about Confederation and the future of Christian Canada.

In the towns and cities, the clergy and the journalists, those two groups that were expected to have great thoughts for public occasions, were busy at their respective callings. The journalists were writing inspiring leading articles for the first Dominion Day; and in many pulpits prayers were being offered and sermons preached for Confederation. In St. Paul's Church, Montreal, the Rev. Mr. Jenkins, apologizing that he could scarcely do justice to this theme in fifty minutes, preached a fine sermon, divided, in good Presbyterian fashion, under four main heads, on the text, 'Blessed is the nation whose God is the Lord'. Church services were, of course, over by the time George Brown, hot, perspiring, and extremely thirsty, arrived at the *Globe* office on King Street, Toronto. He drank copiously, took off his coat, waistcoat, and collar, retired to his inner editorial office, and began to compose the enormous leading article, nine thousand words in length, which was to be the *Globe*'s salute to the 1st of July, 1867. It flowed over into a second huge page of statistics on the population, trade, and navigation of the different uniting provinces. Other editors were impressively reviewing the new Dominion's human and natural resources and speculating generously about its prospects of material advancement. They were also making sober appeals to the new nation's consciousness of maturity and its sense of obligation. 'Colony implies the political status of adolescence,' reflected the Montreal *Gazette*, 'but Dominion implies power and the political status of manhood; it implies also responsibility.'

As midnight and the new day drew closer, people were thinking a good deal less about responsibility and much more about celebration, in even the soberest of Canadian towns and cities. In the central streets of Toronto, strangely gay Sunday groups began to gather; and in Ottawa, an hour before twelve o'clock, large crowds were beginning to assemble on Major's Hill and on the Ordnance Lands beyond the Cathedral. The bells of St. James' Cathedral in Toronto began to peal at midnight; impromptu parades of citizens, led by fifes and drums, were marching happily up

George Brown by J. W. Bengough
A Caricature History of Canadian Politics, *Vol. I, Toronto, 1886*

and down; and in King Street a huge bonfire was kindled. An even more splendid bonfire, a 'huge, pyramidal pile', constructed of firewood, packing-cases, and tar barrels, had been reared, the previous Saturday, on the Ordnance Lands in Ottawa; and at the Cathedral clock's final stroke of twelve, it was fired. There were cheers for the Queen and the Dominion; the church bells chimed; rockets soared into the air and fell in showers of coloured lights; and the Ottawa Field Battery—the capital might be forgiven a rather grandiose expression of enthusiasm—wakened the whole town with the prolonged din of a one-hundred-gun salute.

Little by little, the laughing crowds came home. The gaslit streets grew silent; and one by one, the house lights went out. Long before that, oil lamps had been turned down and candles blown out in the parlours and bedrooms of farmhouses. Still earlier, the trundle beds had been pulled out, and the children, including perhaps a few small visitors from across the townline or the county boundary, had been put to bed. For a while their elders had sat on in the big winter-kitchen, enjoying the cool of the summer night and gossiping about the future. Everybody was eager for tomorrow; everything was ready for the picnic that was to be held in the nearby fair grounds, or on the common under the elm trees beside the drowsy inland river. The children had picked a great mound of wild strawberries; bottles of the best raspberry cordial had been selected; two plump chickens had been roasted and were waiting in the cellar; there were pans of gingerbread, and crocks of lemon biscuits and twisted fried cakes; and two of the girls had been deputed to start a freezerful of frozen cream immediately after breakfast. All the preparations had been made. The lights were out now along the quiet, starlit concession roads. And for a few hours, on that brief summer night, the Canadians slept.

Their land slept too. They had occupied such a small part—such a mere fringe—of its grand totality. The great wheatlands of the North-West, which only the stars looked down on, had never been touched by the plough; and beneath the unbroken prairies and the scarred, primordial contours of the Precambrian Shield there lay untouched and sunk in far more profound slumbers the undreamed-of mineral riches of

the future. No young people had ever looked forward to such a vast inheritance. No new nation had ever begun its existence with such an enormous patrimony. It stretched so far from ocean to ocean that on these longest richest days of summer, the sun ceased to shine on it for only a few hours; and for the whole land the last night before nationhood was brief indeed. It was still bright daylight in the Rocky Mountains and on the Pacific Coast when dusk began to settle down over Nova Scotia and New Brunswick. And it would still be deep night in the far West when the skies began paling over Eastern Canada.

They were paling now; and from Halifax to Sarnia, the Canadians were beginning to bestir themselves. The military —British regulars, volunteers, and home guards—were among the first to rise, for it was their duty to greet the day with gun salutes. All over the country, by forts, on grand parades, barrack squares, and garrison grounds, the great cannon would, as *Le Journal des Trois Rivières* put it, announce to the world 'que nous pouvions maintenant prendre place parmi les nations de la terre'. The volunteers were putting the last touches to their dress uniforms. 'Nos volontaires sont sortis en grande tenue,' the St. Hyacinthe journalist declared proudly. The streets were still nearly deserted in some places as the soldiers moved quickly towards the rendezvous; but in other towns the citizens had risen early to greet the day and watch the guns go off. At Saint John, New Brunswick, the streets were crowded with people before dawn. The shops and houses were ablaze with flags; and great transparencies promised 'success to the Confederacy' and 'Bienvenue à la nouvelle Puissance'.

It was very early yet, the morning was still dull; but though the sky was pale and ashen, it was clear, and there was no doubt that the day would be warm and brilliant. Now the soldiers were all at their posts, beside the guns, waiting for the moment; and from a score of different stations scattered across Canada they looked out over the varying landscapes of their country—past rocky headlands towards the sea, down the St. Lawrence, the River of Canada, over the Great Lakes, or into the green abundance of orchards and farmlands. The sun had risen now; daybreak was on their faces; and the great guns roared their salute into the pale blue sky of morning.

The Road to Confederation, Toronto, 1964

FRANK H. UNDERHILL

The essential work of the Fathers of Confederation was to weld the scattered British possessions in North America into a unity within which Canadian capitalism could expand and consolidate its power, to provide for the capitalist *entrepreneurs* of Montreal and Toronto a half-continent in which they could realize their dreams and ambitions. The dynamic drive which brought Confederation about had its centre in Montreal among the railway and banking magnates who were dreaming of new fields to conquer. It was for this purpose, and not merely to illustrate the abstract beauties of brotherly love, that Macdonald and Cartier built up their Anglo-French *entente*; it was for this purpose that Galt and Head and Monck drafted their paper schemes of British-American union and carried on their obscure negotiations behind the scenes. Federalism was only an accident imposed by the circumstances of the time; union was the essential achievement. In brief, what Macdonald and his associates accomplished in the 1860s in the northern half of this continent was an exact parallel to what Lincoln and Co. were accomplishing at the same time in the southern half. The two sets of statesmen worked with materials which were superficially very different; the incidentals of their statesmanship seem to have nothing in common; but the fundamental objectives were the same. It was Lincoln's function to eliminate the southern planter aristocracy, the only effective rival to northern industrial capitalism; to preserve the Union intact as a continental field of operations for the subsequent triumphant advance of American industrialism; in short, to establish the political framework within which the present economic empire of New York could be built up. Macdonald and Co. had not to save a union but to create one. But the ultimate end of their activities, of which they themselves were quite sufficiently conscious, was to capture and pre-empt for Montreal the opportunity of building up another similar economic empire extending across half a continent.

Since the 1860s these two economic empires have gone through a rapid expansion. The frontiers of settlement and exploitation have been steadily pushed back to the ultimate territorial limits of each empire. More important, there has gone on simultaneously a steady process of economic integration, of concentration of control at the centre. And this process of concentration has been accompanied inevitably by a distribution of income in which the increasingly larger share has been apportioned to the small group who sit with their hands upon the levers of power in the great metropolitan centres. This point as to the increasing concentration of economic power which characterizes all modern national capitalist systems does not need to be laboured here. It is the theme of innumerable books and studies in the United States and elsewhere; and the recent investigations of the Price Spreads Commission have thrown considerable light upon some aspects of it in Canada. Moreover—and here again I repeat an accepted commonplace which does not need to be developed or illustrated—this increasing concentration of economic power has been accompanied by a similar concentration of political power. The federal form of our institutions masks this process to some extent; but it is now fairly well recognized by all except a few incurable liberal romantics that political institutions on the whole only operate so as to express the economic balance of power within any given society. The individual citizen and his fellows who are without economic power gradually become the forgotten men of politics. And the more narrowly economic power tends to be monopolized in the hands of a small group, the more widely will the forgotten men of politics be distributed throughout the other classes of the community.

In Search of Canadian Liberalism, Toronto, 1960

GOLDWIN SMITH

Confederation, so far, has done nothing to fuse the races, and very little even to unite the provinces. . . . From the composition of a cabinet to the composition of a rifle team, sectionalism is the rule.

The Political Destiny of Canada, Toronto, 1878

The ultimate Union of this Northern Continent seems to me as certain as the rising of tomorrow's sun. It may be distant; it is not likely to come in my time; but it will come. Nature has made up her mind, and in the end she will have her way.

Goldwin Smith's Correspondence, comprising letters, chiefly to and from his English friends, written between the years 1846 and 1910, Toronto, 1913

S. D. CLARK

The Canadian political community was not the creation of a people seeking a distinctive national identity. It was the creation rather of certain business, political, religious and cultural interests, seeking the establishment of a monopolistic system of control.

Canada and The American Value System, a paper at the Congrès des Affaires Canadiennes, Laval University, November 19, 1964

NICHOLAS FLOOD DAVIN

We are a happy people. We are a contented people. We are a prosperous people. We are a loyal people. If there is anything old-fashioned in being loyal, we are content to be old-fashioned. We have a country whose extent and riches it would not be easy to surpass. . . . We have the best form of government in the world, at once the freest, the most Democratic, and the most Conservative. We have no universal suffrage; we have no aristocracy; we have no agitators because we have no grievances. . . .

"The Future of Canada", *Rose Belfort's Canadian Monthly and National Review* 6 (1891)

ADDISON F. BROWNE

In a few more decades every grant of available land will be taken up, and the streams of immigration now flowing to our shores will be turned in other directions, and then the peoples of different languages and national ancestry must lose all separating characteristics, and, under the modifying influence of climate and situation, so blend together that a new race will finally appear, which should present the very highest type of natural ability. In its veins will flow the life-currents of all the northern European countries, with a slight but sure tincture of Indian blood. Such a people, dwelling amid the sublime natural aspects of this Dominion, and possessing here marvellous resources of soil, mineral, forest, lake and river, are sure to occupy the loftiest planes of human intelligence, and only receive acceptable control in a government created and managed entirely by themselves.

"The Future of Canada", *The Week* (Jan. 14, 1886)

SIR JOHN A. MACDONALD

I have no accord with the desire expressed in some quarters that by any mode whatever there should be an attempt made to oppress the one language or to render it inferior to the other; I believe that would be impossible if it were tried, and it would be foolish and wicked if it were possible.

House of Commons Debates, Feb. 17, 1890

SIR WILFRID LAURIER

Any policy which appeals to a class, to a creed, to a race, or which does not appeal to the better instincts to be found in all classes, in all creeds, and in all races, is stamped with the stamp of inferiority. The French-Canadian who appeals to his fellow-countrymen to stand by themselves, aloof from the rest of the continent; the English-Canadian who appeals to his fellow-countrymen on grounds affecting them alone, may, perhaps, win the applause of those whom they may be addressing, but impartial history will pronounce their work as vicious in conception as it is mischievous and wicked in its tendency.

Patriotic Recitations, 1893

GOLDWIN SMITH

There is no use in attempting manifest impossibilities, and no impossibility apparently can be more manifest than that of fusing or even harmonizing a French and Papal and a British and Protestant community.

The Bystander, December, 1889

French Canada is a relic of the historical past preserved by isolation, as Siberian mammoths are preserved in ice.

Political Destiny of Canada, Toronto, 1878

THE PRELIMINARY REPORT OF THE ROYAL COMMISSION ON BILINGUALISM AND BICULTURALISM, OTTAWA, 1965

Ten Canadians travelled through the country for months, met thousands of their fellow citizens, heard and read what they had to say. The ten do not now claim that they are relying on this as a scientific investigation, nor do they have solutions to propose at this stage. All they say is this: here is what we saw and heard, and here is the preliminary—but unanimous—conclusion we have drawn.

The members of the Commission feel the need to share with their fellow citizens the experience they have been through, and the lessons they have so far taken from it. This experience may be summarized very simply. The Commissioners, like all Canadians who read newspapers, fully expected to find themselves confronted by tensions and conflicts. They knew that there have been strains throughout the history of Confederation; and that difficulties can be expected in a country where cultures exist side by side. What the Commissioners have discovered little by little, however, is very different: they have been driven to the conclusion that Canada, without being fully conscious of the fact, is passing through the greatest crisis in its history.

The source of the crisis lies in the Province of Quebec; that fact could be established without an extensive inquiry. There are other secondary sources in the French-speaking minorities of the other provinces and in the "ethnic minorities"—although this does not mean in any way that to us such problems are in themselves secondary. But, although a provincial crisis at the outset, it has become a Canadian crisis, because of the size and strategic importance of Quebec, and because it has inevitably set off a series of chain reactions elsewhere.

What does the crisis spring from? Our inquiry is not far enough advanced to enable us to establish exactly its underlying causes and its extent. All we can do is describe it as we see it now: *it would appear from what is happening that the state of affairs established in 1867, and never since seriously challenged, is now for the first time being rejected by the French Canadians of Quebec.*

Who is right and who is wrong? We do not even ask ourselves that question; we simply record the existence of a crisis which we believe to be very serious. If it should persist and gather momentum it could destroy Canada. On the other hand, if it is overcome, it will have contributed to the rebirth of a richer and more dynamic Canada. But this will be possible only if we face the reality of the crisis and grapple with it in time.

That is why we believe it necessary to make this statement to Canadians.

We have to communicate an experience through which we have actually lived, and to show that simple realities of everyday life came to reveal the existence, the depth and the sharpness of the crisis.

Moreover, we are going to have to put our country's divisions on display, and we appreciate the dangers of doing so. But the feeling of the Commission is that at this point the danger of a clear and frank statement is less than the danger of silence; this type of disease cannot be cured by keeping it hidden indefinitely from the patient. Above all the Commissioners are convinced that they are demonstrating a supreme confidence in Canada; because to tell a people plainly, even bluntly, what you believe to be the truth is to show your own conviction that it is strong enough to face the truth. It is in fact to say to the country that you have faith in it and in its future.

Preamble to *A Preliminary Report of the Royal Commission on Bilingualism and Biculturalism*, Ottawa, 1965

MAURICE HUTTON

Canada's history is as dull as ditchwater and her politics is full of it.

Quoted, *Canadian Historical Review*, 1935

HAROLD A. INNIS

The political party is apparently no longer able to provide necessary compromise without the sacrifice of principles. The absence of consistency in the attitude of any English-Canadian party or public leader points to the fundamental corruption of Canadian political life.

Political Economy in the Modern State, Toronto, 1946

W. L. MORTON

To compromise, no doubt, is to corrupt—to corrupt the simplicity of principle, the clarity of policy—but if so, then all politics corrupt and federal politics, the politics of the vast sectional and communal aggregations, especially so. To this conclusion all purists, all doctrinaires, and all Progressives, must ultimately come or abstain from power.

The Progressive Party, Toronto, 1950

FRANK H. UNDERHILL

At this point [1900] we reach the golden age in the evolution of the Canadian two-party system. Both parties were now completely national in the North American sense; that is, both appealed for support to all sections and classes of the nation and both preached the same policy—the continuous fostering of material prosperity through the incitement and patronage of government. The class differences which had been discernible between the original Liberal-Conservatives and the original Reformers in the 1850s had disappeared; class conflicts and sectional conflicts were now reconciled and settled within each party rather than as between the two parties. All that remained to distinguish the parties were the two old English names. Not even in the United States had the functioning of the North American two-party system achieved a greater degree of perfection than this.

In Search of Canadian Liberalism, Toronto, 1960

DONALD CREIGHTON

Although, on occasion, he could quote authorities and appeal to abstract ideas, these references back to a fundamental political and social philosophy were usually implied rather than explicit. Unlike the formidable Brown, who appeared in parliament for the first time in the session of 1852-53, he was not a crusader with a mission. Equally he was not a rationalist who believed that government was a series of general objectives which could be attained by the application of timeless and universal rules. He thumped no tubs and banged no pulpits. He was far too concerned with the intricate details of concrete problems, far too interested in the curious and manifold complexities of human situations, to follow an ideal faithfully or to settle everything by scrupulous reference to a given set of rules. For him government was neither a quest for political justice nor an exercise in political arithmetic. Government was a craft, which one learnt chiefly by doing and by watching others do—a craft which consisted essentially in managing a small group of men which a far larger group of men had selected to govern them. There were no textbooks and no divine revelations. The craft had its traditions, its conventions, its techniques, its stock of forms and variations—all of which were historical products. It found its raw material in the problems of a particular landscape and a particular people. It was the task of a politician to work within the tradition, and to respect the limitations and exploit the possibilities of the medium. He might remain a competent craftsman; he might become a great, creative artist. But he should never aspire to the alien roles of prophet, philosopher, or engineer.

John A. Macdonald: The Young Politician, Toronto, 1952

FRANK H. UNDERHILL

His statesmanship has been a more subtly accurate, a more flexibly adjustable Gallup poll of Canadian public opinion than statisticians will ever be able to devise. He has been the representative Canadian, the typical Canadian, the essential Canadian, the ideal Canadian, the Canadian as he exists in the mind of God.

Two specific achievements will always be associated with Mr. King's name. He brought us out of Dominion Status, the halfway house in which Laurier and Borden had left us; and we face the 1950s as an independent nation, making our own policy, prepared to undertake the responsibilities of an adult people in world politics. He carried us through the strain of a second world war without precipitating an irreconcilable split between French and English Canadians; he avoided the kind of mistakes which, repeated in the 1940s,

Mackenzie King by John Collins
The Gazette, *Montreal, 1960*

would have had more fatal consequences than they had in 1917.

Laurier defeated the earlier efforts of British imperialists to construct a British Empire holding-company with a single foreign policy directed from London. Mr. King's long period of office has given him the opportunity of leading us to the goal towards which Laurier's policy pointed, of an independent Canada within a British Commonwealth which is no longer an exclusive association, which has no central organs for making military or economic policy, and which tends more and more to merge itself into the larger more comprehensive Atlantic Community that is developing under our eyes. Mr. King has always been aware that no form of international organization could meet Canada's needs in which the United States is not a full partner. In peace and in war he has remained firm in this understanding of the realities of our situation. And now today this Atlantic Community under American leadership provides the solution for the difficulties of both the older British Commonwealth and the newer West European Union.

Canada has been able to play a significant part in these recent developments because during the King era we have been gradually equipped with a well-staffed Department of External Affairs. We can now participate in the hard day-to-day practice of international diplomacy. Before we had a diplomatic service of our own, most of the talk of the Laurier and Borden days about our equality of status with Britain was largely in the nature of rhetorical flourish. We have not solved all our practical problems by any means. Evidently there are elements in the British Foreign Office who still labour under the delusion that it is the function of Downing Street to provide the policy and the function of Canada to provide the transport planes; and there are still a few colonial Canadians who agree with them. But these are mere vestigial survivals.

Also it should be remarked that the usefulness of Mr. King's clear-cut conception of the nature of the British Commonwealth has been weakened in recent years by his going soft over the Monarchy, at the very time when the Commonwealth is expanding to include members such as India and Pakistan for whom the Monarchy will never mean what it means to us sentimental Canadians.

However, his essential achievement remains. He has led us irrevocably past the stage at which it was possible to

think of Canada as a junior partner in some Britannic firm. And he has assisted us to some of his own understanding that neither Canada nor Britain can get along in the twentieth-century world except in close co-operation with the United States. His successors will still have plenty to do in emancipating us from our inherited anti-American phobias. One of Mr. King's incidental successes is that he has brought us through a couple of decades without an outbreak of the fever of 1891 and 1911. If we can get through another twenty or thirty years without some impassioned patriots winning a general election by saving us from the United States, this will afford the ultimate proof that we have at last grown up.

One of the fashionable criticisms in academic circles of Mr. King's external policy is that it was isolationist in the 1920s and 1930s, and therefore adolescent and irresponsible. This is to miss the essential conditions under which Canadian policy is carried on. In the inter-war decades we were isolationist in the same way that Great Britain and the United States were. We refused commitments in a collective-security system just as they did. At present we have committed ourselves to far-reaching actions in world politics just as the British and American peoples have done. If the world comes to show signs of a little more stability, the Canadian people, like the British and Americans, will become more absorbed in their own local concerns. In whatever direction we move, it will be along lines already being traced out by British and American policy.

To keep French and English in Canada working together has been the basis of Mr. King's policy, both in external and in domestic affairs, as it must be the basis of the policy of every responsible-minded statesman. The division between these two communities is the deepest division in our national life.

Now, the classical institutional procedure by which French-English co-operation has been achieved in Canadian history has been that of a national political party. For the decade before Confederation and for two decades after Confederation Macdonald worked through the Liberal-Conservative party. Laurier succeeded him, after a transitional period of bitterness and confusion, with the Liberal party till 1911. The ten years from 1911 to 1921 form a unique period in our history when an attempt was made to govern Canada without the effective co-operation of Quebec. Mr.

King's life has been devoted to the restoration of a working national harmony of the two racial communities through a revived Liberal party.

In Search of Canadian Liberalism, Toronto, 1960

H. BLAIR NEATBY

The Prime Minister, for all his difficulties at the time, could still be whimsical when he felt so inclined. The sober intensity of the dedicated public servant was occasionally belied by a lighter touch in his private correspondence. While the Petersen contract was still being debated in the House, King received an awkwardly printed letter addressed to "Dear Government" from a little girl in South Africa who was worried about the redskins being locked up on reserves and not being allowed to shoot "Grizzily Bears." King's reply was worthy of A. A. Milne:

Ottawa, March 28th, 1925.
Dear Elizabeth:

I cannot begin to tell you how very pleased the members of the Government of Canada were when they received your letter.

Some of the letters they receive are so very hard to read—not beautifully written as yours was—and sometimes people ask for the most extraordinary things! You would hardly believe me, I am sure, were I to tell you all the things the people in Canada ask for!

The only difficulty about your letter was that each Minister thought *he* should answer it. However, I was very firm and told them I was the one to do it.

I then spoke, at once, to the Minister of the Interior, who looks after Indians, and he tells me, Elizabeth, that there is nothing you need worry about. It's like this. Supposing the Indians had all gone a-hunting, someone might come and settle on their lands or steal their tents—all kinds of dreadful things—while they were away. So the Government just puts up big signs "This land is reserved for our Indians"—and no one dares to touch anything. But the Indians are never shut up, Elizabeth, and if any Grizzly Bears come, they can always shoot them if they feel like doing so. You say you are coming to Canada when you are fifteen. That is splendid. The Minister of the Interior says that if he is still Minister of the Interior (you never can be *quite* sure), he will see that we have a good supply of Indians on hand.

The Minister of Defence says that if *he* is still Minister of Defence, he will give them plenty of ammunition with which to shoot the bears. And I feel sure that someone else—probably the Minister of Agriculture—will arrange for the Grizzly Bears—so that's all right, Elizabeth.

But there is something I want you to tell me—about South Africa. This Government has never been there but perhaps some day they might feel like going. Now is it true, Elizabeth, that when you have your tea in the garden, lions sometimes come and sit down beside you?

And when you go for a walk, do you have to be *very* careful, for fear a rhinoceros or a hippopotamus might want to walk with you?

It would be apt to make the Government *very nervous*. There is so much you must tell me when you come. Of course, I know you always ride on elephants.

But I shall have to say good-bye now. It was very nice of you to write (we all thought the letter paper beautiful!)

Will you let me thank you again for the Government and, with all good wishes, say at present Good-bye Elizabeth.

Yours sincerely,
W. L. Mackenzie King.

William Lyon Mackenzie King, II, Toronto

JOHN W. DAFOE

A prime minister under the party system as we have had it in Canada is of necessity an egotist and autocrat. If he comes to office without these characteristics his environment equips him with them as surely as a diet of royal jelly transforms a worker into a queen bee.

Laurier, Toronto, 1922

Sir Wilfrid Laurier by Spy, 1897

STEPHEN LEACOCK

The old-time Canadian parties, gentlemen, have had their day. What we need is new life, new energy and, above all, if I may say so, a new Working of the Spirit." —From any soapbox, Halifax to Vancouver.

It is a great pleasure—indeed it gives me a thrill—to be able to announce to the public through the kindly medium of this journal that at last the New Party has come! The hope, the promise, contained in such words as those above is fulfilled. The thing is here. I saw its inception. I was present at it myself no later than last night. All that is now needed is to keep it incepted . . .

Now please, don't ask me for details, for names and places and all that; everything will appear in the full publicity of the newspapers.

It came about this way. I'm not in politics but I have many friends who are—some on one side, some on the other, some on both . . . naturally I hear of the new movements. So when Hoggitt called on the phone to me to come down and join him at the Piccadilly I knew that the big stuff was on.

I found him there at a table and he began to talk, right away and with the greatest enthusiasm, about the new Party. You know Hoggitt. He's all right. He's got a sort of fierce way of talking, but he's all right. He's a big dark fellow and he always seems to be threatening but he isn't—that is he is in a way, but he's all right. Anyway I'd no sooner sat down than he was talking full speed of the Party—with a sort of inspiration.

"It's the real thing," he said, "it's based on human sympathy and equality—where's that damn waiter?—We're aiming at what the old parties never had—social cohesion—I'd like to fire that fellow—and the right of every man to a voice . . . Gimme that check and don't talk back to me . . ."

He was still muttering at the waiter when we left . . .

So we walked. In any case it was only four blocks and I was glad because it gave Hoggitt a chance to explain to me all about the new party. I must say it sounded fine—no more of that miserable intrigue and crookedness of the old parties . . . things done in the dark . . . no more leaning on the "interest" for money; just straight honesty. Hoggitt said that when we got to the hall, he'd introduce me to the chairman, but not to pay too much attention to him as they were going to ease him out. Of course he doesn't know it. They'll keep him while they still need him. Hoggitt said he's not sufficiently genial—that was it, or, no, I've got it wrong—too genial.

The meeting was in a pretty big hall. There must have been well over a hundred, most of them smoking and standing round. They looked all right, too. I've been to a good many political meetings but I couldn't see anything wrong with them. Some of them looked mighty decent fellers, you know—educated, not like what you'd imagine at all. It seemed a kind of free and easy crowd. The chairman was just going to the platform so I only had time to shake hands with him, a middle-aged-looking man, quite well dressed—in fact I couldn't see a thing wrong with him.

Anyway he got up to talk, but they didn't listen much; they went on talking in groups round the room. Hoggitt said that's the way they do; they find they can get through more business if they don't listen. Hoggitt says that's the curse of Ottawa—one of them; he named quite a few.

The chairman was talking about the name of the party. He said, "Gentlemen, you'll be glad to know we've succeeded in getting a name for our party. You remember last week our difficulty over the proposal to christen the party the Forward Party . . ."

There was noise and applause which Hoggitt explained to me was because some of the members—people of fine old U.E. Loyalist families who'd never moved since they came—

thought that the Backward Party would be better, a finer ideal.

"We tried," the chairman went on, "both the name Forward Party and the name Backward Party, and, as you recall, the name Backwards-and-Forwards Party. We wanted something that would mean progressive and yet mean conservative . . . but we couldn't get it . . . We left, as you will remember, a committee sitting on it and they sat, at the Piccadilly, all that night but failed to find it. I'm glad to say that there has since come in the brilliant suggestion of a member—I won't name him but you all know him—who gives us the title the Non-Party Party . . ."

Great applause . . . and cries . . . "Carried! Carried!"

Hoggitt explained to me on the side that the name came from Professor Woodstick, professor of Greek, who's in the party. In fact some of them call him the "brains of the party." Hoggitt thinks they'll probably have to drop him. People don't like the idea of brains running a party. Look at Ottawa—at the successful parties . . . Still I'll say in favour of Professor Woodstick, he doesn't look educated . . .

The chairman came and sat with us, while a man—I didn't catch his name—was talking on what shall we do to get the farmer's vote. It seems he's a member of the platform committee (subsection farming), but Mr. Mills the chairman says they'll probably have to shift him off. He looks too countrified. Anyway nobody listened much.

There was a lot of unanimity and good feeling over that but on the other hand a lot of difficulty over the question of labour. The man who got up to talk (I didn't catch his name, something like Fitkin, or Delbosse—a name like that)—anyway, he said he was a lawyer and couldn't pretend to speak of labour but he said he had the deepest sympathy for labour but all the same it was hard even for a lawyer to get a formula to satisfy labour. A lot of the labour men now, he explained, are mighty well educated and it's hard to put anything past them; difficult to find words for a platform that they wouldn't see through. He'd made, he said, a conscientious attempt at some honest direct statement but everything seemed to have the same fault of giving away its meaning. He had had with him on the committee, he said, the Reverend Canon Sip . . .

There was applause at that, because everybody knows the Canon and he was sitting right there anyway. Hoggitt explained that they had tried to keep him away. Hoggitt says it's all right to talk of popularity but the Canon makes a bad impression—too damn simple and friendly, Hoggitt said. "It won't go over with the plain people . . ."

Well he'd had with him, the lawyer said, Canon Sip and their friend Mr. Vault, who as they all knew was a bank manager, or rather an ex-bank manager, whom we were all glad to see back again with us, but with all that the three of them could do, it was hard to find any adequate words that wouldn't right away show what was meant. It was no use, he said, to advocate a "just reward" for labour. That might be all right for farmers, probably too much, but labour would see through it right away. But he was glad to say that Canon Sip had suggested a labour platform that he believed would carry the country. "We propose to give to labour everywhere an entire freedom from work."

There was a lot of applause, and I must say I realized the party had hit it this time—here you had all the old slogans, "freedom to work" and "freedom from work" subsumed—that was the word the speaker used—into one lucid thought.

It was a great hit for the Canon—no wonder he's popular.

You see he's not a bit like what you'd expect from a religious man—he's always cheerful, takes a drink any time, in fact he was quite tight at Peggy Sherar's wedding the other day, smokes a cigar, indeed as someone said at the meeting, he just seems the ideal of an early Christian, you know, the kind they used to burn at Rome. All the same, some of them are a little afraid of it. They say if people get the idea that a party stands for religion, it's all over with it. So Mills and Hoggitt both talk of easing Canon Sip out of the party. They would, except that having him may help to bring in the liquor interest. It seems you can't possibly hope to get anything out of the liquor interest unless you have with you some sort of showing of clergymen and professors. Lawyers don't help much for that.

Mentioning that reminds me of the main thing of the evening, the really crucial stuff, when they all sat and listened—the discussion of ways and means, how to get the money to carry on.

The chairman of the interim finance committee read a report.

They had done their best in the direction of both the liquor interests and the churches. But as members present would realize, it is very hard to attract the interest of these unless you get them together. They go, as we all know, hand in hand. Any large, really large contribution from a liquor source will bring the clergy round us at once.

I was driven home after the meeting by one of the younger members who had a car—a college boy, keen as anything on politics, enthusiastic and, I could see by his talk, straight as a string. He said he thought there were too many older men in the thing; he was trying to engineer an inside troupe of young men to get them out. That was queer, wasn't it. Because Hoggitt had told me they'd have to get rid of a lot of the younger men. . . .

Anyway, there's no doubt what the party means.

Saturday Night, March 20, 1943

BRUCE HUTCHISON

I have prepared the following address to the electors of Saanich, where I hope some day to be elected to some high public office like the School Board:

"Ladies and gentlemen: In these grave times it is necessary for a public man to speak out frankly the faith that is in him and declare the policies by which he stands. I must tell you, therefore, that I stand unequivocally for general prosperity and a higher standard of living for everyone. For this reason I shall oppose depressions. I am a disbeliever in hard times.

"I stand for the right of every man to have a job, a wife, two children, a home, a car and vigorous health. I stand for the right of every man to be insured against all the hazards of life, but I object to any deductions from his pay for these purposes. Nor should insurance be a charge on industry. To be fair, it must be financed without expense to anyone.

"I stand for the right of every man to high wages. At the same time, I insist on low prices. As for inflation, I shall be frank. I am against it.

"I believe in the right of capital to earn a fair income on its investment provided, of course, that the public does not have to pay it.

"I favour private initiative. But on the other hand, I have an abiding faith in socialism, applied with discretion. Private initiative must be given every opportunity to expand, unmolested by the state. But the state must certainly remove the last vestige of the profit motive.

"I may be called a Liberal. Or if you prefer, call me a Conservative. I am also a member of the CCF in good standing, with strong leanings towards Social Credit, technocracy, communism, British Israelism and somnambulism. Also I am an Elk and an ARP warden.

"As to Canada at large, I take the view that it is a great country of abundant resources, a variable climate, a substantial area and covers a good deal of geography. If these facts are courageously faced at the start, they will be understood. But if we refuse to face them, we cannot expect to see them.

"In international affairs it is my opinion we should have world peace, after this war. Speaking bluntly, I think we should seek to avoid world wars. I also deprecate famine and pestilence. I stand for collective security. But I am opposed to any reduction of Canada's sovereignty. I want a strong League of Nations but I certainly would refuse to give it any power.

"Provided our own industries can be protected from the competition of cheap foreign goods, I strongly advocate a reduction in tariffs. World trade must be restored but not, of course, at the risk of importing foreign commodities.

"Concerning the future relationship between the Dominion and the Provinces, as discussed in the Rowell-Sirois Report, I take the view that this is a very serious question indeed and will require most earnest consideration.

"In provincial affairs, I favour a coalition government composed of Liberals, Conservatives, members of the CCF and anyone else who cares to join it, so long as I am in it.

"While I am a Prohibitionist, I am not a fussy one and favour more beer for the public, at less cost.

"All provincial health, education and other services should be expanded. More roads should be built. Taxes should be reduced as part of the same programme and the budget balanced. The government should take over the B.C. Electric Company, provided the management remains in private hands and is kept out of politics.

"As a farmer I insist on higher prices for all farm products. But, of course, the consumer must not pay more for his food.

"In all such problems I believe in long-range national planning, a programme which will cover every part of the whole country. But I shall oppose to the last the centralization of authority in the government of Ottawa. What we need is control of and regulation of our whole economic system, without bureaucracy.

"Summing up my views as to the future, I should say that the future undoubtedly lies before us. Let us face that fact boldly.

"These are my considered opinions and lifelong principles. If they are not acceptable to the electors of Saanich they can, of course, be altered to suit. That is the democratic way. If I am elected, I shall do whatever seems like a good idea at the time. It will be too late then for you to do anything about it. If you elect me to the School Board, you will show yourselves just as intelligent as I believe you to be. I thank you."

Winnipeg Free Press, June 5, 1943

PETER McARTHUR

Since moving to the country I have been greatly impressed by the spread of education. Those who are set in authority over us seem to think that education is a remedy for everything. If the farmers are not prospering the cry goes forth, "Educate them." When the high cost of living begins to pinch in the cities they trace the whole trouble to the farmer, and then someone yells, "Educate him!" If the farmer complains about the exactions of the middlemen, the answer invariably is "Educate him." No matter what goes wrong, the only solution that occurs to anyone is to "educate the farmer."

Once in a while a reporter representing the press, our modern palladium of freedom, calls on a canning magnate and tells him in a deferential tone that the farmers are complaining because he is not paying enough for tomatoes on the hoof and is charging altogether too much for catsup. The great man looks at the paragraphical serf with a baleful eye, scatters some benzoate of soda on a pile of bills, puts them into his vault and snarls: "The farmer is grumbling, is he? Then ejjercate him."

Another trembling representative of the above-mentioned palladium calls on a high financier and tells him that the farmers are complaining because the last issue of watered stock he unloaded on them had typhoid germs in it.

"Oh, they are, are they?" sneers the plutocrat as he packs a tainted million in a deposit vault and wipes his hands on his overalls. "Then why don't you educate them?"

Up to a certain point this attitude is a good thing for the farmer. In the past he has been woefully lacking in education. But now he is being educated so thoroughly that almost any farmer I meet is ready to sit down and have a breezy chat about the way the soil particles are held together by the water menisci or to discuss intelligently the value of $PbHAsO_4$ in destroying codling moths. The farmer is getting his education all right, and it is a good thing, even though it might be better adapted to his needs than it is. Moreover, if you would only increase his opportunities a little he would clamour for more education. But that is not what is bothering me.

While I sat on a corner of the voluminous report of the Department of Education meditating on these deep matters in a playful spirit I began to wonder what would happen if the farmers got to thinking, like everyone else, that education is a national cure-all. If they once get this into their heads they will want to educate a few other people who are standing in the way of progress. They will want to start night schools in Toronto and Montreal to educate a few plutocrats into right ways of thinking. Does not your imagination kindle at the prospect? The classroom would be the smoking-room of the Millionaires' Club, and the little scholars would be sitting around in large, kind-looking armchairs, smoking expensive cigars, toying with slim-necked glasses, and letting their second chins rest comfortably on the bosoms of their dress shirts. Unobtrusive imported waiters would be flitting about noiselessly, taking orders and promoting good cheer. Enter Bill Simmons, instructor in true economic doctrines. Bill's necktie is climbing over his collar, but no one dares to smile, for he is carrying a well-oiled harness tug in his brawny right hand. Hanging the tug suggestively over the corner of the mahogany desk, he takes his place on the costly Ispahan rug, thrusts out his chin truculently, and opens the proceedings with a few well-chosen words. Thus Simmons:

"The House Committee informs me that after last night's session some of the hollow-stemmed glasses were full of cigarette ashes, and that there were cigar stubs in the silver-plated champagne-coolers. Now, I want it distinctly understood that if I catch any dollar-besotted financial degenerate up to tricks like that I shall dust his swallow-tails so that he will eat his meals off the onyx mantelpiece for the next week and then I shall kick him several parasangs down the street. Do you get me?" (Oh, yes, he would talk like that. You have been educating him, you know.) "The class in elementary economics will now step forward."

Prompt at the word Sir Philabeg McSporran, Senator Redneck, Mr. Gosh Whatawad, and a few others step to the edge of the rug, where they stand with thumbs at the seams of their trousers legs, heels together, and their toes well apart.

"Now, my pretty ones," says Bill, "if a railroad is built under a government charter, with the assistance of the public treasury, and is then presented to the company that built it, to whom should that railroad finally belong?"

"To me," pipes Sir Philabeg, who is a High Financier and understands how to manipulate the market.

"Wrong," says our bold bucko from lot 17, seventh concession of Alfalfa township. "It will belong to the peepul—at least sufficiently so to justify them in regulating its operations so that it will serve the best interests of the community. You may go to your seat, Sir Philabeg, and figure it out, and I will come around with the tug in a few minutes and see that you have it right."

Then the grim instructor goes on:

"What is a Big Interest?"

"A corporation that contributes liberally to our campaign fund," says Senator Redneck, with a knowing smile.

"Wrong!" booms Simmons. "The Biggest Interest in this country is farming and after that comes labour—both engaged in producing the real wealth of the country. If anyone is to get special privileges the farmers are the ones that should get them. You may go to your seat and figure that out, and I will see you when I get through with Sir Philabeg."

Again Simmons:

"If a farmer builds a new bank barn and silo, how much should he be fined in the shape of taxes for showing so much enterprise?"

And so it would go through the whole educative evening.

Of course it is not likely that we shall ever have any educational developments along the lines suggested, but why not? If education will cure all the troubles of the farmers, why shouldn't it be tried on a few other problems? When the promoters of mergers and combines begin to do things that are against the best interests of the country, why shouldn't the farmers all yell: "Educate them!" When politicians become subservient to the powers that prey on the resources of the country, why shouldn't we all start to "educate them"? It wouldn't be so very hard. A few well-placed votes at the right time would do wonders in the way of giving light and leading to those who are making trouble for us. Let the work of educating the farmers go right on, but I hope the farmers will soon feel that they have enough and to spare, and that they can devote a few hours to educating their leaders. "Educate him" is a beautiful cry for a campaign of education of the right kind, and as there are a lot of people besides the farmers who need education, I hope that it will soon swell to a fine chorus. Don't get mad at the people who are bamboozling you. Just give them a good dose of the medicine they are so fond of giving you. "Educate them."

In Pastures Green, London, 1915

LOUIS RIEL

Your Honours, gentlemen of the jury: It would be easy for me today to play insanity, because the circumstances are such as to excite any man and under the natural excitement of what is taking place today (I cannot speak English very well, but I am trying to do so, because most of those here speak English). Under the excitement which my trial causes me would justify me not to appear as usual, but with my mind out of its ordinary condition. I hope, with the help of God, I will maintain calmness and decorum as suits the honourable court, this honourable jury. You have seen by the papers in the hands of the Crown that I am naturally inclined to think of God as the beginning of my actions. I wish, if I do it, you won't take it as a mark of insanity, that you won't take it as part of a play of insanity. Oh my God! Help me through Thy grace and the divine influence of Jesus Christ. Oh my God! Bless me, bless this honourable court, bless this honourable jury, bless my good lawyers who have come 700 leagues to try to save my life, bless also the lawyers for the Crown, because they have done, I am sure, what they thought their duty. They have shown me fairness which at first I did not expect from them. Oh my God! Bless all those who are around me through the grace and influence of Jesus Christ Our Saviour, change the curiosity of those who are paying attention to me, change that curiosity into sympathy with me. The day of my birth I was helpless and my mother took care of me although she was not able to do it alone, there was someone to help her to take care of me and I lived. Today, although a man, I am as helpless before this court, in the Dominion of Canada and in this world as I was helpless on the knees of my mother the day of my birth. The North-West is also my mother, it is my mother country, and although my mother country is sick and confined in a certain way, there are some from Lower Canada who came to help her to take care of me during her sickness, and I am sure that my mother country will not kill me more than my mother did forty years ago, when I came into the world, because a mother is always a mother, and even if I have my faults, if she can see I am true, she will be full of love for me. When I came into the North-West in July, the first of July 1884, I found the Indians suffering, I found the halfbreeds eating the rotten pork of the Hudson's Bay Company, and getting sick and weak every day. Although a halfbreed and having no pretension to help the whites, I also paid attention to them, I saw they were deprived of responsible government. I saw that they were deprived of their public liberties, I remembered that halfbreed meant white and Indian and while I paid attention to the suffering Indians and the half-breeds, I remembered that the greatest part of my heart and blood was white, and I have directed my attention to help the Indians, to help the half-breeds and to help the whites to the best of my ability. We have made petitions, I have made petitions with others to the Canadian Government, asking to

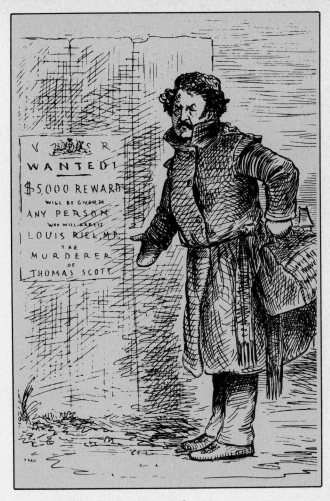

Louis Riel by J. W. Bengough
A Caricature History of Canadian Politics, *Vol. I, Toronto, 1886*

relieve the condition of this country. We have taken time, we have tried to unite all classes even, if I may so speak, all parties. Those who have been in close communication with me know I have suffered, that I have waited months to bring some of the people of the Saskatchewan to an understanding of certain important points in our petitions to the Canadian Government and I have done my duty. It has been said in this box that I had been egotistic. Perhaps I am egotistic. A man cannot be an individualty without paying attention to himself, he cannot generalize himself though he may be general. I have done all I could to make good petitions with others and we have sent them to the Canadian Government, and when the Canadian Government did answer through the undersecretary of state to the secretary of the joint committee of the Saskatchewan, then I began to speak of myself, not before. So my particular interest passed after the public interest.

For fifteen years I have been neglecting myself; even one of the most hard witnesses on me said that with all my vanity I never was particular as to my clothing; yes, because I never had much to buy any clothing. The Reverend Father André has often had the kindness to feed my family with a sack of flour and Father Fourmond; my wife and children are without means, while I am working more than any representative in the North-West although I am simply a guest of this country, a guest of the halfbreeds of the Saskatchewan. Although as a simple guest I work to better the condition of the people of the Saskatchewan, at the risk of my life, to better condition of the people of the North-West, I have never had any pay. It has always been my hope to have a fair living one day. It will be for you to pronounce. If you say I was right, you can conscientiously acquit me, as I hope through the help of God you will. You will console those who have been fifteen years around me, only partaking in my sufferings; what you will do in justice to me, in justice to my family, in justice to my friends, in justice to the North-West, will be rendered a hundred times to you in this world, and to use a sacred expression, life everlasting in the other.

I thank Your Honours for the favour you have granted me in speaking, I thank you for the attention you have given me, gentlemen of the jury, and I thank those who have had the kindness to encourage my imperfect way of speaking the English language by their good attention. I put my speech under the protection of my God, my Saviour, He is the only one who can make it effective; it is possible it should become effective as it is proposed to good men, to good people, and to good ladies also.

Report of The Trial of Louis Riel, Ottawa, 1886

ARTHUR MEIGHEN

If the government of Sir Robert Borden, after manfully making its own decision and acting on that decision, had gone to the people of Canada in 1914 and had said, as it would have said – "We believe this war to be a righteous and a necessary war; we believe the very destiny of Canada is in the balance; we believe the life of the Empire is at stake; we have committed this country to the conflict and we come to you and we ask you to ratify our course; we ask you to proclaim to the world that Canada will do her duty; we ask you to add to the strength of our arms the sanction of the Canadian nation"–if the government of Sir Robert Borden had done that, who is there who would have said: "It is not British"; who is there who would have dared to say: "It is an invitation to separation"? (Applause) But that is the very language that has been applied to me for saying that we would be better to do it in the years to come. In the long journey through the vicissitudes of that war there were hundreds, if not thousands, of Conservatives who said to me that it would have been better for the whole of this country if that step had been taken and the mandate of the people secured in the early days of the war. Recrimination, which afterwards disturbed the unity of our country, would then have been silenced by the most potent voice, the most authoritative voice that a democracy can utter.

Now, it is my province to ask you what is the inference which arises from those accepted truths? I have not asked you to accept any argument up to now, only facts. Would that I could stand before any of you and ask you to deny a single one. Suffice to say that, in my own mind, they are established by experience and are incontestable. Now then,

what is the object to be served? What is there worth while? Surely, it is worth while in any British country to have the people understand, once and for all, that their control of the great policies of that country is real, and not merely a sham. There may be countries where an autocracy is possible, but not in any British country. I know nobody is talking autocracy in Canada, but what I do say is that it is tremendously important that the people do not harbour the idea that their control is merely nominal and farcical, or applies only to matters of minor concern. There is nothing that breeds discontent faster than the feeling down in the heart of a people that they are not being trusted in matters of great policy of state; that they are the victims of a pretence; that democratic control is not permitted by those in the party and that, while they may be consulted in matters of trivial consequence, they are not consulted – and not even warned in advance that they would not be consulted – in matters of great and momentous import. It is feelings of that kind which have been the prolific mother of discontent and suspicion in all democratic countries, often the prolific mother of disturbance itself. So, I say, it is surely worth while that there should go forth the assurance that where the people can be consulted on a matter of transcendent consequence, without delay, without impairment of effort and without danger to the state, there is no justification for not consulting them on the part of any government, and especially, here in Canada with our varied racial position and the presence of propaganda long carried on – designed to establish in the hearts of a great section of our people distrust in the Conservative majority on this very issue. Surely, it is doubly important that the word shall go forth that the people – the whole people – are in real control, and where there is danger involved in great as well as in small things, they will be allowed to decide. It goes, I think, without interpolation, that if a Parliament is elected on issues where the question of war is involved, then that Parliament won't need to be dissolved and another Parliament be elected, but, where a Parliament is elected on issues wholly remote from the question of any participation, then when that mandate of the people can be secured without peril to the state or weakening of the arm of our country, there is no justification for refusing the people the right to speak and to do it will contribute to the unity, the harmony, and the goodwill of this Dominion. You can only justify refusal in the case of a matter so transcendently important – only justify refusal by showing that it can be exercised only with danger to the state, and the experience of that war proves that you cannot show anything to the contrary: it cannot be shown because it is not true. This is the object to be served.

Now I proceed, and with this I close, in an endeavour to answer some of the objections which have been raised – many of them in good faith – against the proposal which I make. In the first place, let me say that almost all – not all, but almost all – the objections advanced have been based upon a wholly inadequate and wrongful impression of what I said. The impression was sounded forth – throughout the country given to our people – that I had said something of a general nature antagonistic to participation in any future war, that I had given expression to a sort of frigid and disdainful indifference to Empire responsibility, that the corner-stone of Conservative faith had been shattered and the very flag hauled down. The impression was given out, as well, that what I had proposed was something in the nature of a plebiscite with a Conservative government looking quietly and indifferently on, not caring what the result! Suffer me, if I read the utterance once more, but only a sentence: here is what I said in this very respect:

I believe it would be best not only that Parliament should be called but that the decision of the government – which, of course, would have to be given promptly – should be submitted to the choice of the people at a general election before troops should leave our shores. This would contribute to the unity of our country in the months to come and would enable us best to do our duty. It would not mean delay – under the stress of war, delay would be fatal. The government would have to decide, and decide quickly, what is best in the interests of Canada; the government would have to act on its judgment, but, before there was anything in the way of participation involving the dispatch of troops, the will of the people should first be obtained. I have, myself, not the slightest fear but that if danger threatened the Empire and therefore Canada again, this country would respond as it responded in 1914.

Now, I ask you first to note that in so far as those words touch the question of Empire responsibility, I took precisely the same stand that the Conservative government has always taken and that the Conservative party has always taken, that, in so far as they affect the question of what Canada ought to do while declaring that the control was in Canada of Canada's conduct – as surely everybody admits and some proclaim – that while declaring that, it was also declared that Canada would never shirk her responsibility. Though there was not one article of our tenets shattered; our flag had not one shred of it been furled; and, so far from advocating a plebiscite, what I stated was that a Conservative government, after taking the full responsibility, would undertake to get the approval of the country for its course and would make that undertaking at the peril of its governmental life.

Then what are the objections? The first advanced, and persisted in, is this: that what was advocated at Hamilton was in reality an invitation to separate from the motherland, or that it would give the opportunity to sever. My first comment is this: I could not give Canada that opportunity. The tie that binds us to the motherland has depended upon the goodwill of this country for over a quarter of a century. It has depended on nothing else. Canada has always, at least for that time and more, had that opportunity, and, because the bond is founded on goodwill, the link that ties us to the motherland is today as strong as it was in the days of Macdonald. It would not likely be a matter of such pride to us – our Imperial position – if the bond depended on anything but goodwill. No, the opportunity could not be given. But was it an invitation to sever? What was said at Hamilton was not that Canada in the event of a struggle involving the motherland would be invited to separate: what was said at Hamilton was this: that in the event of a Conservative government determining that it was the duty of Canada to participate, the people of Canada would not be invited to separate but would be invited to seal the bond again with blood for the security of this country and the security of the Empire. What was said at Hamilton was that if in that event the forces of separation were to succeed they would have to defeat the mass strength of the Conservative party and the last ounce of its forces. What was said at Hamilton was that if the forces of separation were to succeed, they would have to succeed over the prostrate body of the Conservative party: and this is the declaration for which I have been arraigned by ribald newspapers as guilty of disloyalty and treason. This is the declaration on account of which I have had to listen to the gibes of a Lapointe and the silly clackery of a Motherwell. If what I had stated had been that, in this event, a Conservative government would go to a plebiscite and sit by quietly and indifferently to the results, then that would have been repugnant to the Conservative faith and I would justly have been condemned. What I said was, that a Conservative government would take its life in its hands and get the mandate of the people to pay for it.

Now the next objection urged is this: that the very thought of submitting such a question to the electorate contemplates the idea, the possibility, that the electorate might decide adversely and then the consequences would be terrible. Frankly, let me say, it is true. You may measure the possibility in any terms you like: you cannot deny that it is there; but, let me inquire, is there anybody in this Dominion who in this day and generation would suggest that the government of a country could commit this country to war in any part of the world without going to Parliament and getting the mandate of Parliament? I don't hear any. Does not that involve and contemplate the idea that Parliament might reverse the government? Then I want to ask, if it is all right to contemplate a reversal at the hands of a Parliament – if that is righteous and constitutional – then how is it going to end the British Empire to contemplate reversal at the hands of the people? You can trust the people in these matters as in everything else if you give the people the truth, if you bring down on them the direct and immediate responsibility of ratifying the government or not; bring that right down into the hearts of the people and the people of this country you can trust. I would not like to think that, in the confession of faith of the Conservative party, to trust the people was an act of heresy!

But let us inquire further. Some will say, "Well, you may trust them but suppose the result that comes is not enough – it means separation." It might. That far I will go. "And," you say, "it might?" It might, yes. "Well then," you say, "why incur it?" My answer is this: that if under the leadership, the inspiration, the impetus of a great party the people cannot be brought to see the need of war, then you cannot bludgeon them into it – and I tremble for the government that would try. As a matter of fact, if you look back over the history of Britain for fifty years or a century, you will never find a single war launched by the government where the overwhelming mass of the people was not in favour at the commencement of the war at least. And in Canada you certainly would never find a case where the government would take that awful responsibility unless certain, not only that the majority but that the overwhelming mass of the people were behind the state. Unless it is the fact – unless it is the fact, then the share of this country in the conflict could never be made a success.

Now I come to another objection. There are those who say: "We are quite ready to agree" – I have many letters to that effect – "that you must obtain a mandate to send any except volunteers, but we would agree to the necessity of a mandate to send non-volunteers." That is something worth examining. Analyse it carefully. Doesn't it mean this: that there is no objection to Parliament and the government taking the responsibility of launching into war providing only that military service is governed by caprice and chance? Put it another way: doesn't it mean this: that there is no objection to launching on war without a mandate of the nation providing it is a limited liability war, that you go so far and no further? Carefully thought out, I don't think anyone will support that proposition. For my part, I do not contemplate any such thing as a "limited-liability" war. If ever we are forced into conflict again, which God forbid, let us go at it man-fashion from the first, and we can do that better if we go to the people. I want this to be pronounced with all the emphasis in my power. When a government takes the responsibility of sending the troops of a country to far-off theatres of war, it also incurs the responsibility of supporting them there with reinforcements, and with everything else. Now, I ask, how is it that a mandate is not necessary to send troops to far-off theatres and compel others to pay, but a mandate is necessary to support them there, and compel others to go? How is it that without a mandate you can incur the responsibility but you have to have a mandate to discharge the responsibility?

Still further: it has been said to me by those whose judgment ordinarily I respect, that, "in the case of these great things involving war, there are facts known to the government that dare not be disclosed to the people and, therefore, the people without those facts might go wrong." I do not believe it. In the last war, it was not true. All that the people needed to know to come to a decision, the people could know. Nobody would deny for a moment that the people came to their decision blindly. I believe the time has gone by when any government can say to the people of a country – "Blindfold your eyes, see only a piece, and put your sons into uniform." It cannot be done.

Now, I have something further to add. This I have been asked to make a statement regarding since coming to Winnipeg. It is said: "Wasn't your speech at Hamilton inconsistent with your utterance in the City of Toronto, when you uttered the famous expression, "Ready, aye, ready"? Well, my task in this is as simple as in all the rest. I have not the text of my speech at Toronto in my possession but my memory is fairly good. I will tell you what was said there, and the text can afterwards be published and check what I say. That speech was made at a time when a treaty to which Canada was a party – upon which the seal of Canada was affixed – was threatened with violation at the hands of another power. A message was sent to the Government of Canada asking, in the event of that violation, would Canada care to be represented? I took the position that there was no question involved yet affecting the dispatch of troops: I took the position that Canada was being asked for a declaration of solidarity in respect of a threatened violation of the peace, relying on a treaty which Canada had signed. And I said: "When we were asked where we stood in that matter, the answer should have gone forth on the part of the government: 'Ready, aye, ready'." I was discussing what stand the government should take on the government responsibility. Had it been taken and it eventuated later – as it did not – that there was any necessity of any country sending troops, there would have been ample time to get the judgment of the people of Canada – ample time to put into effect the commitment which I made at Hamilton – and so, when the signature of this country is attested to a treaty (unless all honour is dead in the hearts of the nation) you can trust the people just as much as you can trust yourself. My object was not to throw a shadow of doubt or indifference over the obligations of this country as a member of the British Empire. My object was not to sow disaffection in the heart of any Canadian. My object was to plant the seeds of contentment and thereby to establish on firmer and more lasting foundations British institution and British fidelity.

> from verbatim report of the "Responsible Government, Defence of the Hamilton Speech" (delivered October 10, 1927, at the opening of the Winnipeg Conservative Convention)

Arthur Meighen by Gitano   Maclean's, *1933*

5

THE CRITICAL AND THE CONTEMPLATIVE

it
is not much
wonder if Canada
developed with the
bewilderment of
a neglected
child...

preoccupied with trying to define its own identity, alternately bumptious and diffident about its own achievements. Adolescent dreams of glory haunt the Canadian consciousness (and unconsciousness), some naïve and some sophisticated. In the naïve area are the predictions that the twentieth century belongs to Canada, that our cities will become much bigger than they ought to be, or, like Edmonton and Vancouver, "gateways" to somewhere else, reconstructed Northwest Passages. The more sophisticated usually take the form of a Messianic complex about Canadian culture, for Canadian culture, no less than Alberta, has always been "next-year country." The myth of the hero brought up in the forest retreat, awaiting the moment when his giant strength will be fully grown and he can emerge into the world, informs a good deal of Canadian criticism down to our own time.

NORTHROP FRYE "Conclusion" from *Literary History of Canada*, ed. Carl F. Klinck, Toronto, 1965

G. MERCER ADAM

In Canada . . . there is, in the ebbing out of national spirit, a growing intellectual callousness, and a deadening of interest in the things that make for the nation's higher life. Native literature, with nothing to interest it, is fast losing the power to arrest attention and is perceptibly dying of inanition. In higher education the sympathies of our people are only languidly engaged; and but for denominational pride our universities would be in danger of becoming extinct.

"An Interregnum in Literature"
The Week
I (June 12, 1884)

SARA JEANNETTE DUNCAN

Here people are well educated, well read, and, on the whole, well mannered. Here aristocracy of birth is so slender, and here aristocracy of wealth so small, that, while the influence of both is, of course, unmistakably felt, neither of these invidiously operating castes obtains here to any very damaging extent. While we are largely governed by the social traditions that obtain in England, we are so far from the autocratic code of insular dictation, and so near the somewhat lax and liberal system that prevails among our cousins of the Republic, that repressive austerities are somewhat softened among us with the result of a decided gain in individuality. Canadians, as a rule, talk well, and—laus Deo!—not through their noses, except in Toronto, where this distinctively democratic characteristic appears to be rapidly gaining ground. Culture they have, if riches they have not; and the social atmosphere of Eastern Canada, where the inhabitants have had a little more time to grow than we in Ontario, and where already some optimistic sky-searchers see a brightening of our literary horizon, is said by competent critics to be as charming as any, anywhere.

The Week
III (Oct. 14, 1886)

ARCHIBALD LAMPMAN

How utterly destitute of all light and charm are the intellectual conditions of our people and the institutions of our public life! How barren! How barbarous!

The Globe, Feb. 27, 1892

GOLDWIN SMITH

A literature there is fully as large and as high in quality as could be reasonably looked for, and of a character thoroughly healthy. Perhaps a kind critic might say that it still retains something of the old English sobriety of style, and is comparatively free from the straining for effect which is the bane of the best literature of the United States.

Canada and the Canadian Question, Toronto, 1891

J. D. LOGAN

Canadian poetry is such definitively, not because its authors or its material (subject, theme) or even its form, colour and music are Canadian. It is such only by virtue of some distinctive 'note' in it. That note is not Imperialism, as some allege; it is not individual nationhood, as others submit; it is not even Confederate Unity, as others say. It is this and this alone—*an inexpugnable Faith in ourselves.*

And so if you will examine the best Canadian poetry, whether it be hymns, nature songs, or war lyrics, you will find an undertone of a consciousness of self-controlled destiny, which passes from Cheerful Faith (before Confederation) to Triumphant Exultation (since Confederation). . . . And it is this Faith which now guides us, with undoubted energy and serenity, onward to a humane and happy federation of many races in a land still unassoiled and free. Our poetry may not be great in finished perfection of form, in subtle nuances of thought and emotion; but it is of high rank in these social qualities—sane and cheerful Faith in our ideals, restrained but inexpugnable Self-confidence in our power eventually to effect, undirected and unassisted by others, a genuinely mundane, human, and practical Democracy, and Courage to undertake the accomplishment of our predestined task.

Introduction to the *Songs of the Makers of Canada*,
Toronto, 1911

WILLIAM ARTHUR DEACON

Of the improvement in Canadian literature there is no doubt. One can almost see the difference from year to year; at five-year intervals the steps are quite visible. But it is not enough. Pedestrian efforts will not avail for the final elevation, where the wall rises sheer, and only sound craftsmanship, propelled by inspiration, can make the final leap to the top.

As a people, we have never known a cultural youth, with its exuberance and apparent irresponsibility. We have grown up with older people, listening respectfully to them, adopting their ways, effacing ourselves modestly; and we have been old, who were never young.

He would be, I think, blind, deaf and mindless, who could not see and feel the stirrings of the new nationalism. Canadians are starting to know pride; the empty North is beckoning imperatively. From various causes, some roots very far back, out of diverse elements, a mingling of peoples, a growing consciousness of common aim and actual power, a nation is being born as I write. Gestation is over. Independent life moves at last. A new vision, a new impulse, a new courage and a wholly new self-assurance, and will to go our own way, is inherently part of the new Canada, emerging before our eyes.

As surely as China, slumbering giant of Asia, has stirred in his sleep, and is about to resume his rightful place as leader of the Orient, Canada is quietly shaking off the grave-clothes of its European cultural inheritance. Through rebirth, it is now, this hour, becoming a nation; and as a young country—young and brave and hopeful and joyous—it will most surely produce a great literature.

"The Fallacy of Youth" in *Open House*,
ed. Deacon and Reeves, Ottawa, 1931

WILSON MacDONALD

Genius is not always born in a large country. Nor does it always appear in cultured communities. If the size of a country or the culture of a community had anything to do with the divine fires of inspiration, then China or Russia would produce most of our poets and the majority of the bards of England would come from Oxford or Cambridge. "Can any good thing come out of Nazareth?" is still the cry of humanity and no literature in the world has suffered more from this fallacy than has the literature of Canada. The next great genius may come from Mattawa, or Alberni or from Oxford, England. He may see the light of day in the Fiji Islands or in Southampton. There are no border lines, there are no nations where genius is concerned. It comes to us from the clear air of Sinai, from the groves of Greece or from the swamps of Central Africa. Let us then, now and forever, put aside this foolishness of tongue which forbids genius to a young country.

Canadian literature has suffered less from foreign unfairness than from those internal fault-finders who abound in Canada and whose stock-in-trade is the inferiority of colonialism. These critics are for the most part university professors who know as much about the soul of Canada as a stoker at sea knows about the beauty of a storm. The analogy is perfect, for when multitudinous lakes and countless rivers are calling upon the interpreters to proclaim their beauty these academy-prisoned gentlemen are wrestling with vellum in the stolid atmosphere of classrooms.

No university professor ever discovered a genius nor will this ever happen now or in the days to be. After one of the stormiest meetings in history, a group of professors from Oxford and Cambridge decreed that either Browning was insane or they were insane. When Harvard and Yale made merry jests at the expense of Whitman a group of common people discovered the tremendous passion of his song. It has always been the same; and here in Toronto we have witnessed the indifference of Toronto University as far as Carman and Roberts are concerned. It is time we called academic snobbery by its right name for it is academic dishonesty. Matthew Arnold alone escaped it, not because of his genius but because he was a professor himself.

The universities of Canada, apart from the colleges of the Maritimes, have scarcely made a gesture of friendship towards Canadian genius. This attitude inspires many critics who wish to bask in the sunshine of academic approval. The critic who discovers a flaw in Canadian literature is considered very clever; but the critic who discovers genius in our poetry or prose is immediately taunted with nationalistic prejudice.

The attitude of England towards Canadian literature is moulded by the condemnation or praise of a few of our university men, after whose names are an array of imposing letters. Thus the Canadian contempt for herself becomes the world's contempt for Canada. And before I proceed to condemn English indifference towards all colonial art, let me condemn the inspiration of that indifference—the attitude of a group of Canadian literary snobs towards the best that we have produced. If this antagonism were directed at our numerous writers of mediocre talent it would be excusable, but it is nearly always hurled at genius.

If I might describe a colonial, I would describe a citizen who, because of his contempt for himself, inspires the contempt of everyone. As long as Canadians are colonials they will have this inferiority fixation. I say definitely and without any hesitation that no country under the *aegis* of another country ever believed in herself. And I am very positive that England will be indifferent to Canadian literature until the Dominion of Canada has complete independence.

"The Stigma of Colonialism" in *Open House*,
ed. Deacon and Reeves, Ottawa, 1931

PAUL HIEBERT

It is claimed by some writers that Sarah Binks sprang spontaneously from Saskatchewan's alkaline soil, that she was an isolated genius such as the ages have produced from time to time with no significance beyond her unparalleled talent. With this view the Author takes exception. Sarah Binks was the product of her soil and her roots go deep. But more than that, she was an expression of her environment and her age. Without Saskatchewan at its greatest, at its golden age, Sarah would have been just another poetess. Sarah was the daughter and the grand-daughter of a dirt farmer; she loved the soil and much of Jacob Binks' passion for another quarter section flowed in her veins. Her love for the paternal acres was a real love, she believed in the rotation of crops, and in the fall, after the ploughing was done, she spread the fertilizer with a lavish hand. "The farmer is king," she cries,

The farmer is king of his packer and plow,
Of his harrows and binders and breakers,
He is lord of the pig, and Czar of the cow
On his hundred and sixty-odd acres.

The farmer is monarch in high estate,
Of his barn and his back-house and byre,
And all the buildings behind the gate
Of his two-odd miles of barbed wire.

The farmer is even Cæsar of freight
And tariff and tax, comes election,
And from then until then he can abdicate,
And be king on his own quarter section.

The farmer is king, oh, the farmer is king,
And except for his wife and his daughter,
Who boss him around, he runs the thing,
Come drought, come hell or high water.

Before midsummer she had completed *The Farmer and the Farmer's Wife*. It is one of the greatest of her short poems. It was first published in the Piecemeal *Excelsior*, but was immediately copied by *The Times* of Protuberance, Sask., and *The Beam*, of Vigil, N.W.T. She received no royalties from this piracy of an author's rights, but she expected none at this stage of her career. Hers were still the pleasures of giving. She did, however, write to the manager of the Lax Cosmetics Company at Saskatoon, who had used some of her lines in one of their advertisements, calling attention to the fact that her name was spelled with an I instead of a U, but received no reply.

The Farmer and the Farmer's Wife

The farmer and the farmer's wife
Lead frolicsome and carefree lives,
And all their work is but in play,
Their labours only exercise.

The farmer leaps from bed to board,
And board to binder on the land;
His wife awakes with shouts of joy,
And milks a cow with either hand.

Then all in fun they feed the pigs,
And plough the soil in reckless glee,
And play the quaint old-fashioned game
Of mortgagor and mortgagee.

And all day long they dash about,
In barn and pasture, field and heath;
He sings a merry roundelay,
She whistles gaily through her teeth.

And when at night the chores are done,
And hand in hand they sit and beam,
He helps himself to applejack,
And she to Paris Green.

The Farmer and the Farmer's Wife stands pre-eminent in the annals of Saskatchewan lyricism. Marrowfat gives it his unstinted praise. He says in part: "I like The Farmer's Wife. She starts out well and ends on a high note." Inspector Peeker, probably the most outstanding critic in several school districts, says of this poem: "The teachers of Baal and Cactus Lake have asked that this poem be put on the list of supplementary reading."

Sarah Binks, Toronto, 1947

FREDERICK PHILIP GROVE

The Canadian public is ignorant, cowardly, and snobbish; it is mortally afraid of ideas and considers the discussion of first principles as a betrayal of bad manners.

Unless they are very sure that it is socially disgraceful not to own a given book, they refuse to buy it. If it is imperative, socially, that they be able to talk about it, they borrow it. Even in order to own it, you don't necessarily have to buy it; you write to the author, and if the author knows what is what, he will send it to you with his autograph!

To how many people in Canada are books the daily companions they ought to be? Shall we say five hundred? Or is that too flattering? I mean, of course, outside of educational institutions.

Here is the point: any nation has the literature which it deserves; and no false enthusiasm, such as Mr. Callaghan treats to his scorn as one of the "boosting" activities of his country, can alter that fact. More appallingly, Canadians are at bottom not interested in their own country; I honestly believe they prefer to read about dukes and lords, or about the civil war in the United States. They are supposed to be born explorers; but they have not yet heard that the human heart and soul are perhaps the only corners in this universe where unexplored and undiscovered continents are still abounding.

This lack of mental aliveness is fundamental. Canada is a non-conductor for any sort of intellectual current.

"The Plight of Canadian Fiction? a Reply",
University of Toronto Quarterly (July, 1938)

ARTHUR R. M. LOWER

There are times when every people serve false gods. Equality, a god with aspects of beneficence, could easily become one of them, for if the supporting intellectual and philosophical elements are taken from his worship, the slope goes quickly down to that bog which might be called "simpleton democracy", and from this men have always been fished up via the route of demagoguery and tyranny. At mid-century the bog had not yet been reached but only self-conscious and effective inquiry into the deeper aspects of our religion of Equality would save us from it. Our people would have to learn to tolerate men who were not afraid, for the sake of equality, of being 'unequal', for

*"When everybody's somebody
Then no one's anybody."*

Logic carries the worship of the god Equality into all spheres: age, sex, race, nation, body, mind. As a result many temples were consecrated in North America to Equality in regions where it is hard to see that that worship was justified. One of these regions, a strategic one, was education. It is good Christian teaching that every soul is worth as much as every other soul. But it is a far cry from equality of souls to equality of minds. Yet many managed to convert the one belief into the other, and most of those who did so probably were indirectly influenced by the old Christian doctrine. Once the mind and soul were equally caught up into the theology of Equality, however, the door was open to every absurdity as oblation to the great god.

In a country like Canada, where the background of most people has been narrow and the opportunities they have had for learning something about the great world few, it is the mass gods who must be worshipped. There was a time in the old pioneer days when men could be individuals but when the bush was cut away and no longer hid them from each other, deviation easily became heresy: it offended the worshippers of the great god Equality. Today, as yesterday, deviations are reprobated by the average man, precisely because he senses that they stand for an order of things which would displace him from his representative position and threaten his power. 'Democracy,' the average man would say, 'has no room for the fellow who wants to be different.' The problem is a vast one: how to maintain a society with the equalitarian values of the pioneer and at the same time gradually build a national culture which in the distinctions it makes is not concerned overmuch with the shrine of Equality.

Canadians in the Making, Toronto, 1958

FRANK H. UNDERHILL

Now it seems to me . . . that this intellectual weakness of Canada is a quality which shows itself through all our history. In particular it is to be discerned in that process of democratization which is the most important thing that has happened to us, as to other kindred peoples, during the last hundred years. When we compare ourselves with Britain and the United States there is one striking contrast. Those two countries, since the end of the eighteenth century, have abounded in prophets and philosophers who have made articulate the idea of a liberal and equalitarian society. Their political history displays also a succession of practical politicians who have not merely performed the functions of manipulating and manoeuvring masses of men and groups which every politician performs, but whose careers have struck the imagination of both contemporaries and descendants as symbolizing certain great inspiring ideas. We in Canada have produced few such figures. Where are the classics in our political literature which embody our Canadian version of liberalism and democracy? Our party struggles have never been raised to the higher intellectual plane at which they become of universal interest by the presence of a Canadian Jefferson and a Canadian Hamilton in opposing parties. We have had no Canadian Burke or Mill to perform the social function of the political philosopher in action. We have had no Canadian Carlyle or Ruskin or Arnold to ask searching questions about the ultimate values embodied in our political or economic practice. We lack a Canadian Walt Whitman or Mark Twain to give literary expression to the democratic way of life. The student in search of illustrative material on the growth of Canadian political ideas during the great century of liberalism and democracy has to content himself mainly with a collection of extracts from more or less forgotten speeches and pamphlets and newspaper editorials. Whatever urge may have, at any time, possessed any Canadian to philosophize upon politics did not lead to much writing whose intrinsic worth helped to preserve it in our memory.

In Search of Canadian Liberalism, Toronto, 1960

FRANK H. UNDERHILL

For this weakness of the Left in Canada, the ultimate explanation would seem to be that we never had an eighteenth century of our own. The intellectual life of our politics has not been periodically revived by fresh drafts from the invigorating fountain of eighteenth-century Enlightenment. In Catholic French Canada the doctrines of the rights of man and of Liberty Equality Fraternity were rejected from the start, and to this day they have never penetrated, save surreptitiously or spasmodically. The mental climate of English Canada in its early formative years was determined by men who were fleeing from the practical application of the doctrines that all men are born equal and are endowed by their Creator with certain unalienable rights amongst which are life, liberty and the pursuit of happiness. All effective liberal and radical democratic movements in the nineteenth century have had their roots in this fertile eighteenth-century soil. But our ancestors made the great refusal in the eighteenth century. In Canada we have no revolutionary tradition; and our historians, political scientists, and philosophers have assiduously tried to educate us to be proud of this fact. How can such a people expect their democracy to be as dynamic as the democracies of Britain and France and the United States have been?

In Search of Canadian Liberalism, Toronto, 1960

JOHN CONWAY

Canada is the product of the pragmatic nineteenth century rather than of the ideological eighteenth. We are not children of the age of revolution. In our formative period our metaphysics was provided by the dominant Roman Catholic, Anglican, and Presbyterian theologies. We had no occasion to construct a metaphysics of politics. We too have become secularized, but the habit of mind persists. Our history has not conditioned us to vest any one political doctrine with universality. On the contrary, absolutes were not to be found in temporal things. Political and social forms could be no more than relative, all touched with imperfection, even though in varying degrees. Nor were we obliged by an act of revolution to set up a polarity between the individual and the state. We are indebted to our continuity with Europe and in particular with Great Britain for our natural assumption that authority complements and is necessary to freedom. We would, I think, agree with Burke that the limitations upon our liberties are to be counted among our rights. We accept diversity despite our present quarrels, for on the principle of diversity our country rests and must continue to rest. As their history has made Americans primarily individualists and absolutists, so a different history has made Canadians primarily organicists and relativists in national and international politics.

"What Is Canada?"

NORTHROP FRYE

The simultaneous influence of two larger nations speaking the same language has been practically beneficial to English Canada, but theoretically confusing. It is often suggested that Canada's identity is to be found in some *via media*, or *via mediocris*, between the other two. This has the disadvantage that the British and American cultures have to be defined as extremes. Haliburton seems to have believed that the ideal for Nova Scotia would be a combination of American energy and British

social structure, but such a chimera, or synthetic monster, is hard to achieve in practice. It is simpler merely to notice the alternating current in the Canadian mind, as reflected in its writing, between two moods, one romantic, traditional and idealistic, the other shrewd, observant and humorous. Canada in its attitude to Britain tends to be more royalist than the Queen, in the sense that it is more attracted to it as a symbol of tradition than as a fellow-nation. The Canadian attitude to the United States is typically that of a smaller country to a much bigger neighbour, sharing in its material civilization but anxious to keep clear of the huge mass movements that drive a great imperial power. The United States, being founded on a revolution and a written constitution, has introduced a deductive or *a priori* pattern into its cultural life that tends to define an American way of life and mark it off from anti-American heresies. Canada, having a seat on the sidelines of the American Revolution, adheres more to the inductive and the expedient. The Canadian genius for compromise is reflected in the existence of Canada itself.

"Conclusion" from *Literary History of Canada*, ed. Carl F. Klinck, Toronto, 1965

MALCOLM LOWRY

No matter what yoke they were reeling under, no matter how starved, I believe you would never see in France, or among Frenchmen, the appalling sights of despair and degradation to be met with daily in the streets of Vancouver, Canada, where man, having turned his back on nature, and having no heritage of beauty else, and no faith in a civilization where God has become an American washing machine, or a car he refuses even to drive properly—and not possessing the American élan which arises from a faith in the very act of taming nature herself, because America having run out of a supply of nature to tame is turning on Canada, so that Canada feels herself at bay, while a Canadian might be described as a conservationist divided against himself—falls to pieces before your eyes. Report has nothing to do with navigation. Instead of ill this very extremity in Canada probably presages an important new birth of wisdom in that country, for which America herself will be grateful.

"Through the Panama"
in *Hear Us O Lord From Heaven Thy Dwelling Place*,
Philadelphia, 1961

ARTHUR R. M. LOWER

In the societies with which our own has been most intimately associated, the domination of the great centre has long been complete. France and England (which country itself remained for long culturally provincial to Paris) emerged from the Middle Ages as the two nations *par excellence* and their undisputed foci were their capital cities, Paris and London. After the English Conquest, New France slowly found a new metropolitan centre in Rome, and gradually New York—or even Hollywood—usurped London's hegemony over English Canada. It is the failure of modern Canada to find a satisfactory centre within itself which leads to ambiguities in its structure and doubts about its future.

Canadians in the Making, Toronto, 1958

NORTHROP FRYE

Small and isolated communities surrounded with a physical or psychological "frontier," separated from one another and from their American and British cultural sources: communities that provide all that their members have in the way of distinctively human values, and that are compelled to feel a great respect for the law and order that holds them together, yet confronted with a huge, unthinking, menacing, and formidable physical setting—such communities are bound to develop what we may provisionally call a garrison mentality. In the earliest maps of the country the only inhabited centres are forts, and that remains true of the cultural maps for a much later time. Frances Brooke, in her eighteenth-century *Emily Montague*, wrote of what was literally a garrison; novelists of our day studying the impact of Montreal on Westmount write of a psychological one.

A garrison is a closely knit and beleaguered society, and its moral and social values are unquestionable. In a perilous enterprise one does not discuss causes or motives: one is either a fighter or a deserter. Here again we may turn to Pratt, with his infallible instinct for what is central in the Canadian imagination. The societies in Pratt's poems are always tense and tight groups engaged in war, rescue, martyrdom, or crisis, and the moral values expressed are simply those of that group. In such a society the terror is not for the common enemy, even when the enemy is or seems victorious, as in the extermination of the Jesuit missionaries or the crew of Franklin (a great Canadian theme . . . that Pratt pondered but never completed). The real terror comes when the individual feels himself becoming an individual, pulling away from the group, losing the sense of driving power that the group gives him, aware of a conflict within himself far subtler than the struggle of morality against evil. It is much easier to multiply garrisons, and when that happens, something anti-cultural comes into Canadian life, a dominating herd-mind in which nothing original can grow. The intensity of the sectarian divisiveness in Canadian towns, both religious and political, is an example: what such groups represent, of course, vis-à-vis one another, is "two solitudes," the death of communication and dialogue. Separatism, whether English or French, is culturally the most sterile of all creeds.

"Conclusion" from *Literary History of Canada*, ed. Carl F. Klinck, Toronto, 1965

HUGH MacLENNAN

"I'd like to see this country get stirred up about something to find out what goes on underneath. Because a lot must go on. Jim Craig told me how many of your young people were killed in the war. A thing like that means something. Myself, I like a dramatic country, and most of the United States is dramatic. There's something crazy and dangerous about it, but it makes you feel alive. You can get into the deadest town—so long as it's west of the Appalachians or south of the Mason-Dixon—and you can imagine anything happening in it. My father came from a tank town in the plains, but he saw his own father help string up a rustler. Up here I bet you never had any rustlers to string up. Down in the South you can go along a little dirt road and there's nothing to see in the daytime. But at night you go along it. You can pretty easily imagine a lynching party, if you're in the right district of the right state. And you ought to see the Middle West in a fall thunderstorm. No wonder the small-town people in the Middle West have that strained look about their eyes. People here haven't got it. But you're not soft, either. I've found out you don't dent easily. You're just different—as if you'd never got started, somehow. You don't make the money you should because you don't think big enough. You're too content to take what people give you. You're too polite."

The Precipice, Toronto, 1948

ROYAL COMMISSION ON
NATIONAL DEVELOPMENT IN THE ARTS,
LETTERS AND SCIENCES, 1949-51

The task assigned to this Royal Commission was conceived by its authors in the Government with imagination and boldness, and this throughout our work we have found stimulating. We have been more and more impressed by the timeliness, indeed by the urgency, of our inquiry. If, at the outset, we were convinced of the importance of what we were to do, as we proceeded this conviction deepened. The work with which we have been entrusted is concerned with nothing less than the spiritual foundations of our national life. Canadian achievement in every field depends mainly on the quality of the Canadian mind and spirit. This quality is determined by what Canadians think, and think about; by the books they read, the pictures they see and the programmes they hear. These things, whether we call them arts and letters or use other words to describe them, we believe to lie at the roots of our life as a nation.

They are also the foundations of national unity. We thought it deeply significant to hear repeatedly from representatives of the two Canadian cultures expressions of hope and of confidence that in our common cultivation of the things of the mind, Canadians—French and English-speaking—can find true "Canadianism". Through this shared confidence we can nurture what we have in common and resist those influences which could impair, and even destroy, our integrity. In our search we have thus been made aware of what can serve our country in a double sense: what can make it great, and what can make it one.

The American invasion by film, radio and periodical is formidable. Much of what comes to us is good and of this we shall be speaking presently. It has, however, been represented to us that many of the radio programmes have in fact no particular application to Canada or to Canadian conditions and that some of them, including certain children's programmes of the "crime" and "horror" type, are positively harmful. News commentaries too, and even live broadcasts from American sources, are designed for American ears and are almost certain to have an American slant and emphasis by reason of what they include or omit, as well as because of the opinions expressed. We think it permissible to record these comments on American radio since we observe that in the United States many radio programmes and American broadcasting in general have recently been severely criticized. It will, we think, be readily agreed that we in Canada should take measures to avoid in our radio, and in our television, at least those aspects of American broadcasting which have provoked in the United States the most outspoken and the sharpest opposition.

American influences on Canadian life to say the least are impressive. There should be no thought of interfering with the liberty of all Canadians to enjoy them. Cultural exchanges are excellent in themselves. They widen the choice of the consumer and provide stimulating competition for the producer. It cannot be denied, however, that a vast and disproportionate amount of material coming from a single alien source may stifle rather than stimulate our own creative effort; and, passively accepted without any standard of comparison, this may weaken critical faculties. We are now spending millions to maintain a national independence which would be nothing but an empty shell without a vigorous and distinctive cultural life. We have seen that we have its elements in our traditions and in our history; we have made important progress, often aided by American generosity. We must not be blind, however, to the very present danger of permanent dependence.

Royal Commission on National Development in the Arts, Letters and Sciences, 1949-1951

FRANK H. UNDERHILL

T... here is one theme in the report about which some searching questions should be asked. The commissioners seek a national Canadian culture which shall be independent of American influences. Several times they speak of these influences as "alien". This use of the word "alien" seems to me to reveal a fallacy that runs through much of Canadian nationalistic discussion. For we cannot escape the fact that we live on the same continent as the Americans, and that the longer we live here the more we are going to be affected by the same continental influences which affect them. It is too late now for a Canadian cultural nationalism to develop in the kind of medieval isolation in which English or French nationalism was nurtured. The so-called alien American influences are not alien at all; they are just the natural forces that operate on a continental scale in the conditions of our twentieth-century civilization.

The fact is that, if we produced Canadian movies for our own mass consumption, they would be as sentimental and vulgar and escapist as are the Hollywood variety; and they would be sentimental, vulgar and escapist in the American way, not in the English or French or Italian way. Our newspapers, which are an independent local product, do not differ essentially from the American ones. The kind of news which the Canadian Press circulates on its own origination is exactly like that originated by AP or UP. Like the American ones, our papers become progressively worse as the size of the city increases, up to a certain point. Somewhere between the size of Chicago and the size of New York another force comes into operation, producing a different kind of newspaper. We haven't any daily as bad as the *Chicago Tribune*, because we haven't any city as big as Chicago; but also we haven't anything as good as the *New York Times.* . . . It is mass-consumption and the North American continental environment which produce the undesirable aspects of mass-communications, not some sinister influences in the United States.

If we could get off by ourselves on a continental island, far away from the wicked Americans, all we should achieve would be to become a people like the Australians. (And even then the American goblin would get us in the end, as he is getting the Australians.) Let us be thankful, then, that we live next door to the Americans. But if we allow ourselves to be obsessed by the danger of American cultural annexation, so that the thought preys on us day and night, we shall only become a slightly bigger Ulster. The idea that by taking thought, and with the help of some government subventions, we can become another England—which, one suspects, is Mr. Massey's ultimate idea—is purely fantastic. No sane Canadian wants us to become a nation of Australians or Ulsterites. So, if we will only be natural, and stop going about in this eternal defensive fear of being ourselves, we shall discover that we are very like the Americans, both in our good qualities and in our bad qualities. Young Canadians who are really alive make this discovery now without going through any great spiritual crisis.

The root cultural problem in our modern mass-democracies is this relationship between the mass culture, which is in danger of being further debased with every new invention in mass-communications, and the culture of the few. The United States is facing this problem at a rather more advanced stage than we have yet reached; and the more intimately we study American experience the more we shall profit. What we need, we, the minority of Canadians who care for the culture of the few, is closer contact with the *finest* expressions of the American mind. The fear that what will result from such contact will be our own absorption is pure defeatism. We need closer touch with the best American universities (*not* Teachers College) and research institutions, closer touch with

American experimental music and poetry and theatre and painting, closer personal touch with the men who are leaders in these activities. The Americans are now mature enough to have come through this adolescent phase of believing that the best way to become mature is to cut yourself off from older people who are more mature than you are. It is about time that we grew out of it also. I think the Massey commissioners should use their leisure now to study the Americans much more closely than they seem to have done hitherto.

In Search of Canadian Liberalism, Toronto, 1960

DOUGLAS LE PAN

but perhaps there is something that can be plucked and rescued from the encompassing dimness. An image, a conjoined image of bourgeois and voyageur: the Nor'wester who in youth travels the canoe routes westward and lives on Lake Athabasca or Great Slave Lake as a wintering partner, and who only when he is middle-aged returns to settle permanently in Montreal and to build himself a big house on the side of the mountain where he can look out and see the River of Canada flowing by and remember when he was young and lived hard and was ready for anything that might come at the next portage or the next turn of the river. Bourgeois and voyageur: it is a phrase that can be coaxed into summing up much in Canadian history, making long stretches of it seem more evocative and attractive than they would be otherwise; and sometimes the two qualities can be miraculously combined in the one person. So it must have been with many of the fur traders. And even with Louis Riel, that baffling, rebellious spirit, of whom it is related that when he would receive official visitors at Fort Garry as the leader of the provisional government of the North-west in 1869, he would be wearing leather moccasins and a frock coat. It will be a long time before either of those trappings will have altogether ceased to indicate something about the Canadian scene and the Canadian consciousness.

"The Dilemma of the Canadian Author",
The Atlantic Monthly, November, 1964

CANADA COUNCIL
SEVENTH ANNUAL REPORT, 1963-64

Contemplating the arts in Canada at the moment is (as Kingsley Amis has observed in another context) like listening to Mozart while suffering from toothache. There is a most agreeable background distorted by sensations of acute discomfort. The background is created by our artists and the organizations which employ them. The latter continue to grow in size and scope, and sometimes in stature. The discomfort is caused by a lack of funds adequate to maintain even a reasonable rate of growth. We are not suggesting that some companies of performing artists should be fed by subsidy to become fatted calves. It is simply that, at Canada's stage of development in the arts, if you do not grow you are a dead duck. It may be that the Council's brief recently presented to the government will in due course help to correct the present disagreeable state of affairs. At the moment Mozart can be heard in the background playing second fiddle while the abscess of deficit continues to swell.

For we think it should be known that a number of organizations, particularly those devoted to music and the theatre arts, have in our opinion been forced into carrying deficits which are growing beyond their capacity. The fact that they *are* carrying them shows that a good measure of confidence is given to the organizations by the communities they serve. But this display of optimism does not balance the books. The spectre of bankruptcy rather than the *spectre de la rose* is what haunts some of our stages.

It is not infrequently argued from an editorial chair, or from behind the bland refusal to provide a donation, that the arts should live within their income as well-run businesses must do. This point of view has been fearlessly* expressed and it carries with it a measure of short-range common sense. The situation, however, requires the application of uncommon sense. The performing arts are caught in a kind of squeeze not unknown in the world of commerce. The better you get and the more you have to offer, the more your audience expects of you; for its appetite grows by what it feeds on. If a performing organization resists the temptation to bring in a new production, or to invite this or that glamorous soloist to perform with it, on the grounds that it wishes to balance its budget, the result is often a falling off of the audience on which it depends for a large part of its revenue.

We are not suggesting that the arts are an infinitely expanding universe with galaxies of orchestras, operas, ballets and drama flying onwards and outwards forever. Sooner or later, as we can observe in some of the older countries, organizations mature and come to some semblance of rest. The point is that we have not yet reached this state in Canada, and that until we do the pressures of growth and expansion are difficult to resist.

*fearless: "a word now restricted to journalistic usage where it signifies the noisy expression of views already known to be popular." (Beachcomber)

The Canada Council Seventh Annual Report, 1963-64

NORTHROP FRYE

Our principle is, then, that literature can only derive its forms from itself: they can't exist outside literature, any more than musical forms like the sonata and the fugue can exist outside music. This principle is important for understanding what's happened in Canadian literature. When Canada was still a country for pioneers, it was assumed that a new country, a new society, new things to look at and new experiences would produce a new literature. So Canadian writers ever since, including me, have been saying that Canada was just about to get itself a brand-new literature. But these new things provide only content; they don't provide new literary forms. Those can come only from the literature Canadians already know. People coming to Canada from, say, England in 1830 started writing in the conventions of English literature in 1830. They couldn't possibly have done anything else: they weren't primitives, and could never have looked at the world the way the Indians did. When they wrote, they produced second-hand imitations of Byron and Scott and Tom Moore, because that was what they had been reading; Canadian writers today produce imitations of D. H. Lawrence and W. H. Auden for the same reason.

The same thing happened in the States, and people predicted that new Iliads and Odysseys would arise in the ancient forests of the new world. The Americans were a little luckier than we were: they really did have writers original enough to give them their national epics. These national epics weren't a bit like the Iliad or the Odyssey; they were such books as *Huckleberry Finn* and *Moby Dick*, which developed out of conventions quite different from Homer's. Or is it really true to say that they're not a bit like the Iliad or the Odyssey? Superficially they're very different, but the better you know both the Odyssey and *Huckleberry Finn*, the more impressed you'll be by the resemblances: the disguises, the ingenious lies to get out of scrapes, the exciting adventures that often suddenly turn tragic, the mingling of the strange and the familiar, the sense of a human comradeship stronger than any disaster. And Melville goes out of his way to explain how his white whale belongs in the same family of sea monsters that turn up in Greek myths and in the Bible.

The Educated Imagination,
CBC Publications, 1963

REID MacCALLUM

this talk of Canadianism has created myths which stand in the way of a proper appreciation of the movement. Take the case of that great and in some ways solitary genius, Tom Thomson. The public has eagerly seized him and built up a myth about him. He has become a national, even a political, symbol, even a symbol of our recent emergence from political tutelage. For here, against a general background of effete academies, especially the Royal Academy, arises a true earth-born artist, untouched by the past, untutored and unspoiled, who depicts Canada in an idiom which is genuinely Canadian, who brings the fire down from heaven in a new land and founds a flourishing native school. It is a curious revenge of facts upon this quasi-political legend that its originators ingenuously take the universal success of the Canadian pictures at Wembley as the climax of their little drama.

Certainly Thomson is amazing, and there is nearly enough truth in the above account to let it pass, but not quite enough. If you examine his early work when first as a member of the commercial art firm of Grip Ltd. he tried his hand at painting the woods, you feel indeed that Thomson is there, but enveloped as it were in a cocoon; moreover, in these large, flat, decorative, rather poster-like, rather flamboyant canvases there is nothing to lead you to expect the cocoon to break. Compare this with the work of his brief maturity, before his lamentably early death in 1917; everything in these intensely felt, luminous, admirably organized, admirably restrained and economical pictures speaks of what he has learned; in the interval he had come in contact with MacDonald, Harris, Lismer, A. Y. Jackson, and through them with the whole of contemporary painting and with the past. For all these men had studied in Europe, all of them show influences of the vital traditions now at work in the world of art. Jackson's delicate and tender colouring, for example, is an individual expression of the influence at work in Morrice, and by him derived from the French. One is often reminded, when confronted with the luminosity of Harris's paintings, and the finish of his forms, of similar qualities in, say, Ingres. And who can observe the deliberately rhythmized hills and clouds of Lismer, or Jackson, without recalling Van Gogh and others whom he influenced, or who influenced him? Here, as everywhere else, scrutiny reveals that true originality is never a break with tradition for the break's sake, but a transformation of the traditional, arising not from contemptuous ignorance but from sympathetic acquaintance with the whole past achievement of the race. Behind the Thomson legend we find a straightforward story of a man of genius springing into virile maturity through contact with the great traditions of Western painting, and, along with his companions, forging them to a new expressiveness; a scholar, rather than a mythical fire-bringer, not so much a founder as a member in full standing, one who has much to take from as well as to give to his group. I avoid the term Group of Seven, except in my title, remembering Wordsworth's difficult wrestling with that number; but from the first the phenomenon has been a group phenomenon, maintaining over twenty years an informal corporate identity. It is precisely in such a grouping that individual achievement is likely to be most incalculable, that the individual is most likely to do better than he knows, since he works along unforeseen lines towards a goal which is not clearly defined in advance, but arises out of the common effort itself. In this sort of group you find marked individual differences in style, temper, and technique, along with that elusive thing, "a marked family resemblance."

The "Canadian" or "Northernist" theory, then, forces its supporters to exaggerate the originality of our artists beyond what is plausible. Whatever point the theory possesses can be retained without transferring the antithesis between Canadian and British from politics, where it originated, to art, where it has little or no meaning; much clearness is gained by substituting the word "provincial" for the word "colonial" in these discussions. For the real antithesis is that of the metropolitan and the provincial, of the life lived at the artistic centre of interest and growth, and the life slept out on the periphery in passive acceptance of time-worn conventions; and England used to be as provincial as Canada. The transformation brought about there by Nash, Fry, Gill, Kennington,

Nevinson, and others is, like our own movement, an abandonment of provincialism under metropolitan influences. Both are significant incidents in the rebirth of the art of painting in the West. Essentially, an art style is a universal spiritual fact, a mode of man's feeling toward his world, and as such is the property of no race or people, but of mankind, originating from and returning to rest in the collective effort of humanity, in the international sense. It follows that any definition, however tentative, of the essential contribution of this school of painting must be in properly aesthetic language.

"The Group of Seven: a Retrospect"
in *Imitation and Design*,
ed. William Blissett, Toronto, 1953

PETER COLLINS

the standards of gastronomy have remained unchanged for two centuries and are uncontested. The standards of architecture might also be uncontested if romantic influences had not, for two centuries, vitiated its theoretical basis, and spread the germs of its debilitating criteria like phylloxera throughout the Western world. It is no coincidence that Anglo-Saxon cooking is proverbially bad, for bad food and bad architecture both derive from the same philosophical disease.

This disease is, quite simply, Romanticism, or the refusal to accept the fact that, in the highest art, sensation must be subordinate to reason. For two centuries Western art has been divisible into two antagonistic categories, which may be described either as romantic versus classical, or emotional versus rational. Now the essential nature of the revolution which took place in French cooking in the mid-eighteenth century was that the coarse and purely sensual methods of Roman, Mediaeval and Renaissance eating were rationalized. "Gastronomy," explained Brillat-Savarin, the father of the new art, "is the rationalized knowledge of everything which relates to man in so far as he nourishes himself." "Only intelligent men," he continued, "honour fine food, because the others are not capable of an operation which consists in a sequence of appreciation and judgements."

In conformity with Brillat-Savarin's philosophy, the leading French architectural theorist of the mid-eighteenth century, namely J. F. Blondel, similarly defined taste as "the fruit of reasoning", and added, in words which almost paraphrase Diderot's definition of a true philosopher, that "taste founded on reason accepts neither ready-made systems nor the authority of private opinions." But in England at this time, the writers on Taste were already rejecting Classicism in favour of Romanticism, and it is doubtless mainly for this reason that Alison, in his *Essay on Taste*, did not mention food at all, since gastronomy clearly did not fit into the romantic aesthetic theory of "the association of ideas".

According to this theory, it will be remembered, man's awareness of the beauty of proportions is due entirely to a mental association of the relationship between form and function, and the appreciation of the beauty of buildings is due entirely to the stimulus given man's imagination by (in the case of Gothic Revival, Greek Revival or Classical designs) the evocation of the lost glories of the Middle Ages, Greece or Rome. Today, we also seem to consider that architectural beauty is based on the idea of functionalism and romantic associations, although nowadays we romanticize the future, rather than the past. In both instances architectural appreciation, being subjective, is primarily governed by fashion, which to the classical theorist was "the tyrant of taste". "Taste, once acquired, should exclude every kind of fashion from architecture as so many obstacles to its progress," J. F. Blondel told his students two centuries ago, and went on to criticize young architects for neglecting sound principles in favour of new inventions, which must inevitably be superseded by other novelties in their turn.

Novel recipes for preparing food are, of course, frequently invented, but the old recipes still retain the same authority and prestige which they had before, because they are, literally, what Frank Lloyd Wright called "in the nature of materials", and thus their aesthetic properties never become stale. The recipes in Viard's *Cuisinier Royal* (a book already printed in ten separate editions by 1820) are all to be found in the latest edition of *L'Art Culinaire Français*, and the latter only supersedes the former because in the latter there are three thousand recipes more. In gastronomy, there is no prestige attached to novelty *per se*, and nobody asks a chef if he can be guaranteed always to provide something "contemporary". Nor would any gastronome ever refuse *filets de volaille à la Bellevue* simply because they were invented by Madame de Pompadour, or angrily ask why he was not getting the latest recipe from the *Ladies' Home Journal* instead. In cooking, as in any art which really flourishes, the only values recognized are those concerned with degrees of excellence, and the decline in architecture occurred when architects forgot this, and started worrying about whether they were being "contemporary" or "reactionary", instead of whether their work was good or bad.

"The Architectonics of Pure Taste", *Journal of The Royal Architectural Institute of Canada*, XXXVIII (1961).

ERIC ARTHUR

in the interval, the city fathers decided that what Toronto needed was not a court house only, but a city hall as well and, in 1887, Lennox was asked to prepare drawings for a building to combine both functions.

He did so superbly well. That it cost $2,500,000, a figure somewhat in excess of the target of $300,000 set by the City, was explained by Mayor John Shaw on opening day, September 18, 1899:

Why people will spend large sums of money on great buildings opens up a wide field of thought. It may, however, be roughly answered that great buildings symbolize a people's deeds and aspirations. It has been said that, wherever a nation had a conscience and a mind, it recorded the evidence of its being in the highest products of this greatest of all arts. Where no such monuments are to be found, the mental and moral natures of the people have not been above the faculties of the beasts.

Toronto: No Mean City, Toronto, 1964

CHARLES NORRIS COCHRANE

The triumph of classical idealism is in no way better illustrated than by the general acceptance of a public discipline such as had been called for on all hands during the revolution and was now to be embodied in the imperial system of education for citizenship. In elaborating this system the Romans were to raise a monument to their genius hardly less significant than that of classical jurisprudence; together with which it was, indeed, to survive the empire itself, in order to provide a legacy of 'commonplaces' to form the core of subsequent European culture. Organized to promote the inculcation and diffusion of classical ideals, it effected its purpose, firstly, by serving as a reagent to dissolve all forms of particularism; secondly, by erecting 'universal' standards of judgement and taste.

The principles of such a public discipline already existed when Augustus began his work, and it remained only to apply them to the conditions of imperial society. It was, perhaps, Cato who had first laid down the outlines of an educational curriculum; but, with the evolution of the humanistic ideal in the last century of the republic, it had assumed a character quite remote from his simple, almost wholly technical and vocational scheme. In so doing it emerged as the system of *bonae* or *liberales artes* which was destined to take such root in the life of the empire and, with necessary modifications, to constitute the basis of training during the Middle Ages. In this transformation we may once more perceive the hand of Cicero.

Cicero had exhorted his son to follow his own example in basing his studies on the two classical languages. At the same time he had insisted upon the advantage of combining literature (grammar and rhetoric) with philosophy; and, in this connection, he recommended the reading of his own works along with those of the Academics, Peripatetics, and Stoics. For the resultant discipline he claimed a sovereign merit; asserting that it fulfilled the double purpose of ensuring right conduct and correct expression. In other words, it satisfied the demands of thought and action implied by life in society. In this programme Cicero claims that the combination of literature and philosophy is peculiarly Roman, i.e. his own contribution to educational theory. Whether or not this was the case, the deliberate substitution of literature for mathematics in what had been the characteristically Platonic combination marks a distinct departure from the spirit and purpose of the Academic discipline, and its historical significance can hardly be exaggerated. For, by imparting to Classicism precisely that 'literary and aesthetic bias' which Plato had so earnestly deprecated, it modified the whole complexion of Western culture, giving to it a rhetorical cast from which it was hardly to free itself even under the powerful stimulus of modern mathematical and physical science.

In seeking to appraise the results of this Latin discipline we can afford to touch lightly upon the more obvious. It served, for example, a useful economic purpose in the training of speakers and writers, the importance of which should not be underestimated, even though the avenues of expression were drastically curtailed with the disappearance of political freedom. In this connection perhaps the most significant development was an exaggeration of the characteristic weaknesses of rhetoric – its preoccupation with form, resulting in rule-ridden traditionalism and the tiresome 'echoing' of Cicero and Vergil, its emphasis upon aesthetic effort, which issued in the manufacture of 'verbal honey-balls', crammed with false sentiment and exhibiting every form of dexterity possible to authors who aspired to virtuosity without any particular regard for truth. These weaknesses reached their climax with the panegyrists, the worthlessness of whose efforts was in direct proportion to their proficiency in fulsome and nauseating adulation.

Christianity and Classical Culture, Oxford, 1940

MARSHALL McLUHAN

Education is ideally civil defence against media fallout. Yet Western man has had, so far, no education or equipment for meeting any of the new media on their own terms. Literate man is not only numb and vague in the presence of film or photo, but he intensifies his ineptness by a defensive arrogance and condescension to "pop kulch" and "mass entertainment." It was in this spirit of bulldog opacity that the scholastic philosophers failed to meet the challenge of the printed book in the sixteenth century. The vested interests of acquired knowledge and conventional wisdom have always been bypassed and engulfed by new media.

Understanding Media, New York, 1964

NORTHROP FRYE

a vast country sparsely inhabited naturally depends on its modes of transportation, whether canoe, railway, or the driving and riding "circuits" of the judge, the Methodist preacher, or the Yankee peddler. The feeling of nomadic movement over great distances persists even into the age of the aeroplane, in a country where writers can hardly meet one another without a social organization that provides travel grants. Pratt's poetry is full of his fascination with means of communication, not simply the physical means of great ships and locomotives, though he is one of the best of all poets on such subjects, but with communication as message, with radar and asdic and wireless signals, and, in his war poems, with the power of rhetoric over fighting men. What is perhaps the most comprehensive structure of ideas yet made by a Canadian thinker, the structure embodied in Innis's *Bias of Communication*, is concerned with the same theme, and a disciple of Innis, Marshall McLuhan, continues to emphasize the unity of communication, as a complex containing both verbal and non-verbal factors, and warns us against making unreal divisions within it.

"Conclusion" from *Literary History of Canada*,
ed. Carl F. Klinck, Toronto, 1965

HAROLD A. INNIS

The concepts of time and space reflect the significance of media to civilization. Media which emphasize time are those which are durable in character such as parchment, clay and stone. The heavy materials are suited to the development of architecture and sculpture. Media which emphasize space are apt to be less durable and light in character such as papyrus and paper. The latter are suited to wide areas in administration and trade. The conquest of Egypt by Rome gave access to supplies of papyrus which became the basis of a large administrative empire. Materials which emphasize time favour decentralization and hierarchical types of institutions, while those which emphasize space favour centralization and systems of government less hierarchical in character. Large-scale political organizations, such as empires, must be considered from the standpoint of two dimensions, those of space and time, and persist by overcoming the bias of media which over-emphasize either dimension. They have tended to flourish under conditions in which civilization reflects the influence of more than one medium and in which the bias of one medium towards decentralization is offset by the bias of another medium towards centralization.

Empire and Communications
Oxford, 1950

MARSHALL McLUHAN

Of the many unforeseen consequences of typography, the emergence of nationalism is, perhaps, the most familiar. Political unification of populations by means of vernacular and language groupings was unthinkable before printing turned each vernacular into an extensive mass medium. The tribe, an extended form of a family of blood relatives, is exploded by print, and is replaced by an association of men homogeneously trained to be individuals. Nationalism itself came as an intense new visual image of group destiny and status, and depended on a speed of information movement unknown before printing. Today nationalism as an image still depends on the press but has all the electric media against it. In business, as in politics, the effect of even jet-plane speeds is to render the older national groupings of social organization quite unworkable. In the Renaissance it was the speed of print and the ensuing market and commercial developments that made nationalism (which is continuity and competition in homogeneous space) as natural as it was new. By the same token, the heterogeneities and non-competitive discontinuities of medieval guilds and family organization had become a great nuisance as speed-up of information by print called for more fragmentation and uniformity of function. The Benvenuto Cellinis, the goldsmith-cum-painter-cum-sculptor-cum-writer-cum-condottiere, became obsolete.

Once a new technology comes into a social milieu it cannot cease to permeate that milieu until every institution is saturated. Typography has permeated every phase of the arts and sciences in the past five hundred years. It would be easy to document the processes by which the principles of continuity, uniformity, and repeatability have become the basis of calculus and of marketing, as of industrial production, entertainment, and science. It will be enough to point out that repeatability conferred on the printed book the strangely novel character of a uniformly priced commodity opening the door to price systems. The printed book had in addition the quality of portability and accessibility that had been lacking in the manuscript.

Directly associated with these expansive qualities was the revolution in expression. Under manuscript conditions the role of being an author was a vague and uncertain one, like that of a minstrel. Hence, self-expression was of little interest. Typography, however, created a medium in which it was possible to speak out loud and bold to the world itself, just as it was possible to circumnavigate the world of books previously locked up in a pluralistic world of monastic cells. Boldness of type created boldness of expression.

Uniformity reached also into areas of speech and writing, leading to a single tone and attitude to reader and subject spread throughout an entire composition. The "man of letters" was born. Extended to the spoken word, this literate *equitone* enabled literate people to maintain a single "high tone" in discourse that was quite devastating, and enabled nineteenth-century prose writers to assume moral qualities that few would now care to simulate. Permeation of the colloquial language with literate uniform qualities has flattened out educated speech till it is a very reasonable acoustic facsimile of the uniform and continuous visual effects of typography. From this technological effect follows the further fact that the humour, slang, and dramatic vigour of American-English speech are monopolies of the semi-literate.

These typographical matters for many people are charged with controversial values. Yet in any approach to understanding print it is necessary to stand aside from the form in question if its typical pressure and life are to be observed. Those who panic now about the threat of the newer media and about the revolution we are forging, vaster in scope than that of Gutenberg, are obviously lacking in cool visual detachment and gratitude for that most potent gift bestowed on Western man by literacy and typography: his power to act without reaction or involvement. It is this kind of specialization by dissociation that has created Western power and efficiency. Without this dissociation of action from feeling and emotion people are hampered and hesitant. Print taught men to say, "Damn the torpedoes. Full steam ahead!"

Understanding Media, New York, 1964

ARCHIBALD LAMPMAN

It always depresses me to go to church. In those prayers and terrible hymns of our service we are in the presence of all the suffering in the world since the beginning of time. . . . Sunday is a day that drives me almost to madness. The prim black and collars, the artificial dress of the women, the slow trouping to church, the bells, the silence, the dreariness, the occasional knots of sallow and unhealthy zealots whom one may meet at street corners whining over some awful point in theology —all that gradually presses me down till by Sunday night I am in despair and would fain issue forth with pot and brush and colour the town crimson.

Letters to E. W. Thomson (1890-98)
Ed. A. S. Bourinot, Ottawa, 1956

SARA JEANNETTE DUNCAN

In wholesome fear of mistake, one would hesitate to put church matters either before or after politics among the preoccupations of Elgin. It would be safer and more indisputable to say that nothing compared with religion but politics, and nothing compared with politics but religion. In offering this proposition also we must think of our dimensions. There is a religious fervour in Oxford, in Mecca, in Benares, and the sign for these

ideas is the same; we have to apply ourselves to the interpretation. In Elgin religious fervour was not beautiful, or dramatic, or self-immolating; it was reasonable. You were perhaps your own first creditor; after that your debt was to your Maker. You discharged this obligation in a spirit of sturdy equity: if the children didn't go to Sunday school you knew the reason why. The habit of church attendance was not only a basis of respectability, but practically the only one: a person who was "never known to put his head inside a church door" could not be more severely reprobated, by Mrs. Murchison at all events. It was the normal thing, the thing which formed the backbone of life, sustaining to the serious, impressive to the light, indispensable to the rest, and the thing that was more than any of these, which you can only know when you stand in the churches among the congregations. Within its prescribed limitations it was for many the intellectual exercise, for more the emotional lift, and for all the unfailing distraction of the week. The repressed magnetic excitement in gatherings of familiar faces, fellow-beings bound by the same convention to the same kind of behaviour, is precious in communities where the human interest is still thin and sparse. It is valuable in itself, and it produces an occasional detached sensation. There was the case, in Dr. Drummond's church, of placid-faced, saintly old Sandy MacQuhot, the epileptic. It used to be a common regret with Lorne Murchison that as sure as he was allowed to stay away from church Sandy would have a fit. That was his little boy's honesty; the elders enjoyed the fit and deprecated the disturbance.

There was a simple and definite family feeling within communions. "They come to our church" was the argument of first force whether for calling or for charity. It was impossible to feel toward a Congregationalist or an Episcopalian as you felt toward one who sang the same hymns and sat under the same admonition week by week, year in and year out, as yourself. "Wesleyans, are they?" a lady of Knox Church would remark of the newly arrived, in whom her interest was suggested. "Then let the Wesleyans look after them." A pew-holder had a distinct status; an "adherent" enjoyed friendly consideration, especially if he adhered faithfully; and stray attendants from other congregations were treated with punctilious hospitality, places being found for them in the Old Testament, as if they could hardly be expected to discover such things for themselves. The religious interest had also the strongest domestic character in quite another sense from that of the family prayers which Dr. Drummond was always enjoying. "Set your own house in order and then your own church" was a wordless working precept in Elgin. Threadbare carpet in the aisles was almost as personal a reproach as a hole under the dining-room table; and self-respect was barely possible to a congregation that sat in faded pews. The minister's gown even was the subject of scrutiny as the years went on. It was an expensive thing to buy, but an oyster supper would do it and leave something over for the organ. Which brings us to the very core and centre of these activities, their pivot, their focus and, in a human sense, their inspiration —the minister himself.

The minister was curiously special among a people so general; he was in a manner raised in life on weekdays as he was in the pulpit on Sundays. He had what one might call prestige; some form of authority still survived in his person, to which the spiritual democracy he presided over gave a humorous, voluntary assent. He was supposed to be a person of undetermined leisure—what was writing two sermons a week to earn your living by?—and he was probably the more reverend, or the more revered, from the fact that he was in the house all day. A particular importance attached to everything he said and did; he was a person whose life answered different springs, and was sustained on quite another principle than that of supply and demand. The province of public criticism was his; but his people made up for the meekness with which they sat under it by a generous use of the corresponding privilege in private. Comments upon the minister partook of hardiness; it was as if the members were determined to live up to the fact that the office-bearers could reduce his salary if they liked. Needless to say, they never did like. Congregations stood loyally by their pastors, and discussion was strictly intramural. If the Methodists handed theirs on at the end of three years with a breath of relief, they exhaled it among themselves; after all, for them it was a matter of luck. The Presbyterians, as in the case of old Mr. Jamesion of St. Andrew's, held on till death, pulling a long upper lip: election was not a thing to be trifled with in heaven or upon earth.

The Imperialist, Toronto, 1904

PIERRE BERTON

One of the minor phenomena of the postwar North American continent has been the so-called religious revival. Statistically it is impressive. Films, books, and articles dealing with religion are such sure-fire successes that the cliché phrase used in a thousand magazine titles "How I . . . Found God" has become a classic joke inside and outside the trade. Columns of religious advice help to sell newspapers. Millions appear to have been influenced by Norman Vincent Peale, Billy Graham, and Fulton J. Sheen. The Church itself has never been financially stronger. In Canada its property values have passed the one-billion mark. The church-building boom, especially in the suburbs, is easily observable: in Metropolitan Toronto, for instance, two hundred new churches have been erected in a decade. The polls reveal that almost everybody—some ninety-four per cent—believes in God, accepts the doctrine of the virgin birth and life after death, and is convinced of the power of prayer. Everybody in short is a Christian. Yet, oddly, the great revival is rarely if ever referred to as a Christian revival. The operative word is *religious*.

There is another apparent paradox. Though the Church has never been statistically fatter, its influence appears to be waning. In the words of Dr. T. W. Adorno, the director of the Institute of Social Research, "Religion does not play such a decisive role within the frame of mind of most people as it once did; only rarely does it seem to account for their social attitudes and opinions." Often, as we have seen, these attitudes and opinions are at cross-purposes with the Christian ethic. The very people who say they are religious will also admit, when

pressed, that their religion has not greatly influenced them. A *Maclean's* survey in 1961, taken in Guelph, Ontario, showed that while most respondents, Catholic and Protestant, attended church regularly and believed it to be "the home and refuge of all mankind," only a small percentage were influenced by it in matters of birth control, sexual behaviour, political decisions, public causes, or business conduct.

And "success" in business and social terms has all too often been the real gospel of the Church. A successful church is like a successful business. If its membership is growing, its budget growing and its program growing, then it is said to be progressing. The Church existed for three centuries without the need for building programs; but a church today without an expensive edifice is becoming unthinkable in the major denominations. Since pre-Renaissance times, the spectacle of a costly and ornate cathedral rising above the most squalid slums has been one of the continuing and paradoxical images of Christianity. It was Janet Lacey, director of Inter-Church Aid and Refugee Service for the British Council of Churches, who raised this question at the 1963 Anglican Congress in Toronto. She asked, tentatively, if the Church was sure its priorities were in the right order: "Do we need new churches? Are there not several half-empty, little-used buildings of all denominations in one town or diocese?" But a glance at the parish and diocesan press indicates just how important buildings are in the great Numbers Game the religious establishment plays. They reinforce the belief that things really are going well with the Church—and, of course, things *are* going well if you accept the social yardstick of success, and not the Christian one.

If he wishes to achieve recognition from the community at large, from the congregation, from his fellow ministers, and from the church hierarchy—and if he wishes to move forward in that hierarchy—the clergyman must be success-motivated. He must bring lustre to the physical look of his church by financing the building of a new one or by refurbishing an old one. To do this he must enlist as many members and as much money as possible. His congregation must grow numerically if not spiritually, and the minister himself must become an organization man. If he can "relate" to people, and not rub them the wrong way with too many awkward questions; if he is good at raising large sums from the more affluent members of the parish—and good at keeping them happy—if he is good at PR; if he "adjusts" to the community and does not come into conflict with it by raising too many abrasive points of Christian conscience; if he can balance a budget, expand facilities, and act as a good executive while developing the relatively innocuous skills of the pulpit—all without stirring up the natives unduly—then he will be counted a success; he will be sought out by better-appointed parishes because of his proven abilities in the Numbers Game; his photograph will appear in the diocesan press with the appropriate statistics below it; and he will be marked for continuing promotion.

The Comfortable Pew, Toronto, 1965

A. M. KLEIN

When as a young boy, the consolations and prophecies of Isaiah before me, I dreamed in the dingy Hebrew school the apocalyptic dream of a renewed Zion, always I imagined it as coming to pass thus: First I heard the roar and thunder of the battle of Gog and Magog; then, as silence fell, I saw through my mind's eye a great black aftermath cloud filling the heavens across the whole length of the humped horizon. The cloud then began to scatter, to be diminished, to subside, until revealed there shone the glory of a burnished dome – Hierosolyma the golden! Then lower it descended and lower, a mere breeze dispersed it, and clear was the horizon and before me there extended an undulating sunlit landscape.

My childhood vision, no doubt the result of a questionable amalgam between Hollywood and Holy Writ, was indeed fulfilled; but not in all its details and particularities. The cataclysmic war was there, the smoke, the thud and brunt of battle; but no golden dome. What was to be seen instead on the fifth day of Iyar was a forgathered company of men hitherto obscure, as anonymous as the *Bnai Brak*, who too had spent a night expatiating upon the miracles of exodus, met in surroundings not palatial, in a city which forty years earlier had had neither being nor name, to announce to the world on behalf of a people for whom they were as yet *noms de plume*, hardly *noms de guerre*, that henceforward in the domain of their forefathers they, nullifying all hiatus, intended to be, beneath the sovereignty of the All-Sovereign, sovereign.

My life was, and is, bound to the country of my father's choice, to Canada; but this intelligence, issuing, as it did, from that quarter of the globe which had ever been to me the holiest of the map's bleeding stigmata, the Palestine whose geography was as intimately known as the lines of the palm of my hand, filled me with pride, with exaltation, with an afflatus odorous of the royal breath of Solomon. I was like one that dreamed. I, surely, had not been of the captivity; but when the Lord turned again the captivity of Zion, I was like one that dreamed.

My dreaming was given a dream's authenticity when after the first year of the Stablishing my publisher invited me to undertake, for my spiritual advantage and his profit, a pilgrimage to Israel.

I did not want to leave Israel without having visited, for my father's sake and my mother's, Mother Rachel's tomb at Bethlehem. A kaddish intoned at that grave, I had gathered from my mother's pious talk, was of the supremest efficacy. The road to Bethlehem from Jerusalem, however, was still held by the soldiers of the Arab Legion. Yet to have left Israel without having stirred its air with the spoken names of my parents would have been most unfilial. I felt that I ought at least to arrange for a chapter of *Mishnaioth* to be read, in memory of my parents, by the students of some devout seminary.

And no better nor holier place could there be to bring my parents' greetings, failing the Western Wall and Rachel's tomb, than the Synagogue of Rabbi Isaac Luria, known honorifically as Adonenu Rabbi Izhak, the which is initialled ARI – the Lion.

It is no magnificent edifice, this synagogue of the padding lion of the Lord, but a humble house, a place of worship such as one finds in the poorer quarters of the world's ghettos. It was high noon when I entered out of the bright sun and the white roofs and terraces into the cool of the synagogue and intruded upon a scene which, I suspected, had been static against that background for centuries. The young boy, no more than thirteen, holding his heavy tome, the tractate *Baba Kama*, might have been there as of some remote century, forever unaging in the study of Torah, which is Life; and the old venerable sage, bearded like antiquity, was, as he murmured over his book of piety, a sort of anticipatory figure, an image of the boy an era hence. They seemed, surely, not of this world: the boy rapt in the analysis of some complicated *Tosforth*, the old man seeking blear-eyed to peer behind the mysteries of the *Pamalyah shel Malah*.

They affirmed it for me, the young boy prodigy and the old man who looked like Elijah: Israel had not only returned back into Time; it still belonged to Eternity.

I hesitated to break upon their studies, but soon the elder, sensing my presence, rose from his bench to greet me. I told him what I wanted and he said that it most certainly could be arranged, not this afternoon, it was Erev Shabbos, but, God willing, on the first day of the week. Our conversation was in Yiddish, for the old man was of those who held that Hebrew would be profaned by secular use.

"From where comes a Jew?" he asked.

"From Canada."

"Canada!" He sucked at his gums. "A great distance!"

"I flew. With the airplane it is not so great a distance."

"True. . . . True. We live in Messiah's days."

"Because the world is all good? Or, *cholila*, all evil?"

"Judgments are for God. It is the Messiah's days because we see his signs and portents everywhere. Thus is it written that when the Messiah will come there will be the wonder of *kvitzath ha-derech*, the curtailment of the route. What does this mean? It means that a route which but yesterday was long and arduous suddenly becomes short and speedy. Is this not the experience of our times? Is it not the experience of the Yemenites who, located as if on another planet, as if in another century, are brought by planes to this our century and to this our planet, our country, our home, in the space of but eight hours? . . . It is written yet again that before the coming of the Messiah there would be the *chevlai yemoth ha-moshiach*, the pain and agony of the days of the Messiah. Has any generation known deeper pain and bitterer agony than our own?"

Obviously excited by his quotations, he found it difficult to keep up with his rejuvenating enthusiasms. He paused for words, he hesitated, his tongue got caught in the weave of his texts. Laboriously he continued:

"It is written also that with the coming of the Messiah there would take place the wonder of *gilgul m'choloth*. A true resurrection! The cadavers and corpses of Jewry deceased in the Diaspora would roll and strive and roll through subterranean passages, through catacomb and grave, directed all to rise at last and stand erect on the heights of Carmel, on the hillocks of the Negev, on the mountains of Galilee. This, too, we have seen. Blessed are my eyes that have seen them, the risen from the dungeons, the pursued through the undergrounds of Europe who have taken up their stand here in Israel. . . . We live in Messiah's days. Do you not see them, these signs, as well as I, an old man, do?"

The Second Scroll, New York, 1951

6
POETRY

E. J. PRATT

Sea-Gulls

For one carved instant as they flew,
The language had no simile—
Silver, crystal, ivory
Were tarnished. Etched upon the horizon blue,
The frieze must go unchallenged, for the lift
And carriage of the wings would stain the drift
Of stars against a tropic indigo
Or dull the parable of snow.

Now settling one by one
Within green hollows or where curled
Crests caught the spectrum from the sun,
A thousand wings are furled.
No clay-born lilies of the world
Could blow as free
As those wild orchids of the sea.

Collected Poems, Toronto, 1944

CHARLES G. D. ROBERTS

The Pea-Fields

These are the fields of light, and laughing air,
And yellow butterflies, and foraging bees,
And whitish, wayward blossoms winged as these,
And pale green tangles like a seamaid's hair.
Pale, pale the blue, but pure beyond compare,
And pale the sparkle of the far-off seas,
A-shimmer like these fluttering slopes of peas,
And pale the open landscape everywhere.

From fence to fence a perfumed breath exhales
O'er the bright pallor of the well-loved fields—
My fields of Tantramar in summer-time;
And, scorning the poor feed their pasture yields,
Up from the bushy lots the cattle climb,
To gaze with longing through the grey, mossed rails.

Selected Poems, Toronto, 1955 (First published, 1893)

BLISS CARMAN

Low Tide on Grand Pré

The sun goes down, and over all
These barren reaches by the tide
Such unelusive glories fall,
I almost dream they yet will bide
Until the coming of the tide.

And yet I know that not for us,
By an ecstasy of dream,
He lingers to keep luminous
A little while the grievous stream,
Which frets, uncomforted of dream—

A grievous stream, that to and fro
Athrough the fields of Acadie
Goes wandering, as if to know
Why one beloved face should be
So long from home and Acadie.

Was it a year or lives ago
We took the grasses in our hands,
And caught the summer flying low
Over the waving meadow lands,
And held it there between our hands?

The while the river at our feet—
A drowsy inland meadow stream—
At set of sun the after-heat
Made running gold, and in the gleam
We freed our birch upon the stream.

There down along the elms at dusk
We lifted dripping blade to drift,
Through twilight scented fine like musk,
Where night and gloom awhile uplift,
Nor sunder soul and soul adrift.

And that we took into our hands
Spirit of life or subtler thing—
Breathed on us there, and loosed the bands
Of death, and taught us, whispering,
The secret of some wonder-thing.

Then all your face grew light, and seemed
To hold the shadow of the sun;
The evening faltered, and I deemed
That time was ripe, and years had done
Their wheeling underneath the sun.

So all desire and all regret,
And fear and memory, were naught;
One to remember or forget
The keen delight our hands had caught;
Morrow and yesterday were naught.

The night has fallen, and the tide . . .
Now and again comes drifting home,
Across these aching barrens wide,
A sigh like driven wind or foam:
In grief the flood is bursting home.

Selected Poems, Toronto, 1958 (First published, 1893)

ROBERT FINCH

Silverthorn Bush

I am a dispossessed Ontario wood
That took the circling weather as my crown,
Now noise makes havoc of my whispered mood
And enterprise has laughed my towers down.

Is there a poem where I blossom still?
Do paintings keep my solitude secure?
Somewhere remote adventure must distil
Part of its fragrance from an air so pure.

I am the springing memory of my past
In vagabond and child who held me dear,
Theirs is the surest witness that I last
In buds of mine that I no longer bear.

If you can overtake their truant youth
Ask them to flash my secret on your sight,
They heard my pensive river spill its truth
And felt my hidden fibres tug the light.

The riddle is how disappearance puts
A dusty end to a green revery
Yet leaves me nourished by so many roots
That I shall never cease ceasing to be.

The Literary Review, Summer, 1965

E. J. PRATT

On the North Shore a reptile lay asleep—
A hybrid that the myths might have conceived,
But not delivered, as progenitor
Of crawling, gliding things upon the earth.
She lay snug in the folds of a huge boa
Whose tail had covered Labrador and swished
Atlantic tides, whose body coiled itself
Around the Hudson Bay, then curled up north
Through Manitoba and Saskatchewan
To Great Slave Lake. In continental reach
The neck went past the Great Bear Lake until
Its head was hidden in the Arctic Seas.

This folded reptile was asleep or dead:
So motionless, she seemed stone dead—just seemed:
She was too old for death, too old for life,
For as if jealous of all living forms
She had lain there before bivalves began
To catacomb their shells on western mountains.
Somewhere within this life-death zone she sprawled,
Torpid upon a rock-and-mineral mattress.
Ice-ages had passed by and over her,
But these, for all their motion, had but sheared
Her spotty carboniferous hair or made
Her ridges stand out like the spikes of molochs.

*"I am the springing memory of my past
In vagabond and child who held me dear...."*

Her back grown stronger every million years,
She had shed water by the longer rivers
To Hudson Bay and by the shorter streams
To the great basins to the south, had filled
Them up, would keep them filled until the end
Of Time.

Towards the Last Spike, Toronto, 1952

GEORGE JOHNSTON

Love of the City

After a week of wandering through the world
Eating wherever we could, sleeping, washing ourselves
Wherever we could, in bars and railway rooms,
We came to this great city. Nothing
Will persuade us ever to leave it again.

The city loves us now it's moved us in:
The yellow sky comes down and fills the room;
Dirt on the floor is kind, the walls are kind,
Everyone's kind to us wherever we go.

And truly when death comes where will he find
A better room than here, better arrangements,
More courtesy, more eager friendliness
Than in this excellent street-scattered city,
This home, this network, this great roof of pity?

The Cruising Auk, Toronto, 1959

*". . . all the city's restless seething
river surges beside you. . . ."*

RAYMOND SOUSTER

Downtown Corner News Stand

It will need all of death to take you from this corner.
It has become your world, and you its unshaved
bleary-eyed, foot-stamping king. In winter
you curse the cold, huddled in your coat from the wind,
you fry in summer like an egg hopping on a griddle;
and always the whining voice, the nervous-flinging arms,
the red face, shifting eyes watching, waiting
under the grimy cap for God knows what
to happen. (But nothing ever does, downtown Toronto
goes to sleep and wakes the next morning
always the same, except a little dirtier.)
And you stand with your armful of Stars and Telys,
the peak of your cap well down against the sun,
and all the city's restless seething river
surges beside you, but not once do you plunge
into its flood, are carried or tossed away:
but reappear always, beard longer than ever, nose running,
to catch the noon editions at King and Bay.

The Colour of the Times, Toronto, 1964

IRVING LAYTON

On Seeing the Statuettes of Ezekiel and Jeremiah in the Church of Notre Dame

They have given you French names
    and made you captive, my rugged
troublesome compatriots;
    your splendid beards, here, are epicene,
plaster white
            and your angers
unclothed with Palestinian hills quite lost
in this immense and ugly edifice.

You are bored—I see it—sultry prophets
    with priests and nuns
(What coarse jokes must pass between you!)
    and with those morbidly religious
i.e. my prize brother-in-law
                ex-Lawrencian
pawing his rosary, and his wife
sick with many guilts.

Believe me I would gladly take you
    from this spidery church
its bad melodrama, its musty smell of candle
    and set you both free again
in no make-believe world
                of sin and penitence
but the sunlit square opposite
alive at noon with arrogant men.

Yet cheer up Ezekiel and you Jeremiah
    who were once cast into a pit;
I shall not leave you here incensed, uneasy
    among alien Catholic saints
but shall bring you from time to time
                my hot Hebrew heart
as passionate as your own, and stand
with you here awhile in aching confraternity.

A Red Carpet for the Sun, Toronto, 1959

A. M. KLEIN

The Rocking Chair

It seconds the crickets of the province. Heard
in the clean lamplit farmhouses of Quebec,—
wooden,—it is no less a national bird;
and rivals, in its cage, the mere stuttering clock.
To its time, the evenings are rolled away;
and in its peace the pensive mother knits
contentment to be worn by her family,
grown-up, but still cradled by the chair in which she sits.

It is also the old man's pet, pair to his pipe,
the two aids of his arithmetic and plans,
plans rocking and puffing into market-shape;
and it is the toddler's game and dangerous dance.
Moved to the verandah, on summer Sundays, it is,
among the hanging plants, the girls, the boy-friends,
sabbatical and clumsy, like the white haloes
dangling above the blue serge suits of the young men.

It has a personality of its own;
is a character (like that old drunk Lacoste,
exhaling amber, and toppling on his pins);
it is alive; individual; and no less
an identity than those about it. And
it is tradition. Centuries have been flicked
from its arcs, alternately flicked and pinned.
It rolls with the gait of St. Malo. It is act

and symbol, symbol of this static folk
which moves in segments, and returns to base,—
a sunken pendulum: *invoke, revoke*;
loosed yon, leashed hither, motion on no space.
O, like some Anjou ballad, all refrain,
which turns about its longing, and seems to move
to make a pleasure out of repeated pain,
its music moves, as if always back to a first love.

The Rocking Chair and Other Poems, Toronto, 1948

MARGARET AVISON

Thaw

Sticky inside their winter suits
The Sunday children stare at pools
In pavement and black ice where roots
Of sky in moodier sky dissolve.

    An empty coach train runs along
    The thin and sooty river flats
    And stick and straw and random stones
    Steam faintly when its steam departs.

Lime-water and licorice light
Wander the tumbled streets. A few
Sparrows gather. A dog barks out
Under the dogless pale pale blue.

    Move your tongue along a slat
    Of a raspberry box from last year's crate.
    Smell a saucepantilt of water
    On the coal-ash in your grate.

Think how the Black Death made men dance,
And from the silt of centuries
The proof is now scraped bare that once
Troy fell and Pompey scorched and froze.

    A boy alone out in the court
    Whacks with his hockey-stick, and whacks
    In the wet, and the pigeons flutter, and rise,
    And settle back.

Winter Sun, Toronto, 1960

ARCHIBALD LAMPMAN

Winter Evening

Tonight the very horses springing by
Toss gold from whitened nostrils. In a dream
The streets that narrow to the westward gleam
Like rows of golden palaces; and high
From all the crowded chimneys tower and die
A thousand aureoles. Down in the west
The brimming plains beneath the sunset rest,
One burning sea of gold. Soon, soon shall fly
The glorious vision, and the hours shall feel
A mightier master; soon from height to height,
With silence and the sharp unpitying stars,
Stern creeping frosts, and winds that touch like steel,
Out of the depth beyond the eastern bars,
Glittering and still shall come the awful night.

Selected Poems, Toronto, 1947 (First published, 1899)

ANNE HÉBERT

Snow

Snow puts us in a dream on vast plains without track or
    colour

Beware, my heart, snow puts us in the saddle on steeds of
    foam

Ring out for a crowned childhood, snow consecrates us on
    high seas, dreams fulfilled, all sails set

Snow puts us in a trance, a widespread whiteness, flaring
    plumes pierced by the red eye of this bird

My heart; a point of fire under palms of frost flows the
    marvelling blood.

From *St. Denys Garneau and Anne Hébert*, Translations by
F. K. Scott, Vancouver, 1962

IRVING LAYTON

The Bull Calf

The thing could barely stand. Yet taken
from his mother and the barn smells
he still impressed with his pride,
with the promise of sovereignty in the way
his head moved to take us in.
The fierce sunlight tugging the maize from the ground
licked at his shapely flanks.
He was too young for all that pride.
I thought of the deposed Richard II.

"No money in bull calves," Freeman had said.
The visiting clergyman rubbed the nostrils
now snuffing pathetically at the windless day.
"A pity," he sighed.
My gaze slipped off his hat toward the empty sky
that circled over the black knot of men,
over us and the calf waiting for the first blow.

Struck,
the bull calf drew in his thin forelegs
as if gathering strength for a mad rush . . .
tottered . . . raised his darkening eyes to us,
and I saw we were at the far end
of his frightened look, growing smaller and smaller
till we were only the ponderous mallet
that flicked his bleeding ear
and pushed him over on his side, stiffly,
like a block of wood.

Below the hill's crest
the river snuffled on the improvised beach.
We dug a deep pit and threw the dead calf into it.
It made a wet sound, a sepulchral gurgle,
as the warm sides bulged and flattened.
Settled, the bull calf lay as if asleep,
one foreleg over the other,
bereft of pride and so beautiful now,
without movement, perfectly still in the cool pit,
I turned away and wept.

> "The Bull Calf" from *The Bull Calf and other Poems*,
> Toronto, 1956

JAMES REANEY

The Katzenjammer Kids

With porcupine locks
And faces which, when
More closely examined,
Are composed of measle-pink specks,
These two dwarf imps,
The Katzenjammer Kids,
Flitter through their Desert Island world.
Sometimes they get so out of hand
That a blue Captain
With stiff whiskers of black wicker
And an orange Inspector
With a black telescope
Pursue them to spank them
All through that land
Where cannibals cut out of brown paper
In cardboard jungles feast and caper,
Where the sea's sharp waves continually
Waver against the shore faithfully
And the yellow sun above is thin and flat
With a collar of black spikes and spines
To tell the innocent childish heart that
It shines
And warms (see where she stands and stammers)
The dear fat mother of the Katzenjammers.

Oh, for years and years she has stood
At the window and kept fairly good
Guard over the fat pies that she bakes
For her two children, those dancing heartaches.
Oh, the blue skies of that funny-paper weather!
The distant birds like two eyebrows close together!

The Red Heart, Toronto, 1949

". . . The dear fat mother of the Katzenjammers."

E. J. PRATT

The Shark

He seemed to know the harbour,
So leisurely he swam;
His fin,
Like a piece of sheet-iron,
Three-cornered,
And with knife-edge,
Stirred not a bubble
As it moved
With its base-line on the water.

His body was tubular
And tapered
And smoke-blue,
And as he passed the wharf
He turned,
And snapped at a flat-fish
That was dead and floating.
And I saw the flash of a white throat,
And a double row of white teeth,
And eyes of metallic grey,
Hard and narrow and slit.

"... with a roar which ... shook the watchers in the boats,
the liner took her thousand fathoms' journey to her grave."

Then out of the harbour,
With that three-cornered fin
Shearing without a bubble the water
Lithely,
Leisurely,
He swam—
That strange fish,
Tubular, tapered, smoke-blue,
Part vulture, part wolf,
Part neither—for his blood was cold.

Collected Poems, Toronto, 1944

E. J. PRATT

Aboard the ship, whatever hope of dawn
Gleamed from the *Carpathia*'s riding lights was gone,
For every knot was matched by each degree
Of list. The stern was lifted bodily
When the bow had sunk three hundred feet, and set
Against the horizon stars in silhouette
Were the blade curves of the screws, hump of the rudder.
The downward pull and after buoyancy
Held her a minute poised but for a shudder
That caught her frame as with the upward stroke
Of the sea a boiler or a bulkhead broke.

Climbing the ladders, gripping shroud and stay,
Storm-rail, ringbolt or fairlead, every place
That might befriend the clutch of hand or brace
Of foot, the fourteen hundred made their way
To the heights of the aft decks, crowding the inches
Around the docking bridge and cargo winches.
And now that last salt tonic which had kept
The valour of the heart alive—the bows
Of the immortal seven that had swept
The strings to outplay, outdie their orders, ceased.
Five minutes more, the angle had increased
From eighty on to ninety when the rows
Of deck and port-hole lights went out, flashed back
A brilliant second and again went black.
Another bulkhead crashed, then following
The passage of the engines as they tore
From their foundations, taking everything
Clean through the bows from 'midships with a roar
Which drowned all cries upon the deck and shook
The watchers in the boats, the liner took
Her thousand fathoms' journey to her grave.

And out there in the starlight, with no trace
Upon it of its deed but the last wave
From the *Titanic* fretting at its base,
Silent, composed, ringed by its icy broods,
The grey shape with the palaeolithic face
Was still the master of the longitudes.

From "The Titanic," *Collected Poems*, Toronto, 1944

Somewhere far-off in that unwavering gloom,
Cramped in the quarters of a wireless room,
A boy was seated, tapping at a key.
Water ran along the floor: his knee
Was braced against a table to resist
The dangerous angle of a starboard list.
Upon his right a wireless log-chart lay
With many entries for so young a day.
He reached and pushed a button and the drone
Of a generator started. A switch thrown,
He rapped the key, then instantly transferred
To the receiving set; listened with keen
Thrust of his face; and with no answer heard,
Changed over, going through the same routine.
But once when on the panel a blue flame,
Crackling like tearing linen at the gap,
Responded to a more than hectic tap
Of the finger, dumb and drowsy symbols came
To life. Through aerials screaming like curlews,
Magnetic messengers carried the name
Of a disabled vessel with the news
Of water in the stokehold and a crew's
Vigil upon a flooded deck. Legions
Unnumbered moving at the rate of light,
Pushed out beyond all navigated regions,
Exploring every cranny of the night,
Reaching out through dusky corridors
Above the sea to uninhabited shores,
Or taking undecoded human cries
Below the keel to the Atlantic crypts.
And millions undulated to the skies,
Through snow and vapour and the cloud eclipse,
Past day and night and the terrestrial air,
To add their wasted sum to a plethora
Of speed and power in those void spaces where
Light-years go drifting by Andromeda.
And yet in all that sterile plenitude
A few were harnessed to a human mood.

From "The Roosevelt and the Antinoe," Collected Poems,
Toronto, 1944

The Gathering

['*Oats—a grain which in England is generally given to horses,
but in Scotland supports the people.* DR. SAMUEL JOHNSON.
'*True, but where will you find such horses, where such men?*'
LORD ELIBANK'S REPLY AS RECORDED BY SIR WALTER SCOTT.]

Oatmeal was in their blood and in their names.
Thrift was the title of their catechism.
It governed all things but their mess of porridge
Which, when it struck the hydrochloric acid
With treacle and skim-milk, became a mash.
Entering the duodenum, it broke up
Into amino acids: then the liver
Took on its natural job as carpenter:
Foreheads grew into cliffs, jaws into juts.
The meal, so changed, engaged the follicles:
Eyebrows came out as gorse, the beards as thistles,
And the chest-hair the fell of Grampian rams.
It stretched and vulcanized the human span:
Nonagenarians worked and thrived upon it.
Out of such chemistry run through by genes,
The food released its fearsome racial products:
The power to strike a bargain like a foe,
To win an argument upon a burr,
Invest the language with a Bannockburn,
Culloden or the warnings of Lochiel,
Weave loyalties and rivalries in tartans,
Present for the amazement of the world
Kilts and the civilized barbaric Fling,
And pipes which, when they acted on the mash,
Fermented lullabies to *Scots wha hae*.

Their names were like a battle-muster—Angus
(He of the Shops) and Fleming (of the Transit),
Hector (of the *Kicking Horse*), Dawson,
"Cromarty" Ross, and Beatty (Ulster Scot),
Bruce, Allan, Galt and Douglas, and the "twa"—
Stephen (Craigellachie) and Smith (Strathcona)—
Who would one day climb from their Gaelic hide-outs,
Take off their plaids and wrap them round the mountains.
And then the everlasting tread of the Macs,
Vanguard, centre and rear, their roving eyes
On summits, rivers, contracts, beaver, ledgers;
Their ears cocked to the skirl of Sir John A.,
The general of the patronymic march.

Towards the Last Spike, Toronto, 1952

"Magnetic messengers carried the name of a disabled vessel. . . ."

DUNCAN CAMPBELL SCOTT

The Half-Breed Girl

She is free of the trap and the paddle,
The portage and the trail,
But something behind her savage life
Shines like a fragile veil.

Her dreams are undiscovered,
Shadows trouble her breast,
When the time for resting cometh
Then least is she at rest.

Oft in the morns of winter,
When she visits the rabbit snares,
An appearance floats in the crystal air
Beyond the balsam firs.

Oft in the summer mornings,
When she strips the nets of fish,
The smell of the dripping net-twine
Gives to her heart a wish.

But she cannot learn the meaning
Of the shadows in her soul,
The lights that break and gather,
The clouds that part and roll,

The reek of rock-built cities,
Where her fathers dwelt of yore,
The gleam of loch and shealing,
The mist on the moor,

Frail traces of kindred kindness,
Of feud by hill and strand,
The heritage of an age-long life
In a legendary land.

She wakes in the stifling wigwam,
Where the air is heavy and wild,
She fears for something or nothing
With the heart of a frightened child.

She sees the stars turn slowly
Past the tangle of the poles,
Through the smoke of the dying embers,
Like the eyes of dead souls.

Her heart is shaken with longing
For the strange, still years,
For what she knows and knows not,
For the wells of ancient tears.

A voice calls from the rapids,
Deep, careless and free,
A voice that is larger than her life
Or than her death shall be.

She covers her face with her blanket,
Her fierce soul hates her breath,
As it cries with a sudden passion
For life or death.

Selected Poems, Toronto, 1954 (First published, 1906)

A. M. KLEIN

Political Meeting
(*For Camillien Houde*)

"he is their idol...."

On the school platform, draping the folding seats,
they wait the chairman's praise and glass of water.
Upon the wall the agonized Y initials their faith.

Here all are laic; the skirted brothers have gone.
Still, their equivocal absence is felt, like a breeze
that gives curtains the sounds of surplices.

The hall is yellow with light, and jocular;
suddenly some one lets loose upon the air
the ritual bird which the crowd in snares of singing

catches and plucks, throat, wings, and little limbs.
Fall the feathers of sound, like *alouette's*.
The chairman, now, is charming, full of asides and wit,

building his orators, and chipping off
the heckling gargoyles popping in the hall.
(Outside, in the dark, the street is body-tall,

flowered with faces intent on the scarecrow thing
that shouts to thousands the echoing
of their own wishes.) The Orator has risen!

Worshipped and loved, their favourite visitor,
a country uncle with sunflower seeds in his pockets,
full of wonderful moods, tricks, imitative talk,

he is their idol: like themselves, not handsome,
not snobbish, not of the *Grande Allée! Un homme!*
Intimate, informal, he makes bear's compliments

to the ladies; is gallant; and grins;
goes for the balloon, his opposition, with pins;
jokes also on himself, speaks of himself

in the third person, slings slang, and winks with folklore;
and knows now that he has them, kith and kin.
Calmly, therefore, he begins to speak of war,

praises the virtue of being *Canadien*,
of being at peace, of faith, of family,
and suddenly his other voice: *Where are your sons?*

He is tearful, choking tears; but not he
would blame the clever English; in their place
he'd do the same; maybe.

Where *are* your sons?
             The whole street wears one face,
shadowed and grim; and in the darkness rises
the body-odour of race.

The Rocking Chair and Other Poems, Toronto, 1948

A. M. KLEIN

For the Sisters of
the Hotel Dieu

In pairs,
as if to illustrate their sisterhood,
the sisters pace the hospital garden walks.
In their robes black and white immaculate hoods
they are like birds,
the safe domestic fowl of the House of God.

O biblic birds,
who fluttered to me in my childhood illnesses
—me little, afraid, ill, not of your race,—
the cool wing for my fever, the hovering solace,
the sense of angels—
be thanked, O plumage of paradise, be praised.

The Rocking Chair and Other Poems, Toronto, 1948

LEONARD COHEN

Cherry Orchards

Canada some wars are waiting for you
some threats
some torn flags
Inheritance is not enough
   Faces must be forged under the hammer
of savage ideas
   Mailboxes will explode
in the cherry orchards
and somebody will wait forever
for his grandfather's fat cheque
   From my deep café I survey the quiet snowfields
like a U.S. promoter
of a new plastic snowshoe
looking for a moving speck
a troika perhaps
an exile
an icy prophet
an Indian insurrection
a burning weather station
   There's a story out there boys
Canada could you bear some folk songs
about freedom and death

Flowers for Hitler, Toronto, 1964

FRANK R. SCOTT

Conflict

When I see the falling bombs
Then I see defended homes.
Men above and men below
Die to save the good they know.

Through the wrong the bullets prove
Shows the bravery of love.
Pro and con have single stem
Half a truth dividing them.

Between the dagger and the breast
The bond is stronger than the beast.
Prison, ghetto, flag and gun
Mark the craving for the One.

Persecution's cruel mouth
Shows a twisted love of truth.
Deeper than the rack and rope
Lies the double human hope.

My good, your good, good we seek
Though we turn no other cheek.
He who slays and he who's slain
Like in purpose, like in pain.

Who shall bend to single plan
The narrow sacrifice of man?
Find the central human urge
To make a thousand roads converge?

Overture, Toronto, 1945

"The hills will fall in folds, the wilderness will be a garment innocent and lustrous. . . ."

DOUGLAS LE PAN

A Country Without a Mythology

No monuments or landmarks guide the stranger
Going among this savage people, masks
Taciturn or babbling out an alien jargon
And moody as barbaric skies are moody.

Berries must be his food. Hurriedly
He shakes the bushes, plucks pickerel from the river,
Forgetting every grace and ceremony,
Feeds like an Indian, and is on his way.

And yet, for all his haste, time is worth nothing.
The abbey clock, the dial in the garden,
Fade like saint's days and festivals.
Months, years, are here unbroken virgin forests.

There is no law—even no atmosphere
To smooth the anger of the flagrant sun.
November skies sting sting like icicles.
The land is open to all violent weathers.

Passion is not more quick. Lightnings in August
Stagger, rocks split, tongues in the forest hiss,
As fire drinks up the lovely sea-dream coolness.
This is the land the passionate man must travel.

Sometimes—perhaps at the tentative fall of twilight—
A belief will settle that waiting around the bend
Are sanctities of childhood, that melting birds
Will sing him into a limpid gracious Presence.

The hills will fall in folds, the wilderness
Will be a garment innocent and lustrous
To wear upon a birthday, under a light
That curls and smiles, a golden-haired Archangel.

And now the channel opens. But nothing alters.
Mile after mile of tangled struggling roots,
Wild-rice, stumps, weeds, that clutch at the canoe,
Wild birds hysterical in tangled trees.

And not a sign, no emblem in the sky
Or boughs to friend him as he goes; for who
Will stop where, clumsily constructed, daubed
With war-paint, teeters some lust-red manitou?

The Wounded Prince, London, 1948

WILFRED WATSON

Emily Carr

Like Jonah in the green belly of the whale
Overwhelmed by Leviathan's lights and liver
Imprisoned and appalled by the belly's wall
Yet inscribing and scoring the uprush
Sink vault and arch of that monstrous cathedral,
Its living bone and its green pulsing flesh—
Old woman, of your three days' anatomy
Leviathan sickened and spewed you forth
In a great vomit on coasts of eternity.
Then, as for John of Patmos, the river of life
Burned for you an emerald and jasper smoke
And down the valley you looked and saw
All wilderness become transparent vapour,
A ghostly underneath a fleshly stroke,
And every bush an apocalypse of leaf.

Friday's Child, London, 1955

ST. DENYS GARNEAU

Bird Cage

I am a bird cage
A cage of bone
With a bird

The bird in the cage of bone
Is death building his nest

When nothing is happening
One can hear him ruffle his wings

And when one has laughed a lot
If one suddenly stops
One hears him cooing
Far down
Like a small bell

It is a bird held captive
This death in my cage of bone

Would he not like to fly away
Is it you who will hold him back
Is it I
What is it

He cannot fly away
Until he has eaten all
My heart
The source of blood
With my life inside

He will have my soul in his beak.

From *St. Denys Garneau and Anne Hébert*, translations by
F. K. Scott, Vancouver, 1962

ANNE WILKINSON

A Cautionary Tale

*. . . we had sold our death . . . for the sum of £70:18:6d and
lent our fear . . . on interest of £3:10:0d per month, so we
did not care about death and we did not fear again.*
FROM *The Palm Wine Drinkard* BY AMOS TUTUOLA

She met a lion face to face
As she went walking
Up to her hips in grass
On the wild savannah.
So close they stood they touched
If she put out her thumb
Or he his soft ferocious paw.
She bore no weight of fear,
For only yesterday
She'd leased it to a rich man, poor
In that commodity.
Without her terror she was free
From the alarming smell
That irritates a lion
And makes him lash his tail.
And so he yawned, and stretched
On the long stemmed grasses,
And in the pouring sun
She sat beside his royalty
And sang to him a tale of moon.
Before he rose to go
He opened wide his jaw
And took between his teeth
Her wishing bone, as if to say,
I could, you know.
A rich man had her caution
So she laughed; cool,
In the lion's ear, her pretty breath.
What happened next happens
To every maiden fair
Who lends her fear
But forgets to sell her death:
The lion ate her up, and down
To the smallest crumb.
Lord have mercy upon
Her sweet white bones. Amen.

Uncollected.

A. J. M. SMITH

The Mermaid

Dark green and seaweed-cold, the snake-bright hair
Streams on the golden-sun-illumined wave
That sways as gently as two bells the grave
Small coral-tinted breasts to starboard there
Where salt translucency's green branches bear
This sea-rose, a lost mermaid, whose cold cave,
Left lightless now, the lapping seatides lave
At base of Okeanos' twisted stair.

She's come where bubbles burst, crisp silver skims;
Where the tall sun stands naked; where he shines;
Where live men walk the shrouds with fork-like limbs.

She smiles: and the head of the shipmite swims;
But the bo'sun bawls for the grappling lines,
And the Chaplain fumbles in his book of hymns.

Collected Poems, Toronto, 1962

E. J. PRATT

The fury of taunt was followed by fury of blow.
Why did not the flesh of Brébeuf cringe to the scourge,
Respond to the heat, for rarely the Iroquois found
A victim that would not cry out in such pain—yet here
The fire was on the wrong fuel. Whenever he spoke,
It was to rally the soul of his friend whose turn
Was to come through the night while the eyes were uplifted
      in prayer,
Imploring the Lady of Sorrows, the mother of Christ,
As pain brimmed over the cup and the will was called
To stand the test of the coals. And sometimes the speech
Of Brébeuf struck out, thundering reproof to his foes,
Half-rebuke, half-defiance, giving them roar for roar.
Was it because the chancel became the arena,
Brébeuf a lion at bay, not a lamb on the altar,
As if the might of a Roman were joined to the cause
Of Judaea? Speech they could stop for they girdled his lips,
But never a moan could they get. Where was the source
Of his strength, the home of his courage that topped the best
Of their braves and even out-fabled the lore of their legends?
In the bunch of his shoulders which often had carried a load
Extorting the envy of guides at an Ottawa portage?
The heat of the hatchets was finding a path to that source.
In the thews of his thighs which had mastered the trails of the
      Neutrals?
They would gash and beribbon those muscles. Was it the
      blood?
They would draw it fresh from its fountain. Was it the heart?
They dug for it, fought for the scraps in the way of the
      wolves.
But not in these was the valour or stamina lodged;
Nor in the symbol of Richelieu's robes or the seals
Of Mazarin's charters, nor in the stir of the *lilies*
Upon the Imperial folds; nor yet in the words
Loyola wrote on a table of lava-stone
In the cave of Manresa—not in these the source—
But in the sound of invisible trumpets blowing
Around two slabs of board, right-angled, hammered
by Roman nails and hung on a Jewish hill.

"Brébeuf and His Brethren," *Collected Poems*, Toronto, 1944

"Brébeuf a lion at bay, not a lamb on the altar. . . ."

A. J. M. SMITH

Ode:

On the Death of William Butler Yeats

An old thorn tree in a stony place
Where the mountain stream has run dry,
Torn in the black wind under the race
Of the icicle-sharp kaleidoscopic white sky,
      Bursts into sudden flower.

Under the central dome of winter and night
A wild swan spreads his fanatic wing.
Ancestralled energy of blood and power
Beats in his sinewy breast. And now the ravening
Soul, fulfilled, his first-last hour
      Upon him, chooses to exult.

Over the edge of shivering Europe,
Over the chalk front of Kent, over Eire,
Dwarfing the crawling waves' amoral savagery,
Daring the hiding clouds' rhetorical tumult,
      The white swan plummets the mountain top.

The stream has suddenly pushed the papery leaves!
It digs a rustling channel of clear water
On the scarred flank of Ben Bulben.
The twisted tree is incandescent with flowers.
The swan leaps singing into the cold air:
      This is a glory not for an hour.

Over the Galway shore
The white bird is flying
Forever, and crying
To the tumultuous throng
Of the sky his cold and passionate song.

News of the Phoenix, Toronto and New York, 1943

LEO KENNEDY

Words for a Resurrection

Each pale Christ stirring underground
Splits the brown casket of its root,
Wherefrom the rousing soil upthrusts
A narrow, pointed shoot,

And bones long quiet under frost
Rejoice as bells precipitate
The loud, ecstatic sundering,
The hour inviolate.

This Man of April walks again—
Such marvel does the time allow—
With laughter in His blessèd bones,
And lilies on His brow.

The Shrouding, Toronto, 1933

JAY MacPHERSON

The Fisherman

The world was first a private park
Until the angel, after dark,
Scattered afar to wests and easts
The lovers and the friendly beasts.

And later still a home-made boat
Contained Creation set afloat,
No rift nor leak that might betray
The creatures to a hostile day.

But now beside the midnight lake
One single fisher sits awake
And casts and fights and hauls to land
A myriad forms upon the sand.

Old Adam on the naming-day
Blessed each and let it slip away:
The fisher of the fallen mind
Sees no occasion to be kind,

But on his catch proceeds to sup;
Then bends, and at one slurp sucks up
The lake and all that therein is
To slake that hungry gut of his,

Then whistling makes for home and bed
As the last morning breaks in red;
But God the Lord with patient grin
Lets down his hook and hoicks him in.

The Boatman, Toronto, 1958

EARLE BIRNEY

El Greco: Espolio

The carpenter is intent on the pressure of his hand
on the awl, and the trick of pinpointing his strength
through the awl to the wood, which is tough.
He has no effort to spare for despoilings
nor to worry if he'll be cut in on the dice.
His skill is vital to the scene, and the safety of the state.
Anyone can perform the indignities; it is his hard arms
and craft that hold the eyes of the convict's women.
There is the problem of getting the holes straight
(in the middle of this shoving crowd)
and deep enough to hold the spikes
after they've sunk through those soft feet
and wrists waiting behind him.

The carpenter isnt aware that one of the hands
is held in a curious beseechment over him—
but what is besought, forgiveness or blessing?—
nor if he saw would he take the time to be puzzled.
Criminals come in all sorts, as anyone knows who makes
            crosses,
are as mad or sane as those who decide on their killings.
Our one at least has been quiet so far
though they say he has talked himself into this trouble—
a carpenter's son who got notions of preaching.
Well here's a carpenter's son who'll have carpenter's sons,
God willing, and build what's wanted, temples or tables,
mangers or crosses, and shape them decently,
working alone in that firm and profound abstraction
which blots out the bawling of rag-snatchers.
To construct with hands, knee-weight, braced thigh,
keeps the back turned from death.
But it's too late now for the other carpenter's boy
to return to this peace before the nails are hammered.

Ice Cod Bell or Stone, Toronto, 1962

ACKNOWLEDGMENTS

The excerpts in the first five chapters of this book are reprinted with the kind permission of the following: From *Barometer Rising* by Hugh MacLennan by permission of Duell, Sloan & Pearce Inc. and the author, copyright 1941 by Hugh MacLennan; from *The Commercial Empire of the St. Lawrence, 1760-1850* by Donald Creighton by permission of The Ryerson Press, Toronto; from *The Innocent Traveller* by Ethel Wilson by permission of the author and The Macmillan Company of Canada Limited; from *Two Solitudes* by Hugh MacLennan by permission of Duell, Sloan & Pearce Inc. and the author, copyright 1945 by Hugh MacLennan; from *Son of a Smaller Hero* by Mordecai Richler by permission of André Deutsch Limited; from *Why Rock the Boat* by William Weintraub by permission of McClelland and Stewart Limited, Little, Brown and Company, copyright © 1961, and the author; from *Flying a Red Kite* by Hugh Hood by permission of The Ryerson Press, Toronto; from *Jalna* by Mazo De La Roche by permission of the author's estate and The Macmillan Company of Canada Limited; Macmillan & Co. Ltd., London; Little, Brown and Company, copyright 1927 by Little, Brown and Company, copyright 1955 by Mazo De La Roche; from *What's Past Is Prologue* by Vincent Massey by permission of the author and The Macmillan Company of Canada Limited; from *Toronto: No Mean City* by Eric Arthur by permission of University of Toronto Press; from *As for Me and My House* by James Sinclair Ross by permission of the author; from *Who Has Seen the Wind* by W. O. Mitchell by permission of the author, Little, Brown and Company and The Macmillan Company of Canada Limited; from *Stone Angel* by Margaret Laurence by permission of McClelland and Stewart Limited; from *Settlers of the Marsh* by Frederick Philip Grove by permission of McClelland and Stewart Limited; from *Hetty Dorval* by Ethel Wilson by permission of the author and The Macmillan Company of Canada Limited; from "The Forest Path to the Spring", "The Bravest Boat", and "Through the Panama" from *Hear Us O Lord from Heaven Thy Dwelling Place* by Malcolm Lowry, copyright © 1961 by Margerie Bonner Lowry, published by J. B. Lippincott Company; from *People of the Deer* by Farley Mowat by permission of Atlantic-Little, Brown and Company and Littauer and Wilkinson, copyright 1951, 1952 by Farley Mowat; from *Arcadian Adventures with the Idle Rich* by Stephen Leacock reprinted by permission of McClelland and Stewart Limited, the Bodley Head Leacock, and Dodd, Mead & Company, copyright 1914 by Dodd, Mead & Company; from *The Equations of Love* by Ethel Wilson by permission of the author and The Macmillan Company of Canada Limited; from *The Mountain and the Valley* by Ernest Buckler by permission of Harold Ober Associates Inc., copyright Ernest Buckler 1952; from *Return to the River* by Roderick L. Haig-Brown by permission of William Morrow & Co. Inc., copyright Roderick L. Haig-Brown 1941; from *Where the High Winds Blow* by David Walker by permission of the author; from *The Nymph and the Lamp* by Thomas H. Raddall reprinted by permission of the author, copyright 1950, Little, Brown and Company and The Hutchinson Publishing Group Ltd.; from *The Watch That Ends the Night* by Hugh MacLennan by permission of the author and The Macmillan Company of Canada Limited; from *The Prospector* by Charles William Gordon (Ralph Connor) by permission of Fleming H. Revell, Company; from *The Loved and the Lost* by Morley Callaghan by permission of the author and The Macmillan Company of Canada Limited; from *Turvey* by Earle Birney by permission of McClelland and Stewart Limited;

from *God's Sparrows* by Philip Child by permission of the author; from *Execution* by Colin McDougall by permission of the author and The Macmillan Company of Canada Limited; from *Remember Me* by Edward Meade by permission of Faber & Faber Limited; from *The Incomplete Angler* by John D. Robins by permission of Mrs. John D. Robins; from *To Be Taken with Salt* by Peter McArthur by permission of his son, D. C. McArthur; from *A Choice of Enemies* by Mordecai Richler by permission of André Deutsch Limited; from *The Luck of Ginger Coffey* by Brian Moore by permission of McClelland and Stewart Limited, Atlantic – Little, Brown and Company and André Deutsch Limited; from *A Mixture of Frailties* by Robertson Davies by permission of the author, The Macmillan Company of Canada Limited and Weidenfeld & Nicholson; from *The Tin Flute* by Gabrielle Roy by permission of McClelland and Stewart Limited; from *Morley Callaghan's Stories* by permission of the author and The Macmillan Company of Canada Limited; from *Canadian Short Stories* by Roger Lemelin by permission of Oxford University Press; from article in *The Canadian Historical Review* by Maurice Hutton by permission of University of Toronto Press; from *Political Economy in the Modern State* by Harold A. Innis by permission of The Ryerson Press; from *The Progressive Party* by W. L. Morton by permission of University of Toronto Press; from *In Search of Canadian Liberalism* by Frank Underhill by permission of the author and The Macmillan Company of Canada Limited; from *John A. Macdonald: The Young Politician* by Donald Creighton by permission of the author and The Macmillan Company of Canada Limited; from *William Lyon Mackenzie King: Vol. 2 1924-1932, The Lonely Heights* by Blair Neatby by permission of the literary executors of Mackenzie King; from an article in *Saturday Night* by Stephen Leacock by permission of Mrs. Barbara Nimmo; from an article in *Winnipeg Free Press* by Bruce Hutchison by permission of the author; from *In Pastures Green* by Peter McArthur by permission of J. M. Dent & Sons (Canada) Ltd.; from a piece from *The Atlantic Monthly* by John Conway reprinted by permission of the author, copyright © 1964 by The Atlantic Monthly Company, Boston, Mass.; from a paper to the Congrès des Affaires Canadiennes, Laval University by permission of the author, S. D. Clark; from *The Road to Confederation* by Donald Creighton by permission of the author and The Macmillan Company of Canada Limited; from *The Literary History of Canada* by Northrop Frye, by permission of University of Toronto Press; from *Songs of the Makers of Canada* by J. D. Logan by permission of The Ryerson Press; from original articles in *The Graphic*, 1931, by permission of the authors, William A. Deacon and Wilson MacDonald; from *Sara Binks* by Paul Hiebert by permission of Oxford University Press; from a piece in the *University of Toronto Quarterly*, 1938, by Frederick Philip Grove by permission of University of Toronto Press; from *Canadians in the Making* by Arthur R. M. Lower by permission of Longmans Canada Limited; from an article in *The Atlantic Monthly*, 1964, by Douglas Le Pan reprinted by permission of the author, copyright © 1964, by The Atlantic Monthly Company, Boston, Mass.; from *The Precipice* by Hugh MacLennan by permission of the author; from *Imitation and Design, the Group of Seven* by Reid MacCallum by permission of University of Toronto Press; from *The Architectonics of Pure Taste* by Peter Collins by permission of the author; from *Christianity and Classical Culture* by Charles Norris Cochrane by permission of Oxford University Press; from *Understanding Media* by Marshall McLuhan by permission of McGraw-Hill Book Company; from

Empire and Communications by Harold A. Innis by permission of Oxford University Press; from *The Imperialist* by Sara Jeannette Duncan by The Copp Clark Publishing Co. Ltd.; from *The Comfortable Pew* by Pierre Berton by permission of McClelland and Stewart Limited; from *The Second Scroll* by A. M. Klein by permission of Alfred A. Knopf Inc., copyright 1951 by A. M. Klein. Sundry quotations and phrases taken from Canadian Quotations and Phrases, compiled by Robert M. Hamilton, by permission of McClelland and Stewart Limited.

The excerpts from Chapter Six of this book are reprinted with the kind permission of the following: quotes reprinted from *Collected Poems of E. J. Pratt* by permission of the estate of E. J. Pratt and The Macmillan Company of Canada Limited; "The Pea Fields" reprinted from *The Selected Poems of Charles G. D. Roberts* by permission of The Ryerson Press, Toronto; "The Silverthorn Bush" by permission of the author, Robert Finch, and *The Literary Review* (Summer 1965) published by Fairleigh Dickinson University, Teaneck, N.J.; "Love of the City" from *The Cruising Auk* by George Johnston by permission of Oxford University Press; "Downtown Corner News Stand" from *The Colour of the Times* by Raymond Souster by permission of The Ryerson Press, Toronto; "On Seeing the Statuettes of Ezekiel and Jeremiah in the Church of Notre Dame" and "The Bull Calf" from *Collected Poems* by Irving Layton by permission of McClelland and Stewart Limited; "The Rocking Chair", "Political Meeting" and "For the Sisters of the Hotel Dieu" from *The Rocking Chair and Other Poems* by A. K. Klein by permission of The Ryerson Press, Toronto; "Thaw" from *Winter Sun* by Margaret Avison by permission of University of Toronto Press and Routledge and Kegan Paul Limited; "Winter Evening" by Archibald Lampman by permission of The Ryerson Press, Toronto; "Snow" by Anne Hébert by courtesy of the author from her book *St. Denys Garneau and Anne Hébert;* "The Katzenjammer Kids" from *The Red Heart and Other Poems* by James Reaney, by permission of Sybil Hutchinson; "The Half-Breed Girl" from *Selected Poems* by Duncan Campbell Scott, by permission of The Ryerson Press; "Cherry Orchards" from *Flowers for Hitler* by Leonard Cohen by permission of McClelland and Stewart; "Conflict" by Frank R. Scott by permission of the author; "A Country without a Mythology" from *The Wounded Prince* by Douglas Le Pan by permission of Chatto and Windus; "Bird Cage" from the book *St. Denys Garneau and Anne Hébert,* translated by Frank R. Scott, Klanak Press, by permission of Les Editions Fides; "Emily Carr" reprinted from *Friday's Child* by Wilfred Watson, by permission of Farrar, Straus & Giroux, Inc., copyright 1955, and Faber & Faber Limited; "A Cautionary Tale" by Anne Wilkinson reprinted by permission of the estate of Anne Wilkinson and The Macmillan Company of Canada Limited; "The Mermaid" and "Ode: On the Death of William Butler Yeats" from *Collected Poems* by A. J. M. Smith by permission of the author and Oxford University Press; "Words for a Resurrection" from *The Shrouding* by Leo Kennedy by permission of The Macmillan Company of Canada Limited; "The Fisherman" from *The Boatman* by Jay Macpherson by permission of the author and Oxford University Press; "El Greco: Espolio" from *Ice Cod Bell or Stone* by Earle Birney by permission of McClelland and Stewart Limited.

Every reasonable care has been taken to make the list of acknowledgments comprehensive, but in a few cases all efforts to trace the owners of copyright have failed. It is hoped that such omissions will be pardoned.

ILLUSTRATION CREDITS

Order of appearance in the text of pictures listed here is left to right, top to bottom. After the first recording, principal sources are credited under these abbreviations: John de Visser, JDV; Jerry Lazare, JL; Maclean's Magazine, MM; Frank Newfeld, FN; Public Archives of Canada, P.A. Illustrations for Section Three commissioned for this book from Jerry Lazare.

Cover   Ray Webber, Toronto.
11   John de Visser, Toronto.
12   Public Archives of Canada; PA.
13   JDV.
14   JDV.
17   Sam Tata, Montreal.
19   Malak, from Miller Services.
22-23   Henri Rossier, New York.
24   National Film Board.
28   Jack Long, Vancouver
29   Richard Harrington, Toronto.
33   JDV.
35   Harold Town.
37   Canadian Audubon Society.
38   Doug Johnson.
43   James Hill, Maclean's Magazine.
46   No credit.
48   Frank Newfeld.
52-53   Alfred Bastien, from The National Gallery of Canada.
54   Huntley Brown.
57   Lawren Harris, from The National Gallery of Canada.
59   Jerry Lazare.
60   JL.
62   JL.
64   JL.

66   JL.
70   JL.
71   JL.
74   JL.
79   PA.
80   Gitano, MM.
82   PA.
85   John Collins, Montreal Gazette, October 29, 1960.
86   PA.
87   PA.
91   PA.
94   Gitano, MM.
111   JDV.
112   JDV.
113   JDV.
114   FN.
116   King Features Syndicate, Inc.
117   The Bettmann Archives Inc.
118   Donald Fernley.
119   Canada Wide Photo.
121   Frank Carmichael, from the Robert McMichael Collection, Kleinburg, Ontario.
123   FN.
124   FN.

PRINTED AND BOUND IN CANADA

TEXT TYPE   Times New Roman

TYPOGRAPHER   The Hunter Rose Co. Ltd.

PAPER   Webcoat

LITHOGRAPHY   Litho-Print Limited

BINDING   *case printed by* Sampson Matthews Limited
case made by The Ryerson Press
bound by T. H. Best Printing Co. Limited

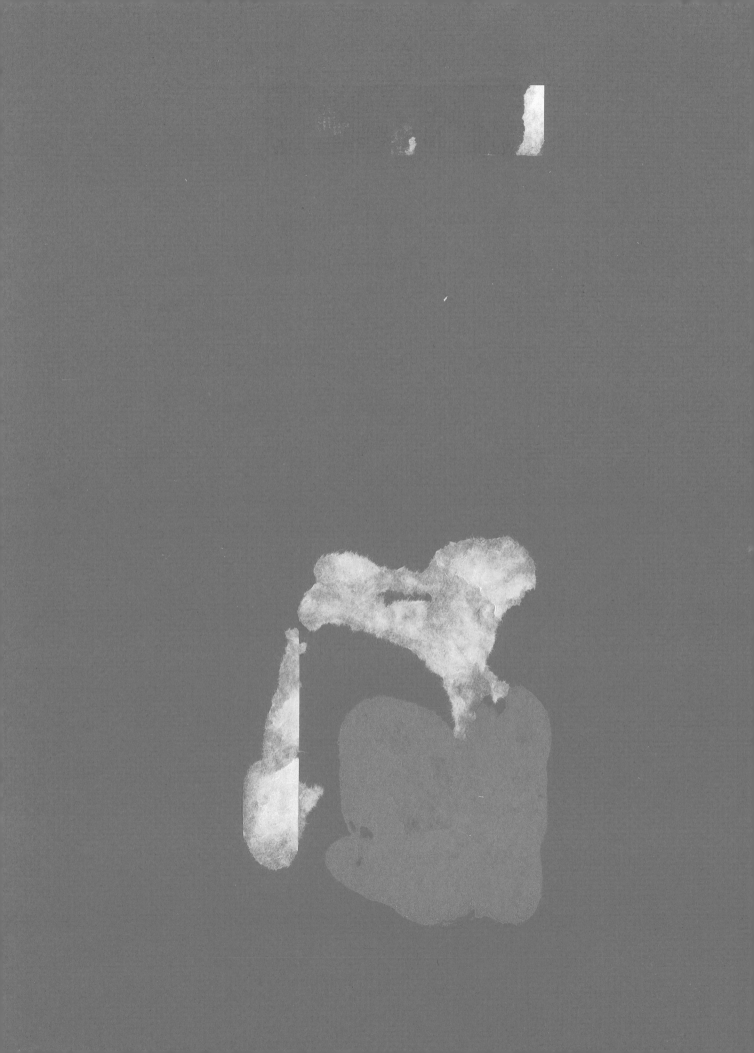